Gift of the

Joan
Thompson
Doll Fund

Many different types of dolls can be thought of as 'famous characters'.

Famous
Character
Dolls

Susan Brewer

First published in Great Britain in 2013 by
Remember When
an imprint of
Pen & Sword Books Ltd
47 Church Street
Barnsley
South Yorkshire
S70 2AS

Copyright © Susan Brewer 2013

ISBN: 978-1-84468-094-8

A CIP catalogue record for this book is available from the British Library.

Typeset in 11pt Ehrhardt by
Mac Style, Driffield, E. Yorkshire

Printed and bound in India by Replika Press Pvt. Ltd.

Pen & Sword Books Ltd incorporates the Imprints of Pen & Sword Aviation, Pen & Sword Family History, Pen & Sword Maritime, Pen & Sword Military, Pen & Sword Discovery, Wharncliffe Local History, Wharncliffe True Crime, Wharncliffe Transport, Pen & Sword Select, Pen & Sword Military Classics, Leo Cooper, The Praetorian Press, Remember When, Seaforth Publishing and Frontline Publishing.

For a complete list of Pen & Sword titles please contact
PEN & SWORD BOOKS LIMITED
47 Church Street, Barnsley, South Yorkshire, S70 2AS, England
E-mail: enquiries@pen-and-sword.co.uk
Website: www.pen-and-sword.co.uk

Contents

Introduction

WHAT MAKES a doll become a famous character? Why should one doll be singled out to receive the acclaim when an almost identical doll is just run-of-the-mill? It's a difficult question, but invariably the answer lies with the doll-buying public. Usually, a 'famous doll' is a doll which has appeared in a book or children's programme and has subsequently been issued in its thousands as an advertising ploy, or in response to consumer demand. However, unlike famous cats, famous dogs, famous horses or famous bears, famous dolls might not actually be dolls at all – which probably sounds something of an oxymoron, but is quite logical when you think about it. Dolls are made in our own image, and so are often made to represent people. For instance, Shirley Temple, Michael Jackson, Queen Victoria, Andy Warhol and Kylie Minogue have all appeared in doll form, yet they are human flesh and blood. A true famous doll is one such as 'Raggedy Ann', who features in many stories. She isn't human, and so representations of her will depict her as she is – a doll. She will not be made as a doll-copy of a human being.

It has therefore been difficult to define the dolls to be included in this book. There are not enough 'Famous Dolls' to fill the pages – but there are thousands and thousands of dolls representing famous characters, or which for some reason or another, have earned their claim to fame. They might have been used to advertise various products or depict characters from films. Maybe they star in children's television programmes, represent popular singers, are likenesses of royalty, wear national costumes, or are classic genres of dolls such as Barbie. They are included here, together with the true famous dolls – Raggedy Ann, Noddy, Hamble, Pinocchio, Hitty, Looby Loo, Tottie, Chucky, and others – who are, and always will be, just dolls.

This book describes some of the dolls that fall into the various categories. The more important and interesting dolls, as well as many additional dolls, will also have an entry in the main dictionary. Furthermore, I have selected several characters who are especially popular for various reasons and have allowed them their own chapters. These range from nursery tale characters through to modern heroes of children's fiction. Inevitably, many dolls fall into several categories. For example, cartoon characters might also appear as film stars, characters from books might be used in greetings cards, or advertising characters might be used in television programmes. Unfortunately, it has not been possible to include more than a fraction of the dolls which come under the category of 'famous characters', but I hope that amongst the hundreds of famous dolls included in this book, you will find some of your favourites too.

Susan Brewer

Red Riding Hood Kickit ('In the Hood') Robert Tonner, with Snow White and Alice, Moxie Girlz.

Chapter One

Dolls in Books

DOLLS FEATURE in hundreds of books, especially those for children, yet only a few of the dolls pictured are actually named. They are frequently included in a general capacity, maybe to illustrate a type of doll, or as an adjunct to a story. Often, they are just referred to as 'doll' or 'dolly', with no specific outstanding qualities and are forgotten as soon as the book is closed. Occasionally though, a book will come along containing a doll-based story that captures the public's imagination. Probably the most famous example is that of 'Raggedy Ann', a rag doll which took America by storm when her stories were first published in 1918, and who is still popular today. Some enthusiasts concentrate solely on Raggedy Ann and build up enormous collections of the dolls and related memorabilia.

The true story of Raggedy Ann's creation is unclear, but the most commonly accepted version is that she was the main character featured in the stories artist Johnny Gruelle told to his young daughter Marcella. Some people believe Raggedy Ann came about when Marcella one day found an old rag doll which had once belonged to her grandmother, in the loft. She showed it to Johnny who drew a face on the doll and called it Raggedy Ann. From then on, the doll became an important part of Johnny's stories and was soon joined by other characters, notably 'Raggedy Andy' and 'Beloved Belindy'. Sadly, Marcella was just 13 years old when she died after being given a smallpox vaccination at school without her parent's consent.

As a tribute to Marcella, her heartbroken father later decided to publish the stories he once told her so that other children could enjoy them. They were an enormous success, and it wasn't long before Raggedy Ann dolls and the other characters were in production. Over the years they have been made by various companies including P. F. Volland, Exposition Dolls, Playskool, Hasbro, Applause, Knickerbocker and Danbury Mint, and Raggedy Ann is still being made today. Legend has it that the earliest dolls, made by the Gruelles themselves, were given a sugar heart, just as Raggedy Ann was in the storybook, but so far, nobody has proved this to be true. Raggedy Ann has red hair, button eyes, a smiling mouth and a distinctive red triangular nose. Her clothing varies; normally a print dress or a skirt and top, but usually with a white apron.

Raggedy Andy looks very similar, but tends to wear blue short trousers, red-checked shirt and red striped socks. The other doll, 'Beloved Belindy', is a chubby black doll dressed in a large pinafore, hoop earrings and a scarf tied around her head. Knickerbocker produced a now much sought-after version of her in the mid-1960s, wearing a brightly-coloured outfit consisting of a red top and yellow skirt – both with white spots – a red scarf, white apron and the typical red-and-white striped stockings. An earlier 1940s 'Beloved Belindy' doll, by Georgene Novelties, wore a red top and floral skirt.

Interestingly, several manufacturers have also produced versions of 'Marcella' dolls, based on the girl who owned Raggedy Ann. The most beautiful is probably the limited edition of 250 created by doll maker R. John Wright which was released in 2005. Wright is a very talented sculptor and his felt creations are deservedly, expensive, but they are stunning and incredibly realistic. His limited edition, well-detailed versions of Christopher Robin, Alice in Wonderland, Flower Fairies, Heidi, Kewpie dolls, Dorothy from the *Wizard of Oz*, Kate Greenaway children and The Little Prince from the book of the same name, are true collectors' items. They are designed by John and Susan Wright and produced at the company's workshop in the New England state of Vermont, America. The felt used is hand painted, and the dolls are sturdy and very beautiful.

Wright's 'Marcella and Raggedy Ann' doll is a 17in-tall, fully jointed doll made from wool felt and with a mohair wig. Marcella's facial features are hand painted and she is dressed in a cotton gauze dress with a felt appliqué pattern. Her straw hat is trimmed with felt flowers and fruit. She has cream cotton stockings and leather slippers, and holds a felt 6in Raggedy Ann doll. Another impressive doll is a 16in porcelain-headed doll on a hand-carved, spring-jointed wooden body, designed by Wendy Lawton in her Childhood Classics series. Called 'Marcella and her Raggedy Family', this beautiful doll with blue eyes and blonde curls, was produced to celebrate the 80th anniversary of Raggedy Ann. Limited to 1,000, Marcella wears an exquisite cream-frilled, lace-trimmed, long-sleeved dress. She holds a 6in Raggedy Ann and a similar size Raggedy Andy. Other Marcella dolls include those by the Madame Alexander Doll Company and Precious Moments. The Madame Alexander version, 'Marcella Loves Raggedy Ann', is one of the 8in sweet-faced Wendy dolls, which are the company's hallmark. Made from vinyl and fully jointed, the doll has blonde hair, blue eyes, and wears a pretty pink coat over a white-skirted outfit. She also has a matching pink hat, white socks, black shoes, and her very own Raggedy Ann doll. The Precious Moments doll 'Marcella tells the Story of Raggedy Ann', is a 12in Marcella designed by Linda Rick. It brings a fresh look to the original Precious Moments face first designed by Sam Butcher more than thirty years ago. Precious Moments dolls are classic 'character face' types.

In 1915 a particularly interesting doll-themed story book, *The Dolls' Day*, by Carine Cadby, was published. It was illustrated with black-and-white photographs of three bisque china dolls. They were shown paddling in a stream,

Raggedy Ann, Knickerbocker.

Raggedy Andy, Knickerbocker.

Marcella and Raggedy Ann, R. John Wright.

Edith the Lonely Doll, Madame Alexander.

climbing trees and precariously dangling from branches, and it's surprising that none of them seemed to be damaged at the end of their adventure. Although the dolls in the book never became household 'famous dolls', they were given names – 'Charles' was the boy, 'Belinda' the girl, and the small one was 'Baby' (whose sex wasn't made clear). Of course, these dolls were already in mass production. Usually when a doll is featured in a book, it is one created especially for the story and then later sold to the public, but in the case of *The Dolls' Day*, it was the other way round. Presumably the author used dolls she already owned, or maybe she bought them from a toyshop especially to use in the book. Nowadays, the dolls depicted in the book are valuable collectors' items, and few of today's collectors would contemplate using their dolls in such a way. In fact, many collectors are horrified when they see the book's illustrations showing the dolls being treated so casually. Yet when we think about it, it is the equivalent of buying a few modern vinyl dolls and using them as models. We wouldn't worry if they became damaged because we know they can be easily and cheaply replaced, just as beautiful bisque dolls could be a hundred years ago!

Author Rumer Godden was fond of writing about dolls, and she used a doll theme for several of her charming children's books. Her most famous creation is 'Tottie', the peg doll who lived in the dolls' house in her 1947 book *The Dolls' House*, along with snooty Marchpane and sweet little Birdie, a celluloid doll which horrifically caught fire. The book was made into a successful television series in 1984, called *Tottie, the Story of a Dolls' House*. It was adapted for television by Peter Firmin and Oliver Postgate, creators of such programmes as *Bagpuss* and *Ivor the Engine* and was narrated by Postgate. The series achieved some notoriety as being the first children's programme to include a murder! A second series of five stories, also made by Smallfilms, was entitled *Tottie, A Doll's Wish*.

Rumer Godden's charming books include several others which feature dolls. Amongst them are *The Story of Holly and Ivy*, *The Fairy Doll*, *Little Plum*, *Miss Happiness and Miss Flower*, and *Home is the Sailor*. Particularly enchanting is *Miss Happiness and Miss Flower*, which tells how a shy little girl built an authentic paper house for two Japanese dolls and gained confidence in the process as it necessitated her researching the details and then buying the required materials. The book *Little Plum* also tells of Japanese dolls, while *The Story of Holly and Ivy* is a Christmas tale about 'Holly', an unsold doll in a toyshop. A cute little rag doll who has plenty of adventures is featured in a trio of books by Modwena Sedgwick. The first in the series was called *The Adventures of Galldora* , but this little doll actually made her first appearance in 1953 in the BBC's *Children's Hour*. Galldora isn't a pretty doll, but she is much loved by Marybell. She was made by Uncle Jack who thought up the name after rearranging the letters in 'a rag doll'.

One of the saddest book dolls must be Edith in the 1957 book *The Lonely Doll*, the first in a series by Dare Wright. The adventures of this small felt doll were shown in photographs taken by Wright which were accompanied by a brief text.

Wright's original 'Edith' was a 'Lenci', a type of felt doll created by Elena Scavini in 1920 but which was discontinued before the book was published. Lenci was the nickname given to Scavini by her husband. *The Lonely Doll* featured Edith wearing a pink gingham frock and white apron. This is the most familiar of the outfits, though she has worn others, and is the outfit in which most manufacturers depict her. The Madame Alexander Doll Company, for example, issued an 8in 'Wendy-type' doll in her pink gingham frock and white apron, and with her blonde hair swept back in a pony tail, revealing tiny gold earrings. Her hair sported a black ribbon which matched her shoes, and she came with a jointed 3in Mr Bear.

Edith appeared in other books, including *Edith and the Duckling, Edith and Midnight* and *A Gift from the Lonely Doll* – in which Edith goes to stay with Mr Bear's cousins, taking with her an extra-long muffler she had knitted as a surprise. Edith tries sledging, ice-skating, and also finds time to decorate the Christmas tree. This book was later issued in a special pack, together with a vinyl Edith who is dressed ready for winter in a warm, blue coat, black hat and fluffy black muff. The doll was made by Kids At Heart in the 1980s. Madame Alexander later issued a doll complete with a duckling from the *Edith and the Duckling* book. Perhaps the most stunning of the Edith dolls are a set of limited editions made by renowned maker R. John Wright in 2007 to commemorate the 50th anniversary of the publication of *The Lonely Doll*. Wright depicts Edith in her characteristic pink-checked gingham frock.

Another very special 'book doll' is 'Hitty', a kind of wooden Dutch doll. She starred in *Hitty: Her First Hundred Years*, written in 1969 by Rachel Field. This unusual book tells of a doll carved from a piece of mountain ash in the early 1800s, for a little girl called Phoebe. The doll's memorable name, Hitty, is actually short for Mehitable, and she is drawn to perfection in a series of pen-and-ink sketches by Dorothy P. Lathrop. Hitty's life is full of adventure, and her escapades include becoming lost in India, being left in a church, going to sea and getting sold at auction. Over the decades many dolls have appeared in Hitty's likeness, including some by the famed American wood-carver Robert Raikes, who issued an open edition of the dolls in 2001. In the United States, various outfits are available to fit Hitty, some of which are 'sew it yourself' kits containing the necessary fabric and patterns. Some people also sell 'Hitty Kits' consisting of wooden forms which need to be carved and assembled into dolls.

The sweet doll which appears in Pamela Scarry's *My Dolly and Me* – one of the American Little Golden Books – was later created as a baby doll figure. Eloise Wilkin's charming illustrations show a little girl and her unnamed doll as they go for a walk, do some washing, play at cowboys, and take a nap. The girl is drawn dressed like 'a grown-up mother' carrying her 'baby' and amazing her mummy who enters into the spirit of the game by pretending she doesn't recognise her daughter. Eloise was responsible for illustrating many books in the Little Golden Books series, one of her most popular being *Baby Dear* which also features a girl copying her mother by taking care of her dolly. The doll was actually designed by Eloise for the Vogue Doll Company in 1960. Called 'Baby Dear', it was a soft-bodied, crumpled-face baby with short hair, and arms with clenched fists. The arms were held upwards, in a very realistic pose. Several versions of this sweet doll were produced over the years, and today she is one of the American classics.

A surreal, rather unnerving family of dolls known as the 'Mennyms', appear in a series of books by Sylvia Waugh. The life-sized cloth dolls with blue faces include 'Sir Magnus', 'Tulip', 'Joshua', 'Vinetta', 'Wimpey', 'Poopie', 'Pilbeam', 'Appleby', 'Soobie', 'Miss Quigley' and baby 'Googles'. The stories tell how these human-sized dolls were made by dressmaker Kate Penshaw who brought them to life. They live amongst humans, though have as little contact with them as possible in case their secret should be guessed. Although the books are intended for children, they are quite scary in parts. Nevertheless, the series is compelling, even for adults. The Mennyms try to act like humans, even to the extent of pretending to eat and drink, going shopping, 'visiting' each other (by slipping out the back way and coming to the front door) and travelling in disguise in taxis. The books contain plenty of food for thought, indirectly dealing with subjects such as death and immortality.

A book written almost 120 years ago has caused considerable controversy over the last few decades by introducing a character doll which many now feel is demeaning. The 1895 book, *The Adventures of Two Dutch Dolls and a Golliwogg*, written by Bertha Upton and illustrated by her daughter Florence, introduced the concept of the golly, a black rag doll with a caricature face, based on a doll Florence had been given. Soon gollies were the favourites of thousands of children, a much-loved toy found in every child's nursery, right up to the 1960s. However, over the last four decades, in some quarters the golly was felt to be offensive to black people, and it hadn't helped that Enid Blyton used gollies as evil characters in her Noddy books. Gradually the toy lost favour and today few children own one, although they are still sold as collectors' items to those who still see the golly for what it once was – a friendly, helpful, lovable doll. The Upton books also featured other characters, notably Sarah Jane, Meg, Weg and Midget, who were based on Florence's childhood peg dolls. For a while the original Golliwog and Dutch dolls resided in a glass case at Chequers, the country home of the Prime Minister, but now they live at the Museum of Childhood in Bethnal Green, London, where they are visited by fans from around the world.

Though maligned by librarians, teachers and golly-lovers, Enid Blyton still seems to be adored by many children today, and the majority of her books have stood the test of time. Her best-loved character is Noddy, who went on to find fame on television. When the first Noddy book, *Noddy Goes To Toyland*, appeared in 1949, it told the story of a wooden boy doll with hair made from cat's fur, who ran away from his maker. After meeting a brownie called Big Ears he was taken to Toyland where he was dressed in his now famous blue hat with a bell, blue shorts and red shirt. He even had a little yellow car to drive. Big Ears named him

Baby Dear, Ideal.

Raggedy Ann & Raggedy Andy, R John Wright.

Mr Plod, McDonald's.

Noddy, Play-By-Play.

Pinocchio, Les Jouets Creation.

'Noddy' because his head was on a spring and wobbled or nodded when it was tapped. Naturally, many Noddy toys have appeared over the years, made by companies such as Golden Bear, Merrythought, Play-By-Play and Bendy Toys, and he is probably the most famous of the British book dolls.

Noddy is friendly and helpful to other characters in the books, though can be a bit silly or naughty sometimes, and he has a habit of breaking into banal verse. Other dolls live in Toyland too, including beautiful 'Angela Goldenhair' – who was cross with Noddy when she thought he had lost her scarf – and the Skittle family, who are, I suppose, not really dolls, but have been depicted with arms. We mustn't forget Mr Plod, the policeman, who constantly has to tell Noddy off for reckless driving. He is a kindly man, though, and the characters all seem to like him. He always looks forward to his cup of cocoa at the end of a busy day. Enid Blyton's Little Noddy character made his television debut in 1955 as a puppet on the new commercial channel.

Enid Blyton was also responsible for creating a very naughty doll, not in Toyland but in a different series of books. The first book was called *Naughty Amelia Jane*. Amelia Jane, who was home-made, was described as 'a big, long-legged doll with an ugly face, a bright-red frock and black curls'. According to her creator, home-made toys are never as well-behaved as those bought in a shop. The series of Blyton's Mary Mouse books, which date from the 1940s, feature a family of dolls who live in a doll's house. Mary Mouse looks after the three children. The family consists of Daddy, who is a sailor doll, Mummy, who wears ankle-length skirts and large bonnets, and the children, Melia, Pip and Roundy. These long, narrow books tell of the dolls' various adventures with Mary. Interestingly, the unusual size of these books (about 5in by 2in) came about because paper was so scarce during and after the Second World War that every scrap needed to be used and offcuts from larger books were utilised. The first Mary Mouse book was *Mary Mouse and the Doll's House* in 1942.

One of Enid Blyton's most appealing tales is about 'a tiny rubber doll, no bigger than your middle finger', who squeaked when she was squeezed. One sad day a mishap caused the squeak to disappear, and her owner declared, 'I don't like you so much now. You don't seem right without a squeak.' The little doll cried bitterly until a kindly mouse squeaked twenty times into a glass of water, and gave it to her to drink. Her squeak came back! This charming tale appears in Blyton's 1964 *Storytime Book*. Even Beatrix Potter, though more well-known for her animal tales, managed to squeeze some dolls into *The Tale of Two Bad Mice*. The mice played havoc in the doll's house belonging to Lucinda, who had a cook named Jane. Lucinda is depicted as a blonde, presumably bisque, girl doll, while Jane is a wooden peg doll. A cloth doll dressed as a policeman is also mentioned in the story.

Another famous 'doll character' is Pinocchio, the puppet made by Geppetto, who first featured in the book by Carlo Collodi before later appearing in a very successful Walt Disney film. Various manufacturers have made versions of this wooden doll puppet. Foremost is probably R. John Wright, who specialises in moulded felt figures. His Pinocchios capture the jaunty puppet boy to perfection. He has also made Geppetto dolls. Pinocchio has also been issued by the Madame Alexander Doll Company which has made many fairy-tale, nursery rhyme and other character dolls. There are plenty of other books which feature dolls, but sadly, unless the book becomes a huge success, or is translated into television or film, it is unlikely that an actual doll representation of the main character will be manufactured.

Chapter Two

Dolls Representing Characters in Print

W^E ARE spoilt for choice here, and this category often overlaps with dolls featured in films, so you will find some book characters in the film chapters. Companies such as Madame Alexander, Mattel, Palitoy, and many others, have produced dolls from much-loved books including *Alice in Wonderland, Anne of Green Gables, Heidi, Little Women, Mary Poppins, Madeline, Peter Pan, Matilda* and, of course, the characters from the Harry Potter books. Characters from comic strips and cartoons also regularly appear in doll form, including Charlie Brown and the rest of the Peanuts gang, Minnie the Minx, Dennis the Menace, Annie, and The Perishers. Some characters are more popular than others. The 'Little Women' girls, Alice in Wonderland, Heidi, Mary Poppins and the Peanuts gang are easier to find, for instance, than Fern from Charlotte's Web or characters from Jane Austen novels. *See also Chapter 7 for dolls from Dickens's novels and Shakespeare's plays.*

The Madame Alexander Doll Company has produced many sets of dolls from the *Little Women* book, the earliest being a set of four 16in fabric dolls in 1933 – although strictly speaking, they were brought out to coincide with the David Selznick-George Cukor movie which starred Katharine Hepburn as Jo. Little Women dolls have been a part of the Madame Alexander line almost continuously ever since, and the company has made the dolls in various sizes in composition (usually a mixture of glue and sawdust), hard plastic and vinyl. The first set of hard plastic dolls appeared in 1948-9.

In 1984 a set of 17in Little Women dolls was issued by Franklin Heirloom. Carefully fashioned in the tradition of the nineteenth-century bisque collector dolls, each was hand-crafted, with meticulous attention to the details of the head, hands and feet. The faces were hand-painted, and the attractive costumes intricately made, such as Beth's hand-tailored tartan-plaid dress trimmed with navy velvet.

Ashton-Drake produced a set of the dolls from *Little Women* in 1995. Created by artist Wendy Lawton, the dolls were 15ins high and made of porcelain. Cleverly, each had an accessory to emphasise her particular talent, so Amy came with her sketchpad, Meg came with her embroidery, Beth had sheet music, and Jo had her *Pilgrim's Progress* book. Each doll was also dressed to echo the girl's personality, so Jo wore a no-nonsense tartan outfit, while Amy was in frills.

Anne of Green Gables,
Mattel.

Jo was also included in a collection of four delightful dolls called 'When I Read, I Dream' made by Mattel in 2001 for its Timeless Treasures series. Each doll stood 8in high, and was made from vinyl. Beautifully dressed, they were packaged in display boxes which complemented the theme of the story. Jo wore a blue gingham and floral lace-trimmed dress with a blue apron. This enchanting series also featured Anne from *Anne of Green Gables*, Fern from *Charlotte's Web* and Heidi from the *Heidi* book.

Mattel's 'When I Read, I Dream' version of Fern stands 8ins high and is dressed in a blue denim pinafore dress over a red gingham shirt. She comes with stout, brown boots and a soft, toy pig which is slightly over one-inch long. Anne (*Anne of Green Gables*), dressed in a peach-coloured outfit adorned with a large green bow, and wearing a straw hat, carries her schoolbooks in a strap, while Heidi wears a traditional Swiss-style outfit of a brightly printed dress, embroidered apron, boots, and has her hair in plaits. Each doll is attractively packaged in a storybook setting. For instance, Anne is shown in a garden with a white fence, trees and blossom. It is a shame that Mattel did not produce more of these small dolls which represent characters from children's fiction, as they were well-thought-out depictions, and provided children with an introduction to various fictional works. Fern has also been made by the Madame Alexander Doll Company, both as a vinyl and cloth doll. The cloth version was 18in tall, and her yellow, plaited hair was made from yarn. She wore a pretty, yellow, frilled cotton frock with puffed sleeves and, as with the Mattel version, carried a little cloth version of Wilbur, her pig.

The Madame Alexander Doll Company has produced dolls celebrating characters from books ever since it first started in 1923, and often covers the unusual titles as well as the more popular books. In recent years, inspired by the series of Eloise books written by Kay Thompson and illustrated by Hilary Knight, the company decided to bring the six-year-old girl to life in doll form. Eloise lives in 'the room on the tippy-top floor' of the Plaza Hotel in New York, together with her Nanny, her pug dog Weenie and her turtle Skipperdee. A portrait of Eloise hung in the lobby of the Plaza until it closed for renovations in 2005, and was subsequently re-hung after three years in storage. The Madame Alexander dolls came in two sizes and forms – 18in cloth or 8in plastic – and in various versions. The basic Eloise wore a white puffed-sleeve blouse, waistcoat and black pleated skirt with straps, and came with a plush Weenie and a Skipperdee on a leash. The 'Eloise in Paris' dolls were dressed in a white-and-blue striped long-sleeved top with a pleated black skirt. There was also 'Eloise in Moscow', who wore a brown, fluffy coat over her black-and-white outfit, with a matching hat and boots. Earlier Eloise dolls were produced by the American Character Company and Hol-Le Toy. This latter company included an Eloise doll which was an enormous 42in-tall doll

A recent popular character doll is Madeline, based on a small girl who first appeared in a book in 1939 by Ludwig Bemelmans. Madeline was a pupil at a Parisienne school run by nuns: '……in an old house in Paris that was covered with vines lived twelve little girls in two straight lines. In two straight lines they broke their bread and brushed their teeth and went to bed.' The smallest little girl was Madeline, probably aged about five, and she and her friends had simple adventures over a series of books. In the first book, Madeline was taken to hospital to be operated on for appendicitis. In 1996, Eden Toys brought out a series of little dolls dressed as Madeline and her friends, though later the dolls were taken over by Learning Curve. Unfortunately, this company altered the traditional faces and made the dolls too modern, losing the nostalgic charm.

The Eden dolls depicting Madeline and her friends stand 8ins high, and are jointed at the neck, shoulders and hips. Just as in the original illustrations, the dolls' faces have simple features with round dots for eyes, blob noses and painted smiles. Although all the dolls look alike, Madeline can always be identified because she has an appendicitis scar on her tummy! The other dolls in the set include Chloe, Danielle, Nicole and the extremely rare Nona. There is also a little boy called Pepito who is the son of the Spanish Ambassador. Miss Clavel, the kindly nun who looked after the girls, was also made in doll form. Most of the dolls are dressed in variations of their school uniform of tartan dresses or skirts. Madeline also wears a blue coat and white gloves. They have large-brimmed yellow hats and look very chic. Miss Clavel wears a traditional nun's black habit with a wimple and white collar, while Pepito wears a red lace-trimmed jacket, red shorts, black hat and cape. Various 'specials' were also released, some commemorating Easter and Christmas, while others included a series of 'International Traveller' dolls. These depicted Madeline dressed in national costumes from various lands including England, Japan, Ireland and Mexico. In recent years a charming Madeline doll was issued by the Madame Alexander Doll Company. Wearing a yellow hat, white gloves and her smart blue coat with its white collar, this Madeline comes with her little dog, Genevieve. Madeline has inset eyes as opposed to the little dots of the Eden dolls, and a pensive half-smile rather than their U-shaped mouths. Madame Alexander has used its popular, delightful Wendy mould for this doll, as they do for many of their doll issues from children's books.

Matilda, the strange little girl who featured in Roald Dahl's book of the same name, was created in doll form by the American company, Horsman, when the movie came out in 1996. This Matilda was made from vinyl with transfer eyes, a pensive face and glossy brown hair. She wore a dark-blue denim short-sleeved dress with a flower-embroidered bodice, trainers and a bright-red hair ribbon. The box bore a photo of Mara Wilson (who played her in the film) with the words 'Mara Wilson plays Matilda – a little girl who finds the courage and strength to stand up for her.' Also available in the same series by Horsman was Matilda's best friend Amanda, a pigtailed, bespectacled blonde in a smocked, floral print dress. A dress and book set was also available, as was the odd-looking doll, Wanda, owned by Matilda.

Another very strange girl appeared in a set of books by prolific Swedish writer Astrid Lindgren. Her name was Pippi Longstocking – apparently short for Pippilotta Delicatessa Windowshade Mackrelmint Efraim's Daughter Longstocking. In Sweden she is known as 'Pippi Langstrump'. Pippi has bright-red hair styled in two heavy plaits that stick out sideways from her head. The first Pippi Longstocking book was published in the 1940s and raised quite a few eyebrows as the title character was a disobedient, rather unconventional, nine-year-old girl who was prone to ridicule adults. Parents and teachers worried that Pippi was too much of a rebel and wasn't setting a good example to other children. Others, however, regarded her as more of a feminist role model; a confident girl who could more than stand up for herself.

The books have been translated into over 70 languages, and the character has appeared in several films. Many different Pippi Longstocking dolls have appeared over the years, amongst them dolls by Horsman, Madame Alexander, Vogue, Semic and Omega. Designer Helen Kish produced a small limited-edition doll based on the character in the late 1990s. This 8in-high interpretation is jointed at the knees and elbows, in addition to the usual neck, shoulder and hip joints. She wears a multicoloured tiered dress over striped stockings and short leather boots; teaming the outfit with an embroidered denim jacket. The Kish Pippi is accompanied by Mr Nilsson, a plush monkey, who is one of her

Madeline, Madame Alexander.

Matilda, Horsman.

Pippi Longstocking.

Tracy Beaker and Gemma, Golden Bear.

Christopher Robin, R. John Wright.

Heidi, R. John Wright.

Peter, R John Wright.

companions in the books. Pippi Longstocking dolls are not so easy to find in the UK, but are colourful and quirky, so are worth looking out for.

Tracey Beaker is a particularly successful children's book character who appears in the Jacqueline Wilson stories which tell of a ten-year-old girl with attitude who lives in a children's home. The first book, *The Story of Tracy Beaker*, was published in 1991. Tracy's adventures as she searches for a real home and family are funny, yet at the same time very touching. Tracy and her friend Gemma have been produced in doll form by Golden Bear. These small, colourful, long-limbed dolls are made from cloth, with yarn hair and embroidered features. From the point of view of the story doll collector, it is refreshing to be able to obtain a modern literary character in doll form.

One of Britain's best-loved children's book characters is Christopher Robin, who was actually a real child, and the owner of Winnie the Pooh. Christopher appears in the poems and stories written by his father A.A.Milne. Although it is usually the animals from the book that are reproduced in toy form, occasionally Christopher Robin is remembered too, such as in the creations dating from 1998 by R John Wright. Perhaps the most evocative, is that showing Christopher in a loose blue smock over brown shorts, and wearing a wide-brimmed sun hat. He has his faithful bear Pooh for company. R. John Wright also was responsible for the production of 'The Little Prince' from the books by Antoine de Saint-Exupery. The doll had tousled blonde hair, over-long coat with epaulettes, cream trousers and shirt, and carried his sword. Madame Alexander too, has produced Christopher Robin dolls, including an 8in 'Jack doll' wearing a yellow mackintosh, sou'wester and wellington boots, as well as a 12in version using a Lissy doll sculpt, but cropping the hair and dressing the resulting boy in blue shorts and a check top.

Sometimes, books, films and personality dolls cross over; for instance, the dolls which feature the 1930s darling of the movies, Shirley Temple. Shirley starred in several book-related productions, amongst them 'Little Princess', based on the novel *A Little Princess* by Frances Hodgson Burnett, *Susannah of the Mounties* by Muriel Dennison, *Rebecca of Sunnybrook Farm* by Kate Douglas Wiggin and Johanna Spyri's *Heidi*. Various Shirley Temple dolls were later issued as tie-ins with the films, and even today are still occasionally produced. (See Chapter 16.) Heidi, in particular, is a character which is quite popular with manufacturers: already mentioned is the Heidi doll included in Mattel's 'When I Read, I Dream' series. Other Heidi representations include a superb creation by Xenis, carved from Canadian maple wood, and several different types of Heidi dolls which have been made over the years by Madame Alexander.

The R John Wright version, dating from 2000, is particularly stunning. It depicts a young girl wearing a coronet of flowers and holding 'Snowflake', her goat, while the companion doll Peter, in his Swiss outfit of muted colours, also has a goat, with impressive curled horns. In 2008, the company issued 'Grandfather', a 27in figure, made, like the others, from moulded felt. He was seated on a wooden stool. The fine details of these R John Wright dolls just can't be surpassed.

A particularly successful story, told in prose, dates from the 1960s. Called *Where the Wild Things Are*, and written by Maurice Sendak, it tells of a boy named Max who dressed in a wolf suit and misbehaved, so he was sent to his room as punishment. The room turned into a forest and he sailed to a magic island where he met up with some monsters. Apparently, the author based the monsters on his own relatives who used to come to dinner. Max and the monsters indulged in a 'Wild Rumpus' dance. This surreal fantasy was subjected to plenty of criticism when first published. Even so, the clever final phrase, 'And it was still hot' (referring to Max's supper), must have soothed many a scared child when they realised that Max was so loved that his mother had kept his meal warm for him. Soft dolls of Max in his white wolf suit, together with the monsters, have been made by various companies, including Crocodile Creek and Medicom, while Madame Alexander recently produced a cloth Max doll, 9in high, which contains a wire armature so that he can be posed.

Many other characters from books have appeared as dolls over the years, though often it is difficult to decide whether the doll is from the book or is based on the subsequent film. Two unusual dolls which need mentioning are the Beatrix Potter Barbie dolls, dating from the early 2000s. These dolls, though not intended to portray Beatrix Potter herself, are tributes to the writer. Both wear skirts with vignettes from *The Tale of Peter Rabbit*, and one doll has a pink-and-white puffed-sleeve satin top, while the other is in a long-sleeved blue top. These lovely Barbies are a good way to remember Beatrix Potter, as although many of her animal creations have been made over the years, there are few dolls. One of the best-loved series of children's books in Britain is the Railway Series, written by the Rev. W. Awdry. The first of the books, *The Three Railway Engines*, appeared in 1945, and although the series is about trains – most noticeably Thomas the Tank Engine – there is a character called the Fat Controller, who has appeared in doll form, as both a vinyl figure and a 12in plush doll. Another classic series of books is the Narnia series by C.S. Lewis, especially his timeless tale *The Lion, the Witch, and the Wardrobe*. When Walt Disney's epic film, *The Chronicles of Narnia* was released in 2008, designer Robert Tonner, through his collection of Tonner Character Figures, released lifelike portraits of the actors who brought the books to life. Amongst them were William Moseley in the role of Peter Pevensie, Anna Popplewell (Susan Pevensie), Skandar Keynes (Edmund Pevensie) and Georgie Henley who played Lucy Pevensie. The dolls ranged from 13-19in tall, and were authentically dressed in costumes displaying such details as real buttons, lace-up shoes and custom-knit sweaters. Separate coronation costumes were also available for the kings and queens of Narnia, which included intricately moulded crowns, hand-embroidery detailing and luxurious fabrics. This is yet another series which could fit into several categories, as could the mystical *Lord of the Rings* dolls which were issued when the epic films of the books were released, starting with *The Fellowship of the Ring* in 2001. This was followed by *The Two Towers* (2002) and *The Return of the King* (2003). Characters such as Aragon, Eowyn, Frodo Baggins, Arwen Evenstar,

Galadriel, Legolas Greenleaf, Bilbo Baggins and others have been expertly modelled by Applause, Toy Biz and Robert Tonner. In addition, Mattel produced a Barbie and Ken version of Galadriel and Legolas.

During the 1920s and 1930s, a series of books of verse appeared, illustrated in exquisite watercolours and written by Cicely Mary Barker. In 1984 a range of Flower Fairies dolls made by Hornby Hobbies was issued, and today the dolls are very collectable, with the rarest fairies changing hands for high sums. These 6in-high, dainty, vinyl dolls were dressed to resemble those as depicted by Cicely, and had names such as 'Narcissus', 'Hellebore', 'Poppy', 'Bluebell', 'Storksbill', 'Plum', 'Guelder Rose' and 'Sweet Pea'. They had pretty faces and pointed ears, and their costumes were made from taffeta and a suede-effect fabric. These charming costumes contained plenty of detail and often the fairy would come with a magic wand, belt or silver headdress. Other dolls/costumes produced included 'English Rose', 'Fuchsia', 'Bindweed', 'Fumitory', 'Laburnum', 'Daisy', 'Rose', 'Harebell', 'Lavender', 'Blackthorn',' Red Clover', 'Marigold', 'Hazelnut' and 'Christmas Tree'. Later, a range of Flower Pixies also based on the paintings, was released. Amongst the first batch of pixies were, 'Elm', 'Pine', 'Plantain', 'Privet' and 'Thistle', and each wore smart suede-effect jerkins over tights and plastic pointed hats. Sometimes they came with

Flower Fairies, Hornby.

Victoria Plum, Telitoy.

Little Red, Applause.

Perishers, Pedigree.

accessories such as watering cans, rakes or flowerpots. Some pixies are very rare, such as Strawberry and Bluebell. One particularly attractive pixie was the 'Self-Heal' or 'healing pixie', which accompanied the fairy of the same name. This small pixie wore a pink suede-look top with blue sleeves, pink shorts, pale-blue tights and pink wings.

In 2002 Alberon issued a beautiful range of nine large porcelain Flower Fairies dolls, based on Cicely Mary Barker's watercolours. These stood around 14ins high, and their well-detailed costumes, designed by Louise Goldsborough, had shimmering wings attached with press fasteners. These were collectors' dolls and came complete with wooden stands bearing a nameplate. The dolls in the series were 'Blackberry', 'Christmas Tree', 'Marigold', 'Lavender', 'Snowdrop' 'Rose', 'Cowslip', 'Poppy' and 'Daisy'. Not long after they issued the Flower Fairy vinyl dolls, Hornby was responsible for a series of 1980s small dolls dressed as Mabel Lucy Attwell's 'Boo Boos' – fairy folk who appeared in her books and art works.

Another fairy character, Victoria Plum, was the subject of a series of books written by broadcaster Angela Rippon during the 1980s. This is another doll which could fit into an alternative category, as she came into being after Angela was shown a series of greetings cards drawn by Roger Hutchings, a director of the W. N. Sharpe Company. Angela was asked to create a background for the character and to write a series of children's stories. The first book was *Victoria Gives a Flying Lesson*, and tells of the novice fairy and her elf friend, Ben. It wasn't long before Victoria Plum appeared in the shops as a doll. Angela's creation had auburn, frizzy hair, a cheeky face, snub nose and no wings – far removed from the traditional concept of a fairy. She was dressed in purple flower petals and wore a large white hat fashioned from the flower of a bindweed. Her pointed shoes had bobbles on the toes. Most of the dolls were made by Telitoy and are distinctive with round, brown eyes and 'water-melon' curved mouths. The dolls have short brown hair and some feature a strangely-shaped flat head. One of the nicest dolls – and the one that bears most resemblance to the character as illustrated in the books – is a 6in-tall Victoria Plum. Wearing the burgundy shade featured in many of the illustrations, she also sports a very realistic large pale-pink-and-white hat, which perfectly resembles a bindweed flower with a green stalk. This doll has curly chestnut hair (as shown in the book) and her box is labelled Telitoy. Other dolls were issued in this range, including an excellent version of Ben.

Dolls depicting characters from comics and newspaper cartoons can sometimes be found, such as Minnie the Minx and Dennis the Menace, both from *The Beano* comic, published by D. C. Thompson. The long-running Peanuts cartoon comic strip, serialised in many newspapers, needs no introduction, and dolls based on the characters are often seen. Charlie Brown, his dog Snoopy and the other members of the gang were created by Charles M. Schulz and made their debut in 1950. Although the main character is Snoopy, a loveable white beagle with black ears, the children have proved almost as popular with manufacturers. Several of them have appeared as vinyl dolls created by

Madame Alexander, United Features, Boucher Associates and others. Additionally, a range of soft-cloth dolls have been made by companies such as Golden Bear and Kohl's. With such an interesting range of children to depict, amongst them Linus, Lucy, Schroeder, Marcie, Peppermint Patty, PigPen, Sally, Franklin and of course, Charlie Brown, it's more than probable that further dolls will appear. Charlie Brown, the main child, has a head shaped like a billiard ball, and usually wears a jumper with a zigzag pattern around the hem. He seems to come off worse in most adventures, and even his dog Snoopy gets the better of him. Lucy bosses him around, while his small sister Sally teases him. Charlie is a kind-hearted boy, and rather vulnerable. Amazingly, the Peanuts gang has appeared in over 2,600 different worldwide newspapers since their debut 60 years ago.

A similar idea to Peanuts was a picture strip called The Perishers, which first appeared in the *Daily Mail* in 1958, written by Maurice Dodd and drawn by Dennis Collins. Centring around a streetwise boy called Wellington, his shaggy dog Boot, and a small gang of children who live in the fictional town of Croynge (a cross between Croydon and Penge), the cartoon strips continued until 2006. The main character, Wellington, is a bit of a worrier, and is a resourceful, thoughtful, rather gloomy boy who lives in a disused railway station with his dog. Wellington earns funds by building and selling soapbox carts, and his friends include Maisie, Marlon, and Baby Grumpling. Maisie loves Marlon, though all Marlon can say about that is 'Yeuk'. Marlon is rather dim, though would quite like to become a brain surgeon, or perhaps 'A-Bloke-What-Goes-Down-Sewers-In-Big-Rubber-Boots'. As for Maisie's little brother, Baby Grumpling, his angelic looks belie a devilish temperament and constant hunger. He enjoys upsetting his cronies, has a neat line in philosophy and is the inventor of such delicacies as the worm sandwich. In the 1970s, Pedigree brought out a delightful set of dolls of the main characters. The dolls were around 15ins tall, and were soft-bodied with vinyl heads and hands. They are fairly difficult to find today.

American comic books, published by such companies as Marvel and D.C. Comics, have spawned a whole range of dolls over the decades, including Batman, Superman, Spiderman, Wonder Woman and others alongside their sidekicks and enemies. Many of the dolls have been sold as children's toys, although some are intended especially for collectors, such as a series of limited editions by the Tonner Doll Company. Most of the toy versions endured rough handling by their young owners, so if you can find pristine or boxed versions, they are certainly worth acquiring for your collection and might even appreciate in value. Another famous American strip cartoon character was Annie, the young girl who lived in an orphanage and was adopted by a millionaire. When the Annie stage musical and the film came out, they were accompanied by plenty of doll memorabilia; so much that Chapter 18 has been devoted to Annie and her friends.

Chapter Three

Dolls Representing Characters in Fairy Tales and Nursery Rhymes

A S YOU might expect, hundreds of different nursery rhyme character dolls have been created over the years – but surprisingly, the vast majority seem intended for adults rather than children. And although so many of them have appeared, most feature the same few favourite rhymes again and again, so it is always exciting to come across dolls dressed as more obscure nursery rhyme characters. Probably the most popular character of all is 'Little Bo Peep'. Additionally, 'Little Miss Muffet', 'Mary, Mary, Quite Contrary' and' Mary Had A Little Lamb', are also regularly portrayed by doll designers. No doubt much of the attraction is because these characters can easily be recognised on account of their props: crook and sheep; spider and bowl; watering can and flowers; lamb.

A series of nursery rhyme dolls were made by the Shallowpool doll company in the 1960s and 70s. Shallowpool was a cottage industry based in Cornwall, which made small costume dolls with plaster faces and padded-wire bodies. Many of their dolls were 7in-high traditional Cornish characters, but the majority of the nursery rhyme dolls were slightly smaller, at 6in. Amongst them, apart from the ubiquitous 'Little Miss Muffet', 'Mary Mary' and 'Little Bo Peep', were 'Tom, Tom the Piper's Son' (complete with pig), and 'Simple Simon'. They had accessories made from plaster of Paris. 'Old Mother Hubbard' was 8in high and came complete with her little dog on a ribbon lead. This rather unusual doll wore a long, floral full-skirted dress with a white lace-edged pinafore and had curly white hair and spectacles.

Companies which manufacturer collectable porcelain and vinyl dolls, such as Knightsbridge, Leonardo, Alberon and Ashton-Drake, regularly turn to the world of nursery rhymes, and renowned doll designer Dianna Effner has been responsible for many series, as has artist Wendy Lawton. Dianna takes inspiration from both popular favourites like 'Jack and Jill' and 'Little Boy Blue' and the more unusual rhymes such as 'Curlylocks, Curlylocks'. She was also responsible for a pair of dolls depicting the good and the bad child from the poem *There Was a Little Girl* by Henry Wadsworth Longfellow. The version we are most familiar with is:

Old Mother Hubbard, Shallowpool.

Mary, Mary, Quite Contrary, (Dianna Effner) Ashton-Drake.

There was a little girl,
And she had a little curl,
Right in the middle of her forehead.
When she was good,
She was very, very good,
But when she was bad she was horrid.

The two little girl dolls Dianna created from this rhyme are both known as 'Girl with a Curl'. One depicts a cross-looking child holding a broken pot of flowers, while the other is a good child with an unbroken pot. Her dolls have appeared in both large and small sizes, and are full of delightful details and appropriate props, such as the rather cheeky red-headed little boy who features in 'Snips and Snails', and holds a bright-green spotted-frog.

What are little boys made of?
Snips and snails and puppy dog's tails.
That's what little boys are made of.

Dianna later went on to produce a set of delightful, quirky, modern, ball-jointed dolls for Ashton-Drake. They are 12in high and trendily dressed, in contrast to the usual nursery rhyme outfits which seem set in the 1800s. Dianna's 'Mary, Mary', inspired by the rhyme 'Mary, Mary, quite contrary, how does your garden grow?' is much more up to date. She wears a tiered, floral dress, blue-striped leggings, a large red hat and has a mass of red curly hair. This Mary is a very modern miss. Others in this unusual series are mentioned further on in this chapter. Dianna also started designing for the American company Nancy Ann Storybook. Her solemn-faced porcelain dolls, just 6¼-in high, include many more difficult to source rhymes, amongst them 'I saw A Ship A-Sailing', 'Roses Are Red, Violets Are Blue', 'Lavender's Blue, Dilly Dilly' and 'Twinkle, Twinkle Little Star'. The company Lee Middleton, makers of large vinyl baby dolls, has included several nursery rhyme inspired babies in its range. The attractive well-made dolls have appeared dressed as characters such as 'Mary Had a Little Lamb'.

One of the most famous nursery rhyme doll characters of recent years is feisty Bo Peep from the animated Disney film *Toy Story*. The doll in the film is far from demure, in spite of her feminine, pink-and-white dress, and all she wants is the hapless cowboy Woody – often using her crook to hook him. Mattel made several versions of the Bo Peep doll wearing her pretty dress and matching bonnet. Another child-friendly doll is Barbie Bo Peep from the Children's Collector Series, which was issued in 1996. Barbie is prettily dressed in a pink gown with a glittery skirt decorated with rosebuds and vines, a lace decorated bonnet and ankle-length pantaloons. Her long hair is styled in ringlets and she carries a white shepherd's crook. Back in the 1950s an unusual little clockwork doll was made by the Wells/Brimtoy company. Just a few inches tall, she represented 'Mary Had a Little Lamb' and her lamb clipped onto her skirt, following her, just as it says in the rhyme. Also in the 1950s, Pedigree manufactured a series of 7in, hard plastic 'Delite' costume dolls with the unusual feature of fingers spread wide, known to today's collectors as 'starfish' hands. These little dolls included 'Mary Had a Little Lamb', 'Wee Willie Winkie' 'Jack and Jill' and 'Little Bo-Peep', while the 1970s saw the introduction of various soft-plastic nursery rhyme characters made by Bluebox, such as 'Jack and Jill'.

The American company, Effanbee, has introduced many attractive vinyl nursery rhyme dolls over the years, including 'Mother Goose' and 'The Queen of Hearts', while the enchanting 7in-high Wendy dolls, from Madame Alexander, often appear dressed as children from nursery rhymes. They feature unusual characters too, for instance, 'Pussycat, Pussycat', 'Rock-a-Bye Baby', 'Three Blind Mice', 'I'm a Little Teapot', 'Pease Pudding Hot', 'Starlight, Starbright', 'Three Little Kittens' and 'Hickory Dickory Dock'. Jellycat, a company who specialise in cloth dolls, has produced several enchanting nursery rhyme characters. All Jellycat dolls are brightly and innovatively dressed, and though their faces are rather unconventional, they are still interesting additions to a nursery rhyme collection. During the 1960s, 70s and 80s, Worthing-based company, Rexard, which specialised in small, hard-plastic souvenir character dolls, distributed hundreds of different designs, usually dressed in national or historical costume, to tourist outlets and corner shops. Later, the company introduced a selection of prettily dressed vinyl nursery rhyme characters designed by Odette Arden. 'Miss Muffet', 'Mary Had A Little Lamb', and 'Mary, Mary' were just a few of the characters available. Each bore a swing tag with the appropriate nursery rhyme inside.

Burbank, a short-lived British company dating from the 1970s, created a range of bean-filled dolls which represented storybook characters and children from nursery rhymes. These cuddly 11in-high characters were very popular, and were packaged in beautifully designed boxes featuring colourful drawings of other dolls available. Although the dolls' heads and hands were made from vinyl, the bodies were cloth and stuffed with beans, so that they could be posed. Characters such as 'Wee Willie Winkie','Little Boy Blue', 'Little Miss Muffet', 'Little Jack Horner', 'Little Bo-Peep' and 'Ring-a-Ring-a-Roses' proved extremely popular, especially with toddlers. Toddlers also like musical dolls, as do many adult collectors, and so Green Tree's soft-bodied nursery character range which plays various nursery rhymes is worth looking out for. An unusual, double-side cloth doll made by Toy Works appeared in the 1980s and was sold together with a rag story book. The doll was based on a traditional rhyme:

> Little Bobby Snooks was fond of his books,
> And loved by his Usher and Master;
> But naughty Jack Spry, he got a black eye,
> And carries his nose in a plaster.

The doll depicted Bobby dressed smartly on one side, carrying his books, but when he was turned over a dishevelled, patched version of Jack with a plaster on his nose was revealed.

It's impossible to include all the types of nursery rhyme dolls available, but those by American designer Suzanne Gibson deserve a mention. Released as vinyl editions in two sizes through Reeves International in the 1980s, the 16in-high dolls included 'Mother Goose' and 'Little Bo Peep', while amongst the 8in range were 'Polly Put the Kettle On', 'Mary Had a Little Lamb' and 'Little Miss Muffet'. In 1998 Suzanne Gibson produced a limited edition vinyl 'Baa Baa Black Sheep' girl doll with an unusual, pointed face and large eyes. She had a mass of curly hair, wore a blue smock over yellow-and-black-check trousers, a large red straw hat, and came with a black Steiff sheep. Felt modeller R John Wright has included many nursery rhyme dolls in his range. Amongst them are 'Jack and Jill', 'Little Boy Blue', 'Little Miss Muffet' and 'Mary, Mary Quite Contrary.' Particularly unusual were the models of 'Wynken, Blynken and Nod', based on a nursery poem written in 1889 by Eugene Field, which tells the story of three fishermen going to sea in a shoe, and begins:

> Wynken, Blynken, and Nod one night
> Sailed off in a wooden shoe
> Sailed on a river of crystal light
> Into a sea of dew.

Bo–Peep from Toy Story, Mattel.

Wynken, Blynken and Nod, R. John Wright.

Bobby Snooks Toy Works.

Red Riding Hood (Dianna Effner), Ashton Drake

Goldilocks and Baby Bear, R. John Wright.

'In the Hood' and 'Breaking and Entering' (Kickits), Robert Tonner.

Goldilocks and Red Riding Hood (Dianna Effner), Ashton–Drake.

Fairy-tale dolls are also popular with designers and manufactures, and probably the most popular character of all is Little Red Riding Hood, presumably because she is easy to recognise in her red cloak and with her basket of goodies. There must be hundreds of depictions of this character in doll form, in all kinds of medium. Other popular fairy-tale dolls are Snow White, Cinderella and Sleeping Beauty. As with the nursery rhyme figures, the dolls are made by many different manufacturers, and although the majority (especially those featuring Disney versions of the characters) are intended for children, there are still many types produced for collectors. Once again, Dianna Effner has produced a quantity of delightful fairy-tale figures for companies such as Ashton-Drake, while Leonardo and other companies have issued characters too.

Effanbee created a delightful range of fairy-tale dolls in the 1990s featuring the favourite solemn-faced Patsy dolls, and the Madame Alexander Doll Company often includes fairy-tale dolls in their Wendy lines. Burbank created a delightful series of fairy-tale, bean-filled vinyl-headed dolls in the 1970s – similar to their nursery rhyme set of dolls – which came in a box shaped like a book. When the box was opened, it revealed the doll in a 3D setting with cardboard cut-outs. For instance, Little Red Riding Hood featured a wolf, and Cinderella, the glass slipper. R John Wright has, as might be expected, made several fairy-tale characters, including some unusual dolls such as 'Babes in the Wood'. These particular felt dolls, which stand 17in tall, were released in 2007, and have mohair wigs and hand-painted features. Made in just 100 sets, they are based on the artwork of American illustrator Jessie Willcox Smith. Their traditional outfits are made from cotton and felt, and their shoes are leather. Also from R John Wright are Goldilocks, Snow White – complete with her seven dwarf friends – Cinderella and Little Red Riding Hood. Needless to say, all are superbly modelled; the Goldilocks doll in particular, is very demure in her smocked dress and carrying a basket of daisies. This doll was released in 2008 in a limited edition of 350.

In the 2000s the White Balloon Company issued a superb and unusual set of four fairy-tale dolls, which were 20in high and made from high-quality vinyl (although the first doll in the series was porcelain). Cinderella, Sleeping Beauty, Snow White and Rapunzel were modelled by Linda Mason, and wore well-detailed costumes with charming accessories, such as a 'glass' slipper for Cinderella. Though rather large to display, they are nice additions to a fairy-tale collection. The auburn-haired Sleeping Beauty doll was particularly attractive. Linda Mason's gorgeous fairy-tale doll wore an elaborate, mauve, shimmery gown with gold highlights, and had a gleaming flower tiara. Even larger were Annette Himstedt's German versions of Cinderella, 'Aschenputtel', which were produced in 2003, and, as with all Himstedt dolls were of exceptional quality and beauty. The two dolls depicted the poor Cinderella and the ball-gowned version. This version of the story had Aschenputtel's stepmother set her the seemingly impossible task of picking peas out of ashes to prevent her from going to the ball. However, a pair of white doves came to her rescue, enabling her to complete the task. Annette Himstedt illustrated this scene in a limited edition of 35in-tall vinyl dolls which wore lilac work dresses and clogs, and came complete with trays of peas. Each doll had a dove to assist her with the task. By contrast, the 'Rich Cinderella', also by Annette Himstedt, wore a sumptuous blue velvet and lace gown, with tulle and metallic lacy wings, and came with white porcelain slippers and a dove. The German version of the folk tale explains how the doves also help Aschenputtel when she is sad because she only has rags to wear. They provide her with beautiful dresses and shoes, thus enabling her to go to the three balls being held for the prince to choose a bride. Sadly, rising costs and falling sales forced Annette Himstedt's factory to close in 2008.

The renowned designer Robert Tonner, who produces many character dolls, has issued his own versions of some of the stories, the most unusual being in the 8in 'Kickits' series, giving different humorous takes on characters from rhyme, story book, legend and tradition. For instance, 'Breaking and Entering' depicts an innocent-looking little girl prettily dressed in white frills and pink-striped socks. She holds a small bear, and though there is no mention of the story, it's obvious that she is meant to represent Goldilocks, and, just as Tonner's punning title suggests, *did* break into their cottage to eat the porridge. Another Tonner Kickits doll is 'In the Hood', which depicts Little Red Riding Hood in a completely different way, in a white, long-sleeved smock over a red-and-yellow floral skirt and matching long bloomers. She has a red cloak, striped stockings and carries a basket. These Kickit dolls are all jointed at the knees, hence the 'Kickits' name, which means they sit well for display.

Dianna Effner's quirky Ashton-Drake 12in ball-joint dolls not only included 'Mary, Mary', but also Goldilocks, Little Red Riding Hood and Alice in Wonderland. Goldilocks, as you have never seen her before, wears a sage-green 'Goldie Girl' T-shirt, with a denim jacket, printed cotton tiered skirt, sage tights and fur-lined boots. She sports a jaunty blue crocheted beret with an orange flower over her tumbling golden locks, and carries a denim bag with a teddy bear motif. Dianna has given her a delightfully cheeky expression with a snub nose and quizzical smile. Solemn-faced Little Red Riding Hood is dressed slightly more traditionally in a cream long-sleeved blouse and brown laced-bodice over a print skirt and apron; though the skirt is far shorter than usually depicted. She also wears lacy cream tights, smart suede lace-up boots, and, of course, her red-hooded cloak. Her hair is a mass of rich brunette curls, and she carries a basket filled with flowers. Alice in Wonderland can be seen in Chapter 19.

Amongst the many fairy-tale offerings from Mattel is a delightful set in the 'Storybook Favourites' range dating from 2001 with Barbie's young sister Kelly dressed as Goldilocks. She is packaged in a window-fronted box together with a bowl of porridge, a baby bear and his tiny chair. Also in the range are Hansel and Gretel and Little Red Riding Hood. Hansel and Gretel are not seen so frequently as character dolls, though Madame Alexander has produced sets. A stunning porcelain, limited edition set consisting of Hansel, Gretel and the Witch, designed by German doll artist Ruth Treffeisen, has the children crafted as 26in-high figures and an admirably warty 33in-high Witch. Ruth Treffeisen has designed many other top-quality collectors' dolls, amongst them Snow White and the dwarfs, the Snow Queen and Alice in Wonderland.

In 1984 Steiff, renowned for its teddy bears, issued a delightful limited edition set of three bears, together with a pretty Goldilocks doll dressed in red. As well as the quirky Dianna Effner Goldilocks referred to earlier, Goldilocks was also the chosen subject of another, earlier, Ashton-Drake production designed by

Cinderella (Dianna Effner), Ashton Drake.

her. Made from porcelain, she was dressed in a blue floral frock with bright-red shoes, and carried a brimming bowl of porridge and a wooden spoon. As mentioned previously, Effner is a particularly renowned designer, and has dozens of character dolls to her credit. All feature her own special distinctive style, combining charm and originality. She has been making dolls for over thirty years, after studying sculpture and ceramics. She has designed for many companies, notably Ashton-Drake, and now has her own company. The Goldilocks doll was in a set called 'Storybook Miniatures', which featured both fairy-tale and nursery rhyme dolls. This set, based on an earlier, larger range of dolls, was produced in the mid-1990s, and amongst the prettiest dolls were the two versions of Cinderella, depicting her in rags and in her ball gown. Wearing an apron over her tattered dress and a headscarf to protect her blonde curls, she busily wielded her broom. The ball gown version was enchanting in a blue satin lace-trimmed gown with a white pannier overskirt trimmed with flowers. She had her glass slipper.

The name invariably linked to fairytales is that of Walt Disney. Over the years the company has made films of many of the great stories, including Snow White, Cinderella, Sleeping Beauty and Rapunzel, and has issued thousands of dolls as tie-ins. (*See Chapter 5.*) Other manufacturers have made character dolls under licence from Disney. Most Disney animated films featuring human characters have a doll tie-in. This tradition started with Disney's first feature film in 1937 starring everyone's favourite heroine, Snow White. Companies such as Chad Valley were quick to capitalise on the idea of media memorabilia. Today, a Chad Valley Snow White, together with her seven dwarfs, in mint condition and boxed, could cost you several thousands of pounds. But don't despair. There are many other versions of Snow White around, including some made by Mattel. One very pretty model has her in her famous blue and yellow gown, but if you remove the skirt and sleeves there she is in her tattered dress, ready to look after the cottage for the dwarfs. (*See Chapter 20.*)

Chapter Four

Dolls Representing Characters in Films

THIS IS a very popular theme for doll makers and covers a bevy of characters, though as usual, there is a cross over, especially with characters from books and cartoons. Some of our most glamorous and iconic film stars are immortalised as dolls; top star names, from Elizabeth Taylor to Bette Davies and from Marilyn Monroe to Audrey Hepburn are usually dressed for one of their most famous roles and can all be found with a bit of searching. Although these are recent dolls, many classic film stars were issued as dolls back in the 1930s – the era of stars such as Deanna Durbin, ice-skater-cum-movie-queen Sonja Henie, and of course, Shirley Temple, who has Chapter 16 devoted to her.

Unlike Shirley Temple, Deanna Durbin (born Edna Mae Durbin in Winnipeg, Canada in 1921) didn't break into movies as a young child. It was when she and her parents moved to California that her light, pure classical-type singing voice started to attract attention. At the age of 14 she signed a contract with MGM which resulted in a 1936 short film, *Every Sunday,* in which she was joined by another newcomer, Judy Garland. She then signed with Universal, and a series of films followed. While still 14, Deanna was tested for the lead voice in the classic animated cartoon *Snow White and the Seven Dwarfs,* but Walt Disney turned her down, saying that she sounded 'too mature'.

It wasn't long before Deanna – 'Winnipeg's Sweetheart' – was a major star, becoming so well-loved that in 1942, a seven-day Deanna Durbin Festival was held throughout Britain, during which her films were screened exclusively on the Odeon Theatre Circuit. This accolade has never been awarded to any other star. In all, Deanna starred in 21 movies in 12 years.

The Ideal Toy Company arranged for famous doll designer, Bernard Lipfert – who had achieved such success with the earlier Shirley Temple dolls – to sculpt Deanna's likeness. Ideal claimed that the resulting doll was the 'first teenage doll in history'. The doll was made of composition and came in various sizes from 15in through to 25in, and was available in a choice of 16 outfits, all based on costumes featured in her various films. Attached to her clothing was a lithographed badge bearing a photo of the star and her signature, and she was packed in a labelled gift box. These very pretty Deanna Durbin dolls had glassene sleep eyes, human-hair wigs and smiling mouths revealing tiny teeth.

They were marked 'Deanna Durbin' on the neck and 'Ideal' on the back, and reached the stores in autumn 1938. That Christmas, it was almost impossible to find one. The dolls were manufactured into the 1940s. Even today vintage Deanna Dolls are in great demand, not only by doll collectors but also by fans of the girl with the beautiful voice. Consequently they are expensive. Despite her amazing success, Deanna was a very private person and she was never happy with the attention she received. At the age of 27, she simply walked away from fame and now lives anonymously in France. According to the BBC, they receive more requests to broadcast Deanna Durbin films and recordings than they do for any other star of Hollywood's Golden Age.

Dolls from the movies is a wide-ranging field and one that becomes more popular all the time, with some designers, such as American Robert Tonner, creating 'mini film epics', often producing several characters from one movie, in all their various costumes. Tonner, who specialises in collectors' dolls, ensures their costumes are as accurate as he can make them, right down to the smallest detail. The faces are skilfully modelled so that they really do resemble the person they portray. His dolls include most of the main characters from the Harry Potter series of films, as well as *The Wizard of Oz, Pirates of the Caribbean, The Lord of the Rings* and many others. In 2009 he introduced a collection of dolls and outfits as tributes to three American iconic film stars, Bette Davies, Ava Gardner and Joan Crawford. The resemblance of the dolls to the stars is unmistakable, and each doll is approximately 16in tall with 13 points of articulation, so that it can recreate the poses of its alter ego.

Another classic actress was the naughty Mae West, darling of 1930s cinema audiences. She whisked them into a frenzy with her sultry, witty phrases, including such gems as 'When I'm good I'm very, very good, but when I'm bad, I'm better'; 'To err is human but it feels divine' and 'I never worry about diets. The only carrots that interest me are the number you get in a diamond'. Perhaps the most famous phrase attributed to her is 'Come up and see me sometime', though this was actually a combination of quotes, so isn't strictly true. The American company Effanbee created Mae West in doll form in their Legends series, in 1982. Labelled the 'Come up and see me sometime gal', this lookalike wears a beautiful long, black lace gown and fur stole. She also has a sparkly necklace, large feather-trimmed hat and carries a cane. In 1991 the Hamilton Collection issued a vinyl-headed soft-body version of a Mae West doll for collectors which was equally stunning.

One of the best-loved classic films is the epic *Gone With the Wind*, which first appeared in 1939. Many of the characters have since been depicted in doll form by various companies, including Mattel which issued a series in their 2001 'Timeless Treasures' range. Amongst them was Vivien Leigh, who was renowned for her performance as Scarlet O'Hara. An earlier series dating from 1994 from Mattel, featured a set of Barbie dolls dressed as Scarlet O'Hara in various outfits, amongst them gowns in black and white, pale-green floral print, green velvet and red velvet, all as seen in the film. The Tonner Doll Company, too, has issued many dolls from *Gone With the Wind*, all with amazing facial

Mary Poppins, Robert Tonner.

Deanna Durbin, Ideal.

Mae West, Effanbee.

Mary Poppins, Effanbee.

My Fair Lady, Mattel.

Gone With The Wind, Mattel.

Brigitta Von Trapp, Madame Alexander.

likeness to the actual actresses – and main actor. For also included is 'Rhett Butler', played in the film by Clark Gable.

An elegant doll wearing the classic, black Givenchy dress, pearl choker and tiara sported by Holly Golightly (Audrey Hepburn) in the 1961 movie *Breakfast at Tiffany's* was issued in 1998 by Mattel. This doll bore a good facial likeness to Hepburn, and was also obtainable in the pink suit from the same film. During the 1990s the Mattel company made dolls depicting her in another of her famous roles – Eliza Doolittle from *My Fair Lady*. These Eliza dolls could be obtained in various costumes, amongst them the frilled, pink tea gown, the flower girl outfit, the ivory gown adorned with rhinestones worn at the Embassy ball, and the iconic black-and-white Ascot costume, complete with enormous hat. In 1996 Mattel came up trumps with an excellent 'Henry Higgins' as played by Rex Harrison. Dressed in his tweeds, Henry is depicted as the typical aristocratic gentleman. A much earlier Rex Harrison doll can sometimes be found; a soft-bodied, dark-suited creation representing his character from the 1967 movie *Doctor Doolittle*. This doll, which was a child's toy rather than a collector's item, was also made by Mattel.

Back in the 1960s there was an enormous furore when Julie Andrews, who starred in the stage version of *My Fair Lady*, lost the film role to Audrey Hepburn. Yet it helped Julie, too, because she was soon starring in the blockbuster *Mary Poppins*. As this film was aimed at children, play dolls appeared on the market, as well as the more expensive collectors' types. Several companies, amongst them Mattel, Effanbee, Peggy Nisbet, Semco, Tonner and Disney, have made Mary Poppins dolls depicting the outfits worn by Julie Andrews in the film. Some of the play dolls didn't have an accurate facial likeness, but the majority of those intended for the collector's market were excellent, such as a pretty 2008 Mattel doll with Mary in the white dress and hat, worn on the day she rode on the carousel. This doll bore a particularly good likeness to Julie Andrews. Her co-star, Dick Van Dyke, as Bert, could be purchased separately, as could the two children, Jane and Michael, which were also excellent replications. The packaging included cardboard horses in the boxes, with the dolls seated upon them. Tonner dolls representing Julie Andrews in her role as Mary Poppins appeared in 2008, and could be obtained with various outfits. Probably the most iconic was a 16in-high model which featured her famous get-up of long coat, large bag, felt hat, knitted scarf and, of course, an umbrella with a parrot-head handle.

Another classic actress from a child's film was Judy Garland in *The Wizard of Oz*, and several companies, amongst them Mattel, Tonner and Ideal, have commemorated her wearing the distinctive blue gingham dress and red sparkly shoes. The very first Judy Garland doll was released by the Ideal Novelty and Toy Company in 1939, and she was made from composition in various sizes. The doll was another designed by Bernard Lipfert, who was responsible for many classic dolls including Shirley Temple, Deanna Durbin and Sonja Henie. Judy's costume was designed by Mary Bauer. The Ideal Judy Garland dolls are very much sought after by Garland fans nowadays. It would be quite possible for a collector to fill several cabinets just with dolls issued over the years dressed in that famous blue gingham dress. It is interesting how some actresses appeal to the manufacturers (and doll enthusiasts) more than others, and how, often, it is one particular costume which makes them 'iconic' and is issued over and over again. For instance, Judy Garland in blue gingham from *The Wizard of Oz*, Marilyn Monroe in her white, pleated dress from *The Seven Year Itch* and Shirley Temple in the red-spotted frock from *Stand Up and Cheer*.

One of the best-loved post-war musicals is *The Sound of Music*, 1965, starring Julie Andrews, though surprisingly, it didn't generate all that many dolls considering there were plenty of children in the film. It was based on the novel *The Story of the Trapp Family Singers* by Maria Von Trapp and contained many, now famous, and favourite, songs. Madame Alexander issued several sets of dolls dressed as characters from *The Sound of Music*, from the mid-1960s onwards. In 1965 a set of large dolls featured a 17in 'Maria' and the children, and was a tie-in with 20th Century- Fox. This pretty doll had blue sleep eyes and dark blonde hair. She wore a full-skirted print dress with an apron, and was marked 'Madame Alexander 1965'. There were seven dolls in the set, the others being the children, Brigitta, Liesel and Louisa at 14in high, and Friedrich, Gretyl, and Marta, at 11in high. All the children were beautifully dressed in typical Swiss cotton skirts, white blouses and colourful bodices. Friedrich wore lederhosen. Sets of smaller dolls were later issued, including ones in the 1970s and 1990s, but none seem to be particularly easy to find today. In 1995 Mattel issued a collectors' edition Barbie doll as Maria in their 'Hollywood Legends' Collection. Dressed in a jacquard brocade top with a floral printed skirt, and with a straw hat as a finishing touch, she had cropped hair as in the film, and carried a guitar.

Elizabeth Taylor was a major, iconic star, and perhaps her most famous role was that of Cleopatra in the 1960s film of the same name. Elizabeth, in her stunning Egyptian-style costume, headdress and extravagant eye make-up had never looked so amazingly beautiful, and the movie was famous for triggering a passionate love affair between Liz and her co-star Richard Burton. The tabloid headlines screamed 'Going For a Burton' as the public followed the blossoming romance between two much-loved film stars. Four decades later Mattel issued a *Cleopatra* Elizabeth Taylor doll wearing her magnificent golden costume re-created in splendid detail, and complete with a dramatic 'feather' cloak that surrounded her like the wings of a bird. According to the Mattel company, 'Her spectacular headdress features cobra symbols that protect royalty, a sun disk enclosed in horns identifying her with the goddess Isis, and a large double feather representing cosmic harmony'. Great pains were taken with the facial likeness, from the incredibly fine glitter eye shadow and heavy kohl liner, to the exact shade of violet for her eyes. The company issued other Elizabeth Taylor dolls too, but nothing as stunning as Cleopatra.

Marilyn Monroe has been depicted many times in doll form, and by far the favourite costume is the white pleated dress she wore in *The Seven Year Itch*, as mentioned above. However, many other costumes have appeared too. Mattel has produced several Barbie-sized versions, amongst them a long, shapely, pink sheath-dress from *Gentlemen Prefer Blondes* and a stunning scarlet Lurex gown with a split front from the same film, as well as the white dress in *The Seven Year Itch* .This set of three was released in 1997 and the facial likeness was excellent. In 2002 Mattel issued a doll wearing the 'Happy Birthday Mr President' gown, and another in the deep magenta evening gown from *How To Marry a Millionaire*. Seven years later along came 'Barbie as Marilyn Monroe' in a plunge-neck gold gown, inspired by one created for her by American costume designer William Travilla.

Another prolific producer of Marilyn Monroe dolls is Franklin Mint, which has produced well over 30 different dolls in both porcelain and vinyl. The dolls feature dresses inspired by many of her films, including some unusual outfits. Amongst them is the dress she wore to make her mark in the cement outside Graumann's Chinese Theatre in Los Angeles, a gown she wore at an awards ceremony, and the white ballerina outfit in the famous photo taken by Milton H. Greene. This latter doll is a seated version and the modelling is superb. Other companies, notably DSI Inc. have issued ranges of Marilyn dolls, too. The prolific Mattel company has also issued dolls that represent James Dean and Grace Kelly, as well as producing a gift set featuring Rock Hudson and Doris Day as they appeared the 1950s movie *Pillow Talk*. Doris Day wears a white gown with a matching clutch bag and elbow-length gloves. Her blonde hair is styled to resemble her movie look. Rock Hudson wears a smart classic suit and white shirt.

Amongst the more quirky famous film star dolls issued over the years is one from Mattel which depicted a scene from Alfred Hitchcock's suspense movie *The Birds*. The doll came out in 1963 and was a model of Tippi Hedron who played the ill-fated heroine Melanie Daniels, wearing her green suit with several menacing black birds attached! (Apparently, that particular scene in the film took almost a week to shoot and the birds were attached to the actress by nylon threads so that they couldn't escape.) Other unusual dolls include the 2011 release from Madame Alexander –Tony Curtis in two outfits from the *Some Like It Hot,* which also starred Marilyn Monroe. The 21in doll is fully articulated, and boasts a Hollywood tan. Dressed in character as Joe, also known as 'Shell Oil Junior', he wears a navy-blue double- breasted blazer with gold buttons, teamed with beige-striped trousers. He comes with a black suitcase with a pink handle and a *Some Like It Hot* logo. Inside is a set of clothes to transform him into his female persona. The clothes include a short-sleeved, black georgette 'flapper' dress trimmed with black sequin insets, beige net neck inset and a black fringe at the hips and hem – and, of course, just like in the movie, a gold saxophone!

Maybe even more quirky – certainly scary – are the 1990s figures made by Sideshow Collectables of actors from famous horror movies. Amongst them is a very creepy 12in Lon Chaney in the starring role in the 1925 film *Phantom of the Opera*. Others in the series include characters from *Frankenstein* and *Dracula*. If you decide to collect this type of doll, it might not be really advisable to display them in a room you use to relax in because you could get a terrible fright if you

Lon Chaney Phantom of the Opera, Sideshow.

Titanic, Mattel.

James Bond Barbie Set, Mattel.

Captain Jack Sparrow, Elizabeth Swann and
Will Turner, Robert Tonner.

look up unexpectedly and see one of these hideous faces leering at you. Perhaps it would be better to wrap them up well and put them in a box out of sight in a spare room!

Jumping a few decades – filmwise, though not historically – blockbuster movie *Titanic* featured one special scene which was to stay in many people's memories. Who can forget the moment when Kate Winslet as Rose DeWitt Bukater stood at the prow of the great ship with her elegant arms outstretched and the wind blowing her hair? The Franklin Mint company produced a 17in porcelain doll wearing the long, midnight-blue velvet gown and cream crepe shawl, just as depicted in that 'flying scene'. The doll came with a faux pearl necklace, earrings and a butterfly hair decoration, and her dress was elaborately embroidered. Mattel later recreated this scene with a beautiful Barbie-sized doll, though this one wore a copy of Kate's elegant wine-red gown with black lace overlay. The doll was cleverly mounted in the box by a cardboard rail that resembled the rail from the ship, posing just as in the film. In 1998 Galoob produced a limited edition 12½in doll in that same iconic gown and which came with a certificate of authenticity, while Franklin Mint created a stunning 16in-high vinyl 'Rose Titanic' doll in the red dress, complete with replica jewellery. Additionally, various costumes from the film were available separately to fit the doll. It is interesting how certain characters fire the public's imagination and cause doll designers to all bring out the same character in the same outfit.

One of the most famous cinema heroes is James Bond, who over the decades, has been played by several actors. The first Bond movie, *Dr No*, appeared in 1962, and starred Sean Connery as James Bond. Since then, there have been over 20 Bond films. Considering this amount, and the popularity of the character, it is surprising that he hasn't been depicted all that often as a doll. Admittedly, female dolls are much more liked than male dolls, but even so, it does seem a surprising omission. In 2003, a Barbie set containing a James Bond doll was issued by Mattel, while a series of Hasbro Action Man special issues were sold in the late nineties, though no attempt was made to capture any of the actors' features. Later, American company, Sideshow Collectables, produced dolls representing James Bond as played by Roger Moore, Pierce Brosnan and Sean Connery. They also have many other characters from the films, such as Honor Blackman as Pussy Galore, Joseph Wiseman as Dr No, Telly Savalas as Ernst Blofeld and Halle Berry as Jinx. Mattel has produced other James Bond related dolls in the Barbie range too, such as a Solitaire *Live And Let Die* Barbie doll and Honey Rider from *Dr No*.

A much more earthy action hero is Indiana Jones, played by Harrison Ford in movies such as *Raiders of the Lost Ark*, issued by Hasbro as a talking character doll. As he repeats such phrases as 'I think we've got a big problem' and 'That's why they call it the jungle, sweetheart', his mouth moves, which makes it an exciting addition to a collection of film character dolls. The doll comes dressed in Jones', typical outfit of leather jacket, coarse trousers and battered hat. Handsome, swashbuckling heroes are always popular in movies, and the *Pirates of the Caribbean* series of films has spawned some excellent dolls, notably a range from Robert Tonner which stand 17in high and have 14 points of articulation. The Tonner version of Captain Jack Sparrow (Johnny Depp) wears an elaborate costume, and the beading in the hair has been painstakingly reproduced. Orlando Bloom as Will Turner, in either his pirate's costume of shirt, breeches and long jacket, or his elegant frock coat, waistcoat, knee breeches and tricorn hat, is also in the collection, as well as Keira Knightly as Elizabeth Swann.

The Tonner 'Elizabeth Swann' dolls from *Pirates of the Caribbean* are made of fine quality vinyl with rooted saran hair, stand 16in high, have 13 joints and beautiful hand-painted faces. The dolls can be obtained in a dramatic, swashbuckling pirate's outfit of cotton knee breeches, pirate's jacket with antique-looking button details, cotton shirt, printed waistcoat, boots and tri-cornered hat, as well as a silk brocade court gown or an exquisite wedding gown. Zizzle Toys produced some 12in-high dolls a few years ago – the one representing Johnny Depp as Captain Jack Sparrow bore an amazing resemblance to the actor, even though the hair was moulded. The costume was extremely intricate too, considering this was really intended as a play doll rather than a collector's item. Zizzle also made an 'Orlando Bloom' as Will Turner, in a choice of outfits – either a 'pirate-type' red shirt, black waistcoat and black trousers, or a black leather outfit with a cream brocade waistcoat. Up until recently, male dolls were very few and far between, but as the trend for character dolls has grown, men have gradually been making their presence felt – though not James Bond, it seems!

Numerous dolls and figures have been inspired by the films *Star Trek* and *Star Wars*. Although those from the former could be regarded as television dolls, most of the dolls were actually issued when the films came into production. In 1977 a series of 12in *Star Wars* dolls was released, which today are a rare collector's item. The dolls in the set comprised such characters as Princess Leia, Obi Wan Kenobi and Luke Skywalker. The likeness to the actors' faces was excellent, and there was plenty of detail. For example, Princess Leia's hair was intricately braided as depicted by Carrie Fisher in the film. Incidentally, it is quite difficult to find one of these first Princess Leia dolls today with perfect hair, as most were bought for young children, and the hair soon became tangled. (It seems practically impossible to get the hair restyled perfectly, as it is difficult to reform the braided coils.) As the series of films progressed, many other dolls (as opposed to the 5in plastic figures with moulded clothing) were issued by various companies. In 1996 a new series of 12in dolls was introduced. This range was more extensive than before and featured characters such as Lando Calrissian, Tusken Raider, Admiral Ackbar and Greedo, as well as the principals. Other characters were remodelled; Chewbacca now had realistic fur rather than the plastic of the 1970s version – though the new version of Princess Leia depicted a startled-faced, rather podgy lady with no neck and broad shoulders, vastly different to the original, pretty 1970s model.

However, as the series progressed, and, presumably, with manufacturers realising that the dolls were being bought by collectors as well as by children, many stunning versions appeared. One of the most iconic of the dolls was the

1990s issue of Princess Leia in her chains and 'bikini' outfit when she was held prisoner by Jabba the Hutt. There was also a 'portrait' doll of her character issued at the same time. These dolls were produced by Hasbro. With the coming of the 'prequel' series of the *Star Wars* films, a whole gamut of new characters emerged, in particular Queen Amidala, played by Natalie Portman, whose outfits were striking. Perhaps the most impressive was the 1999 'Portrait' collectable 12in doll wearing a scarlet 'senate gown' outfit. Amongst the other Queen Amidala dolls of the time was one of her dressed in a black travel gown and another, called 'Hidden Majesty', which depicted the Queen in disguise as Padme, her servant. There are many other *Star Wars* dolls which fit into the scope of this book, but unfortunately, there is not enough room to describe them all.

Earlier *Star Trek* dolls were released to tie in with the television series, but it was when the films were released that the market was flooded. There were several characters issued, including James T. Kirk, as played by William Shatner, and Mr Spock (Leonard Nimroy). There was also a Hasbro Barbie and Ken set of dolls which seemed to relate to the television programme rather than the films. This Barbie/Ken set was issued by Mattel in 1996 and depicts Ken as Captain Kirk while Barbie is dressed as Uhura. In 2009, Barbie was issued again as Uhura, while Ken was dressed as either Captain Kirk or Mr Spock. These dolls were sold separately. Once the films were released many dolls put in an appearance, and it would be possible to form a large collection concentrating solely on *Star Trek*. The dolls were produced by various companies, amongst them Playmates, Mego, Kenner and Hasbro. A new batch of *Star Trek* dolls made by Playmates was called 'The Command Collection', and was from the prequel movie, *Countdown*.

An all-action girl, Lara Croft, starred in the 2001 movie *Tomb Raider*, and eventually appeared in doll form from Robert Tonner. The doll showed Croft as played by Angelina Jolie and was an excellent reproduction of the feisty character. Standing 17in tall, the doll had 14 points of articulation so that she could recreate her most famous action poses, and had rooted saran hair, finely sculpted weapons, and hand-painted facial detail. The most iconic of the Tonner Lara Croft dolls wore an Army-green cropped T-shirt with twill shorts and intricately detailed vinyl boots with working buckles and zips. Additional models have been made too. Other companies which produced *Tomb Raider* dolls include Playmates and Neca.

The highly popular 1978 movie *Grease* set in the 1950s, has spawned a plethora of dolls, amongst them a Franklin Mint 16in 'Sandy' (Olivia Newton John) in her black leather outfit. Sandy could also be purchased in her 'First Day at School' outfit (yellow two-piece), while the Cheerleader outfit was sold without the doll. Mattel issued a range of characters from the film in various outfits, notably Rizzo, Frenchie and Cha Cha, as well as several versions of Sandy. Also available was a set of two miniature Kelly and Tommy dolls dressed as Sandy and Danny (John Travolta).

Grease, 25 Years, Mattel.

More recent very popular dolls are those from the *High School Musical* series of films which started out in 2006 as an American television film, but was later a feature film and stage show. Amongst the numerous dolls issued by Mattel are Troy (Zac Efron), Gabriella Montez (Vanessa Hudgens), Sharpay Evans (Ashley Tisdale), Ryan (Lucas Grabeel), Chad (Corbin Bleu) and Kelsi (Olesya Rulin). Many of these characters are available in various outfits and scenarios.

If you're a fan of comedy, then actor Kenneth Williams was personified a few years ago by BBI Product Enterprises in his famous role of Julius Caesar from the film *Carry On Cleo*. This 12in talking figure was dressed in a white toga and the facial sculpture was excellent. The voice chip was authentic Williams dialogue from the film, and included 'Infamy! Infamy! Infamy! They've all got it in for me!', 'I came, I saw, I...Urrrgh... I conked out!', 'Friends! Romans!', (Interrupting voice: 'Countrymen...'), 'I KNOW!' and 'Atchoo! Oh, even me laurels have wilted'.

There are so many film star dolls around – far too many to mention – so those described here are only a sprinkling of what is available. Interestingly, a collection of famous film star dolls could prove a bit of an investment – especially if you buy some of the cheaper types. If this sounds an odd theory, it's really very simple – there are some wonderful versions of dolls produced by designers such as Robert Tonner. However, these top-of-the-range models are intended for collectors who tend to keep them safe in their boxes. They are unlikely to undress them. In contrast, children will naturally remove the cheaper dolls from their boxes and play with them so they will soon become undressed and scuffed. Character dolls usually have quite a short shelf life because movies are constantly changing and new heroes are produced. So in a few years' time, if you have resisted the temptation to 'de-box' your hero or heroine, you may suddenly find the doll is demand.

Chapter Five

Dolls Representing Characters in Animated Films

W ITHOUT A DOUBT, the most successful and prolific of the animated filmmakers is the Walt Disney Company which made its first full-length cartoon in 1937 and which is still going strong today. Literally thousands of different dolls representing characters from the Disney movies have been released over the years, with a major surge in the 1990s that shows no sign of letting up. By far the majority of the dolls have been intended for children, though many are sought by collectors of the genre too. As well as vinyl dolls, character dolls have appeared in porcelain, cloth and even rubber, so there is a terrific variety. Some of the major films such as *Snow White* (*See Chapter 18*), have so many different versions of dolls that even if a collector concentrated on just the one film, it would be virtually impossible to gather together every kind of doll produced. The boom in the toy collectables market – which really began in the late 1970s with the production of the *Star Wars* figures and dolls – caused manufacturers to look at movies with new eyes and see the huge potential for character dolls.

Films such as *Cinderella, Sleeping Beauty, Pocahontas, Mulan, Beauty and the Beast, The Little Mermaid, Tarzan, Snow White, Hunchback of Notre Dame, Hercules, Aladdin, Peter Pan* and many other productions by Walt Disney, provided inspiration for a vast range of character dolls. In addition, Disney teamed up with Pixar for a series of blockbuster animated movies such as three *Toy Story* films and *Monsters Inc.* Dolls from the *Shrek* series from Dreamworks have also been issued, while Fox Animation Studios had a huge success with *Anastasia* in 1997 which told a story loosely bound up with the Russian Royal Household, based on the legend that Anastasia survived the execution of her family. Anastasia and her grandmother Marie manage to escape through a secret passage but then become separated. For years, Marie searches for her granddaughter, who is tricked by a pair of conmen who want to claim the reward for finding her. One of the men, Dimitri, eventually falls in love with Anastasia. Grandmother is found and all ends well. One of the classic dolls released at the time by Galoob, depicts Anastasia in her blue skating costume, but there were many more, including some collector's editions portraying the Empress and also Czar Nicholas. A particularly impressive doll was 'Her Imperial Royal Highness Anastasia' in a magnificent gown, issued by Galoob in

1997. Other Anastasia dolls include a couple of her in Paris fashions, and some of Dimitri.

Warner Brothers produced dolls for the animated versions of the *King and I* and *Magic Sword: Quest for Camelot*. Interestingly, the Warner Brothers' doll created to represent the King of Siam was an almost-perfect likeness of actor Yul Brynner, who played the original part alongside Deborah Kerr in 1956. The film was based on the stage musical, which in turn was based on the book, *The King and I* by Anna Leonowen. Some of the dolls created from the film were very attractive and several came with musical chips, but they were soon being sold off very cheaply, and presumably bought for children. So the mint condition and boxed ones which occasionally turn up are now beginning to attract high prices. There was also a range of bean-filled soft dolls depicting many of the characters from the film – a trait which is becoming increasingly common as it seems the majority of animated movies are now automatically issuing Beanie dolls to appeal to the younger market. For instance, *Arthur Christmas* (2011) from Sony Pictures Animation and Aardman Animations, saw the release of several Beanie character dolls from the film.

Although most of these vinyl character dolls are intended as playthings for small children, they can be extremely beautiful with their faces bearing an impressive likeness to the various Disney animated film characters. For instance, the classic Greek look of Megara, one of the main characters in the 1997 film *Hercules*, the Chinese features of the heroine in *Mulan* (1998) and the wide-eyed charm of Ariel from *The Little Mermaid* (1989) were (and still are) all faithfully captured in vinyl. The clothes, too, are usually detailed and reflect the various outfits seen in the film. They are often reversible, or the doll comes with a spare outfit so she can be displayed – for instance, in 'peasant dress' or 'princess style', depending on the film. Some of the costumes are little short of ingenious in the way they transform to other styles. The transformation of the Mattel 'Beast' doll into the handsome Prince from *Beauty and the Beast* (1981) was extremely clever. Many of these play dolls were made by toy companies such as Simba, Tyco, Character Options, Mattel and Vivid Imaginations, and stand around 11–12in tall.

As well as the basic 'toy' dolls, there are various limited editions to be found, both in vinyl and porcelain. Usually these are far superior to the play versions of the dolls as they have hand-painted faces and much more detailed costumes. As with film dolls, television character dolls and music dolls, many of the animated cartoon dolls have a fairly short life (apart from those from the major classics films such as *Snow White, Cinderella* and *Sleeping Beauty*). Consequently, it's a good idea for collectors to keep a look out for reductions. Once the dolls have lost their appeal to children, they tend to end up in bargain baskets. Diligent searching might find old stock on toyshop shelves, and although Disney relies on animal characters for child appeal, most of its animated films still feature at least a few human characters, which ensure a doll tie-in. Obviously, with the thousands upon thousands of dolls from this genre, only a few can be mentioned here, so if this is an area of collecting that appeals to you,

Pocahontas and John Smith, Mattel.

Dancing Anastasia and Dimitri, Galoob.

The King and I, Playmates.

Sleeping Beauty, Disney.

a search on the internet or a trip to your local toy store will show the types of dolls available.

Amongst the major Disney classics, *Cinderella* (1950) has never lost its appeal, and in the early 1990s, Mattel produced a Cinderella doll dressed in the pale-blue gown as depicted in the film. Her blonde hair was piled high and around her neck she wore a black choker. Her tiny feet were encased in glass slippers. Additional costumes could be purchased, such as a pink or ragged dress, and it was also possible to buy costumes complete with miniature masks that could transform your Cinderella doll into either the Fairy Godmother or the Wicked Stepmother. These separate costumes and masks are very collectable today.

Cinderella is a popular subject for collector dolls too, and designers such as Annette Himstedt, Dianna Effner, Robert Tonner, White Balloon and many others, have produced their own versions. (*See Chapter 3*). The Cinderella theme dates back hundreds of years and there are numerous stories to be found from around the globe. When Walt Disney was researching the film, he discovered 300 different variations, but finally settled for a French version by Charles Perrault, written in the 1600s, and which introduced the all-important glass slippers. Debate still rages whether this was a deliberate ploy or whether it was a misinterpretation by Perrault. Originally, Cinderella danced the evening away in fur footwear, 'pantouffle en vair', but Perrault described her slippers as 'en verre' (of glass). The fragile, delicate, glass concept appealed to readers' imaginations and became the accepted portrayal. A glass slipper is now symbolic of the Cinderella story, alongside the pumpkin carriage and the clock striking midnight.

Another Disney classic animated cartoon, *Sleeping Beauty* (1957), is also a popular subject with doll manufacturers and artists. The story of the young princess who pricked her finger on a spindle and fell asleep until woken with a kiss from a prince, not only provides scope for the beautiful princess and the handsome prince but, more excitingly, allows for the creation of the evil witch. Disney issued Maleficent, the sorceress in *Sleeping Beauty* in their 'Villains' series in the 1990s. Resplendent in a black-and-purple robe lined with cerise silk, a high collar framing a dramatically made-up face and a headdress forming two curved horns, Maleficent looked chilling. She grasped a staff topped with a magic crystal ball on which reposed her pet raven. In the 1991 Mattel release of *Sleeping Beauty*'s Princess Aurora and Prince Phillip, both characters were dressed in reversible costumes. Princess Aurora had a white ball gown with a blue bodice and iridescent sleeves which cleverly reversed to a pink dress, while her prince reverted to a 'Handsome Horseman'. This was effected by his grey trousers, royal-blue tabard and a red cloak scattered with gold stars which converted to a brown-shirted outfit. Both dolls were the usual 11½in tall. Many of these earlier Mattel dolls bear small gold stars which make it easier to identify outfits should you come across the clothes without the doll. Amongst the other creative 11½in play dolls which have abounded since the film was released, was an intriguing 1990s Disney doll with not only a reversible costume – her gown changed from blue to pink – but also eyes she magically closed when they were dabbed with water.

Over the years many more Disney dolls have been made of dozens of characters from its films, including *Pocahontas*, Esmeralda from *The Hunchback of Notre Dame* (1996) , *Mulan*, and *Hercules*. Certain dolls, such as Ariel from *The Little Mermaid*, have proved so popular that a myriad of styles and costumes have been made. Some of the Tyco range of costumes for Ariel were particularly innovative, amongst them a set of paper mermaid tails which dissolved in water to leave behind a fabric skirt. Many people who collect dolls from the animated movies just stick to accumulating as many different models as they can of one of two of their favourite characters, otherwise they would be inundated. The other way is to choose just one doll to represent each film or each character – but it is often extremely difficult to decide which is the 'best' doll when faced with so many versions.

Perhaps one of the most successful of the animated movies was *Toy Story* (1995), which introduced us to Andy's toys – Woody the Cowboy and Buzz Lightyear, amongst many others. Later, along came *Toy Story 2* (1999) and *Toy Story 3* (2010), when we met Jessie the Cowgirl, Stinky Pete and Big Baby. The first film was released in November 1995 and Buzz Lightyear practically brought toy stores to a halt when parents across the land queued to get him in time for Christmas. The original talking Buzz was the one that caused the initial furore. Moulded in grey plastic with green trim, he looked just as he did in the film and said such things as 'I'm Buzz Lightyear', 'Buzz Lightyear to the rescue', 'I come in Peace', and, of course, 'To Infinity and beyond'. He was fully posable with light and sound 'laser' functions, and pop-out wings. His green trim glowed in the dark. Another version was the 'Intergalactic Buzz', spectacular in a silver space suit, detachable backpack with space-disc-firing-mechanism and a flip-up light and sound arm communicator.

Cowboy Woody, dressed in a yellow-checked shirt, denim jeans, black-and-white 'pony skin' bolero, brown stetson and boots, was 11in high and made by Thinkway Toys. His five sayings included 'Reach for the Sky', 'Howdy, Partner' and 'Look! There's an alien!' Thinkway's cute, green-headed, triple-eyed *Toy Story* Alien repeated phrases from the film such as, 'The claw is my master',

'I have been chosen', and 'Ooooooooh'. Another of Andy's toys from the first film was Bo-Peep, who was originally sold in America as a collector's doll, dressed in her pink-spotted white frock and pink bonnet. (*See Chapter 3.*) When *Toy Story 2* reached the cinema screens, there was another star for people to clamour for – Jessie the cowgirl. Made by Mattel, Jessie had big green eyes, a snub nose and red-brown hair. She wore a white blouse with a yellow trim and red braid, pony skin over-trousers topped with denim, and a bright-red wide-brimmed hat. Soon, the stores sold out of Jessie – it was a repeat of the earlier Buzz shortage. Since then, many different Jessie dolls have been made, not always wearing outfits from the film. Stinky Pete, the Prospector, was also available and, with the release of *Toy Story 3* we had characters such as Big Baby and Dolly.

Betty Boop is an instantly recognisable character from various cartoons – yet she actually began life as a dog, when the artist Grim Natwick, who worked for movie mogul Max Fleischer, drew a canine character based on singer Helen Kane. In 1930 the dog appeared in a film called *Dizzy Dishes*, but was soon morphed into a glamorous, rather raunchy lady. Unfortunately, Helen Kane's career took a turn for the worse, due mainly to a series of uninspired movies, and soon she was a faded star. She bombarded the studios with threats of legal action, convinced she was entitled to a share of the profits for being the original inspiration for the character of Betty Boop. In 1937 Betty was accused of being too risqué and for a brief while her famous garter was removed, but was soon replaced owing to public demand. Even so, the fickleness of the public meant that she was soon to fall from favour, and so the final *Betty Boop* cartoon appeared in 1939. Almost fifty years later, in 1988, our heroine made a cameo appearance in the movie *Who Framed Roger Rabbit?*

Many Betty Boop dolls have been manufactured over the decades, with the earliest being a wood-pulp jointed character doll by the Cameo Doll Company in 1932. Much later, Mattel manufactured a range of attractive Betty Boop vinyl dolls for collectors, all dressed in tight dresses, feather boas and sparkly trims. In addition, various soft-bodied dolls appeared in collectors' shops, as did 'wobbler' or 'nodding' dolls, resin and ceramic dressed-figures, vinyl squeaking dolls and china musical Bettys. Precious Kids company in America issued a range of 12in vinyl Betty Boop dolls wearing a range of outfits, including a GI, nurse, patriotic girl, glamorous Hollywood star and a talking version which said 'I wanna be loved by you' and, of course, 'Boop oop a doop'. The most interesting interpretation of Betty was produced by another American company, Marty Toys, in the early 1990s, using 1980s moulds. These dolls were often trendily dressed, in stripy, knitted jumpers or colourful jogging suits – worlds away from the ubiquitous red dress! Dolls also appeared from the Madame Alexander Doll Company which, while keeping the Betty Boop look, made the face pretty, rather than that of a cartoon character.

Although Betty was a famous cartoon icon in America she wasn't so popular in Britain, and until recently, Betty Boop dolls and memorabilia were extremely difficult to buy over here. A few years ago, all that changed when Americana,

Mulan Matchmaker, Mattel.

Woody, Think Way.

Jessie, Mattel.

Betty Boop, Mattel.

retro-characters and the cartoon cult suddenly became the in-thing. Nowadays, Betty in her red dress is a common sight in our shops.

Amongst the other character dolls made as a tie-in to the animated movies were those from the *Popeye* series of cartoons, including the pipe-smoking, spinach-guzzler himself, Olive Oyl, Baby Swee'pea, Wimpy, Bluto and others. Most of the dolls were soft-bodied plush and by various makers. Popeye started off as a newspaper cartoon figure drawn by Elzie Crisler Segar, and appeared in the daily King Features comic strip 'Thimble Theatre', in 1929. In 1932 Fleischer studios adapted the strip characters into a series of 'Popeye the Sailor' cartoon shorts for Paramount Pictures. The cartoons continued to be produced right up till the late 1950s and were also shown on television. Popeye later appeared in a live-action film in 1980 starring Robin Williams.

Arthur Christmas.

Chapter Six

Dolls Representing Characters in
Television and Radio

TELEVISION IN BRITAIN was available before the war to those who could afford it, but it was really the 1953 Coronation that triggered the television phenomenon. Although children had their own programmes and characters from the late 1940s, it wasn't until the mid-1950s that dolls began appearing on the market, representing the more popular characters such as Andy Pandy and Looby Loo. Nowadays, as soon as a character appears on television, it is also released as a toy, because merchandise is a vital part of the media process. Andy Pandy was strangely dressed in a baggy, striped all-in-one suit and a pompom-decorated hat. He was rumoured to be based on Paul, the small son of puppeteer Audrey Atterbury, who grew up to be one of the *Antique Roadshow* regulars.

The dolls were made by various companies including Chad Valley, Born To Play and Golden Bear. There were also the puppet versions made by Pelham Puppets. Andy Pandy's best friends were Teddy and Looby Loo, and these too, have appeared in toy form. Looby Loo was a rag doll with pigtails, dressed in a spotted skirt with shoulder straps worn over a white blouse. She lived in a large picnic hamper alongside Andy Pandy and Teddy. In 2002 a new TV series of Andy Pandy was launched, prompting something of an Andy Pandy/nostalgia revival and modern versions of the dolls were issued.

Of the same era were television's *Bill and Ben* (the Flowerpot Men), Archie Andrews (*Educating Archie*) Mr Turnip, Twizzle, Torchy, Tex Tucker (*Four Feather Falls*), *Bleep and Booster* and *Hank*, amongst lots of others. Many of these characters were produced as string or glove puppets by Pelham, but some were made as dolls by other companies. Archie Andrews was something of a weird notion as he was a ventriloquist's dummy, operated by Peter Brough – on a radio show! In the late fifties, however, he made the transfer to television. Archie Andrews' dummies were made as a toy by Palitoy and proved very popular. The show, *Educating Archie*, included many people who went on to become household names, such as Tony Hancock, Benny Hill, Beryl Reid and Julie Andrews.

Even in those far-off days when children assumed that television characters were all black and white, enterprising manufacturers realised that television-related toys would be a money-spinner. Today, such toys are very collectable. Not only are today's characters produced in doll form, the nostalgia element is so great that much-loved icons from the 1950s and 60s are also being reproduced. It is still possible to source Andy Pandy, Bill and Ben, Captain Pugwash, Popeye and other favourites, just as easily as it is to buy the more modern Dora the Explorer, Bob the Builder, Fireman Sam, Rosie and Jim, TV Tots, Teletubbies, Fifi and the FlowerTots, Tweenies and characters from *Fetch the Vet* and *In the Night Garden*. Enid Blyton's Little Noddy character made his television debut in 1955 as a puppet on the new commercial channel, so there is a cross-over of toys, both book and film. (*See Chapter 1*.) Other character dolls to look out for include those from *The Flintstones* who made their names in an animated television cartoon before being promoted to the big screen. Bam Bam and Pebbles were made as vinyl dolls in the 1960s by the Hanna Barbera company. Human characters which happen to appear in cartoons with animated creatures can often be found with a bit of searching, such as the Ranger from *Yogi Bear* or the Spotty Man (actually an alien in human form) from *Superted*.

A particularly appealing character created in doll form was called Joe who starred in a series of delightfully unsophisticated still-frame *Joe* animation films shown in the *Watch With Mother* programmes during the late 1960s. The gentle stories, written by Alison Price, were aimed at the very young, and centred on the wide-eyed lad Joe who lived with his rosy-cheeked family. Joe was later created as a 16in-high, sturdy vinyl character doll with large brown eyes and wearing a typical Joe outfit of orange dungarees over a white T-shirt. Television doll spin-offs tend to be made from cloth, as they are often intended for the very young child, so it's good to find all-vinyl versions.

Raggy Dolls, stars of a long-running children's television series in the mid-1980s to mid-1990s, were popular and of course, were ideal to bring out as a range of children's dolls. Manufactured by Pikit, seven of the toys – 'Hi Fi', 'Dotty', 'Princess', 'Sad Sack', 'Claude', 'Lucy' and 'Back To Front' – appeared as colourful soft dolls with yarn hair, as depicted on the programme.

Another doll series, running in the 1990s, was *Tots TV*, made by Ragdoll Productions. It featured three rag doll friends – Tom, a blue-haired boy who wore glasses, Tilly, a red-haired French girl and a green-haired boy called Tiny, who was the smallest of the tots. Interestingly, the programme was written by the actors who voiced the dolls in the show; in the French version, Tilly spoke English while in the US version she spoke Spanish. The dolls were made as sturdy, cloth dolls by Ravensburger, Golden Bear and others.

Two very popular dolls, Rosie and Jim, appeared in the 1990s. This pair of colourful rag dolls lived aboard a canal barge called, appropriately enough, *Ragdoll*. They had interesting adventures which usually involved them spying on the barge's owner, John Cunliffe (later replaced by Pat Coombes and then Neil Brewer). The owners, of course, didn't realise that they were being followed by the cheeky dolls. The *Rosie and Jim* programmes were produced by Ragdoll Productions, which also made *Teletubbies, Tots TV* and *Boohbah*. Naturally, dolls

Looby Loo, Born To Play.

Archie Andrews, Palitoy.

Joe, maker unknown.

Tom (TV Tots), Ravensburger.

Raggy Dolls, Pikit Toys.

Hamble, Winfield.

of all these characters were made, bought by parents so their children could act out the programmes they had watched.

When the *Teletubbies* series was launched in 1997, it created a furore; many parents and teachers were appalled by the characters' babyish speech – for example, they said 'eh-oh' instead of hello. However, when the dolls were released just before Christmas that year, shops sold out instantly. People fought over the dolls in shops, indulging in tug-of-war tussles, and some of the dolls were even stolen from babies' prams. In addition, the dolls changed hands for vastly inflated sums on the secondary market. The four strange beings, Dipsy, Tinky Winky, Laa-Laa and Po, had antennae on their heads and television screens on their tummies. Each character was a different colour; Dipsy was green, Tinky Winky was purple, Laa-Laa was yellow and Po was red, and though intended for toddlers, they became cult viewing with many adults, especially students. The Teletubbies' dolls were produced by Golden Bear as basic soft toys and since then, numerous other versions have been made, including dancing ones by Tomy. There are also many singing and speaking kinds. Teletubbies lived in an eco-friendly underground house with their vacuum cleaner called Noo Noo, and are still one of the most successful and instantly recognisable characters from children's television.

Postman Pat appeared on our television screens in 1981, with scripts written by John Cuncliffe, and his cheery character in his little red Post Office van was an instant success. Pat chugged along the lanes of Greendale accompanied by his cat Jess, and the catchy songs, bright colours and gentle humour of the show, ensured it was one that appealed both to children and grown-ups. Postman Pat dolls, as well as those of others in the cast, such as Mrs Goggins and Ted, were not only made by various companies such as Golden Bear but were knitted in their thousands using the many patterns which appeared at the time. Interestingly, when the programme first appeared, manufacturers still weren't geared up to producing instant tie-ins, and so the only solution for parents was to knit a Postman Pat doll – obviously the knitting wool companies were much more clued up with regards to television characters!

One of the most classic children's television programmes was *Play School*, a much-loved programme intended for the under fives. It was first broadcast in 1964 and ended its run in 1988. The presenters included Brian Cant, Floella Benjamin, Johnny Ball and Derek Griffiths, and amongst the cast of toys were Big Ted, Little Ted, Humpty, Jemima and Hamble. Although Humpty, a big green, egg-shaped soft toy with large eyes, and Jemima, a pretty rag doll, were possibly made especially for the programme, the other toys weren't. Consequently, Hamble, the other doll, was bought from a toyshop. Today, collectors have deduced that Hamble was a doll in the Woolworth's 'Little Beauty' range. In fact, there seem to have been two Hambles because the Little Beauty doll – a soft-bodied toddler type with thick, brown curly hair – was later replaced by an all-vinyl doll with straighter hair, but retaining the Hamble name. Apparently, Hamble was very much disliked by the presenters because she wasn't pretty and her soft body meant that she was inclined to loll about and fall over. In fact, one presenter confessed, 'I did a terrible thing to Hamble. She just would not sit up.....so one day I got a very big knitting needle, a big wooden one, and I stuck it right up her bum, as far as her head. So she was completely rigid, and she was much better after that.'

Today, many nostalgic fans of the show seek out these dolls, which later became known as 'Hamble Dolls' (although they were never sold as this) and consequently they are very collectable. They can be found with brown or blonde hair. Presumably this Hamble eventually deteriorated beyond repair, and so the all-vinyl replacement was used in later programmes, but by the mid-1980s her place was taken by Poppy, a doll with an ethnic look, and Hamble disappeared from the show. Another stalwart of the series, Jemima the rag doll, seemed to be continually replaced, no doubt because she didn't last long with all the rough-and-tumble that the toys received on the show. Poppy resides in the Museum of Film, Photography and Television in Bradford, along with the Teds, Humpty, and a version of Jemima. Accounts suggest that poor Hamble was last seen in a rubbish skip.

Other well-loved classics included *Camberwick Green* and *Trumpton*. Many of the characters featured in the programmes were produced as toys in the 1960s by Marx, in their 'Twistables' series. These Twistables measured around 6½in high and were made from vinyl and plastic, with wired necks, legs and arms which could be posed, hence the name. Much-loved characters such as Chigley, Dr Mopp, PC McGarry, Farmer Brown and others, were popular, though are not particularly easy to come by nowadays as they were vulnerable to breakage. Other companies, including Codeg and Combex, also issued toy dolls from the show, while in recent years collectable figurines have been made by Robert Harrop Designs Ltd, amongst them Pugh, Pugh, Barney McGrew, Cuthbert, Dibble and Grubb! Many characters such as Andy Pandy, Looby Loo and Bill and Ben from early 'classic' children's television programmes have been relaunched as toys in an effort to cash in on the current nostalgia boom. So this is an excellent way of adding to a collection of character toys, as it is often extremely difficult – or expensive – to source original dolls.

No doubt the most successful children's television series of all time is *Doctor Who*, which was first broadcast in 1963. Several 'Time Lords' have appeared over the decade, with dolls made to represent them – one of the classics being a model of Tom Baker which was made in the 1970s by Denys Fisher in collaboration with Mego. At the same time, the company issued a 'Leela' doll, based on his faithful companion, as well as a Cyberman. Other Doctor Who dolls to look out for include Dapol's action figures such as Jon Pertwee, Sylvester McCoy and Bonnie Langford (Melanie Bush). Christopher Eccleston (who played the ninth Doctor) was made by Character Options. The Tonner Doll Company has produced the tenth Doctor Who (David Tennant), and his companion Martha Jones (Freema Agyeman), as excellent 17in-high dolls with hand-painted features and quality outfits, for collectors. Naturally, the Doctor carries his sonic screwdriver, as does the Character Options version, which depicts David

Camberwick Green, Marx.

Bionic Woman,
Denys Fisher.

Tennant as Doctor Who in his battered suit. Both the Tonner doll and the Character Options version bear an excellent likeness to David.

The Avengers, a 1960s slightly eccentric series which featured spies, fantasy and humour, starred Patrick Macnee as John Steed, alongside a series of female sidekicks played by Honor Blackman, Diana Rigg, Joanna Lumley and Linda Thorson. Various dolls have appeared over the years, and the earlier ones are very collectable. Some were produced by Denys Fisher in the 1970s. At the time, this short-lived company seemed to have cornered the market in making niche character dolls, amongst them a rather dashing Joanna Lumley 'Purdey' doll. The Fairylite Company also made some dolls from *The Avengers*, – notably an Emma Peel lookalike – in the mid-sixties. Various other Avengers dolls are around, many made in Hong Kong. Product Enterprises issued a John Steed and Emma Peel 12in-tall talking action-figure set.

The 1970s saw characters from two popular television series, *Six Million Dollar Man* and *Bionic Woman*, appearing as dolls, marketed by Denys Fisher. These dolls were slightly gruesome, as the 'skin' on their bionic limbs could be rolled back. The 12in doll representing the Bionic Woman (played by Lindsay Wagner in the television series) was dressed in a blue jumpsuit and came with a mission purse containing various useful items. The rubber skin on her right arm and flaps on her thighs peeled back to reveal the robotic-type modules. The Six Million Dollar Man (played by Lee Majors in the TV series) was similar and had a bionic arm. He also had a special wide-angle lens fitted into one eye which could be peered through via a hole in his head. These dolls can still be found today, though often the rubber skin flaps have perished.

Denys Fisher produced a set of dolls based on the *Angels* series, which centred around nurses in a hospital called St Angelas. The dolls bear little facial relation to the actresses in the series, but even so are interesting and rare examples of a character spin-off that came with a play set – in this case, a hospital ward. The all-vinyl dolls were 9½in tall, and dressed in various nursing uniforms from the time, including a trainee in lilac stripes and a Sister in blue.

Doctor Who, Character Options.

Chapter Seven

Dolls Representing Characters in the Arts and Sport

THIS CHAPTER looks at dolls which represent famous authors, actors and artists, or which have been created as a tribute to their work. It also looks at dolls from the world of ballet, opera and musical theatre. Britain's greatest and most-respected writer is, without a doubt, William Shakespeare. Yet considering he was such a famous person, it's surprising that so few dolls or models relating to him have been created. It doesn't help that there is still much debate as to whether the accepted image of the great man is actually him or someone else.

Probably one of the most attractive depictions of William Shakespeare is an 8in-high doll created by Peggy Nisbet, taken from the Chandos painting of him in the National Portrait Gallery. The doll features the same high-domed forehead, bald head and pointed beard. Peggy Nisbet dressed the Shakespeare doll in a red waistcoat, black doublet, peacock-blue satin breeches, short, red stockings, and black-and- gold braid-trimmed cloak with a scarlet lining. He carries a scroll, and is instantly recognisable as the accepted image of our most celebrated playwright and poet.

Sporadically, other Shakespeare dolls crop up, often destined for the tourists who flock to his birthplace in Stratford-on-Avon. Amongst these is a 9in soft-bodied seated doll complete with ruff and velvet doublet, in the 'Little Thinkers' series. This doll has a caricature-type face, though is still recognisable as the Bard. Others include various small fabric-hanging dolls, finger puppets, a bobble-head nodder, and paper dolls in a book entitled *Great Characters from Shakespeare Paper Dolls* by Tom Tierney. Incidentally, there is a vast selection of paper doll books now, many of which feature famous people from history, so it is always worth keeping an eye out for them. Peggy Nisbet made a range of 'Shakespeare Characters' dolls, and amongst them were Lady Macbeth, Macbeth, Romeo, Juliet, Falstaff, Ophelia, Hamlet, Bottom, Titania and Oberon. She also included Shakespeare's wife, Anne Hathaway.

Probably the greatest Shakespearean actress was Dame Ellen Terry, of whom George Bernard Shaw once said, 'Ellen Terry is the most beautiful name in the world; it rings like a chime through the last quarter of the nineteenth century'. Ellen Terry was born in 1848, gave her first professional performance aged eight, and performed right through her life until her death, aged 80, in 1928. From 1878 she was considered the finest British Shakespearean actress and worked with renowned actor Sir Henry Irving's company as his leading lady. Her most famed roles were Portia from *The Merchant of Venice* and Beatrice from *Much Ado About Nothing*. Terry was born into an acting family and the tradition lived on through her great nephew, Sir John Geilgud. Peggy Nisbet immortalised Dame Ellen Terry in her series of collectors' dolls.

Shakespeare's *Romeo and Juliet* was 'immortalised' in 1997 when Mattel issued a limited edition set of Barbie and Ken as the two star-crossed lovers in the 'Together Forever Collection'. A few years later, a collector's Barbie doll was issued depicting Juliet in the ballet named after the tragic couple. She wears a soft-pink high-waisted gown with brocade sleeves and a delicate, gold chiffon underskirt. The ballet's famous pas de deux is also depicted by Madame Alexander's collectable 8in-tall Wendy and Jack dolls, both sumptuously dressed in fine fabrics. Barbie appears dressed as Titania, from *A Midsummer Night's Dream* – again depicting the ballet rather than the original play – dressed in a fantasy costume of violet and teal tulle, trimmed with ribbons and flowers.

Jane Austen, another of our national treasures, occasionally appears as a doll. The 'Little Thinkers' series already mentioned, includes an 11in-high cloth version of Jane wearing a pretty, flower-trimmed morning dress. This company, incidentally, seems to have discovered a niche for quirky cloth dolls of writers, artists and other people from history – they even sell a Charles Dickens's puppet. In the 1970s Peggy Nisbet produced a resin doll representing author Charlotte Brontë in their 'Portrait' series. Peggy also created a range of dolls inspired by some of Charles Dickens's characters, all beautifully crafted and instantly recognisable. Amongst the dolls she made were Oliver Twist with other characters from the story; Mr Bumble, the Artful Dodger, Fagin, Bill Sykes and Nancy, and Mr Pickwick from *The Pickwick Papers*. She also produced a figure of Scotland's most famous writer and poet, Robert Burns.

Kate Greenaway was a much-loved nineteenth-century artist and writer specialising in paintings of children dressed in the Regency costumes of a century before. Her book illustrations were printed from hand-engraved wood blocks. During the 1970s Pedigree produced a series of five dolls based on Kate Greenaway children. The dolls' names were Constance, Benjamin, Meg, Nell and Charles. Constance was 15in and the others were 12in. These dolls were made from a porcelain-look high-quality vinyl, with painted eyes and delicate colouring. Each was dressed in velvet or fine floral cotton, and were sold in pretty flower-decorated boxes with an oval window so that the doll could be displayed *in situ* if required. Kate Greenaway children were also made by Peggy Nisbet in collaboration with Royal Doulton in 1981 as a series of 12in porcelain dolls. With names such as 'Winter', 'Pink Ribbons', 'Swansdown' and 'Small Sister', these dolls were limited editions and very popular. The sculptor of the heads and hands was Eric Griffiths (who had previously worked for Pedigree) and the dolls had hand-painted features and mohair wigs. Alison Nisbet, daughter of Peggy, designed the dainty clothing. There were ten dolls in the series all inspired by Kate Greenaway's paintings. Their inventive boxes

William Shakespeare, Peggy Nisbet.

Charlotte Bronte, Peggy Nisbet.

Barbie as Juliet (Ballet), Mattel.

Dame Ellen Terry, Peggy Nisbet.

Charles from Kate Greenaway Collection, Pedigree.

Gibson Girl Barbie, Mattel.

Bubbles, Ridings Craft.

Cries Of London, Peggy Nisbet.

resembled Regency houses with multi-paned perspex bow windows. Some other makers who have included Kate Greenaway-inspired dolls in their range are Madame Alexander, R. John Wright, and Dunedin, the latter produced a series of porcelain doll kits complete with fabric and trims, to enable a collector to create their own Kate Greenaway doll.

During the late nineteenth century and early twentieth century in America, illustrator Charles Dana Gibson came up with the notion of the 'feminine ideal', which he portrayed in a series of satirical pen-and-ink-illustrated stories, and which subsequently became known as the 'Gibson Girl'. He said that the perfect American woman was tall and slender, with an ample bosom, and hips, and her body had an exaggerated S-curve torso shape achieved by wearing a special corset. Her neck was thin and her hair piled high. Dolls depicting this Gibson Girl have subsequently appeared, amongst them a Barbie issue in the 'Great Eras' series dating from 1993. Barbie as a Gibson Girl was dressed in a long, blue gown with matching cape, white blouse and cream hat.

The Madame Alexander Doll Company has transformed one of its 10in Cissette dolls into Margaret Mitchell, the author of *Gone With The Wind*. 'Margaret Mitchell' is dressed in a black-knit ankle-length, sheath dress, trimmed with buttons and with a large white bow, and carries the manuscript for her famous book. Also from Madame Alexander is a charming limited edition doll representing Louisa May Alcott, author of *Little Women*. This doll wears a blue full-skirted gown in a style typical of the late 1860s (Alcott wrote *Little Women* in 1868).

Recently, Barbie dolls have been used by designer Linda Kyaw to depict the possible muses of artists Leonardo da Vinci, Vincent Van Gogh and Gustav Klimt. Consequently, the 'Leonardo' Barbie wears a stunning Renaissance-style gown of green, brown and gold with rich brocade shoulders, and her face bears the enigmatic smile of the Mona Lisa. Vincent Van Gogh's Barbie is dressed to recall his work *The Starry Night* in a dramatic, strapless full-skirted cocktail dress, which skilfully depicts the swirling night sky overlooking Saint-Remy, just as the artist painted it. Finally, the doll inspired by the works of Gustav Klimt, notably *Portrait of Adele Bloch-Bauer 1* not only bears a striking facial resemblance to wealthy industrialist's wife Adele, and has the same thick, curly hair, but her gold outfit is similar to the portrait's design inspired by Byzantine mosaics and Egyptian motifs.

Various other art-related dolls sometimes appear. There are several versions of *Bubbles* dolls which depict the velvet-clad curly-haired boy with a bubble pipe, as painted by Sir John Millais in 1885. The boy was his grandson, Willie James, and originally, the portrait was entitled *A Child's World*. Later, the *Bubbles* portrait was bought by the Pears soap company which added a bar of soap to the foreground and used it for advertising purposes – to the fury of Millais. Dolls featuring the 'Bubbles Boy' have been made by several companies, including a bisque version sold as a kit by Ridings Craft in the 1970s.

Peggy Nisbet produced many dolls connected with the arts, and one of the most famous ranges was called 'The Cries of London', which first appeared in the 1950s and remained in production throughout the life of the company. These dolls were based on a series of paintings featuring street vendors by eighteenth-century artist Frederick Wheatley, who was born in 1747. Peggy studied the paintings and dressed her dolls in outfits based on those the sellers wore. Each doll had an authentically-styled full-skirted dress, frilly cap or hat, and carried a basket of her wares. The range included 'Lavender Girl', 'Turnips and Carrots', 'Cherry Ripe', 'Flower Girl', 'Orange Seller' and 'Strawberries Scarlet'. Other artist dolls from Peggy Nisbet included representations of women from paintings *The Straw Hat* by Reubens, *The Honourable Mrs Graham* by Gainsborough and *The Theatre Box* by Renoir.

Moving slightly more up to date, in 2000 a soft-bodied doll representing Andy Warhol was produced by Merry Makers Inc. This doll, with its shock of white hair and large, round glasses is seated in a Cellophane-fronted box bearing Andy Warhol's signature, and wears jeans, a black leather-look zipped jacket and a T-shirt bearing his famous Campbell's Soup design. In 1999, designers Doug James and Laura Meisner introduced 'Willow' and 'Daisy', two glamorous 16in teen dolls wearing over-the-top outfits. One of the outfits was entitled *An Art Opening With Andy and Edie*. This tribute to Andy Warhol and his muse, Edie Sedgwick, had Daisy wearing a vivid Warhol-print pvc dress, and her black hair cut in a geometric style. The look was completed with a huge pair of turquoise earrings.

Dolls dressed as ballerinas are extremely popular, and though some are more like play dolls, there are others which strive to depict actual stage costumes. One particularly lovely doll, made by the Clea Bella company of America which specialises in ballet dancer and stage dolls, represents the dancers as they are seen in paintings by Degas. With her black curls, choker, long, romantic white tutu and long, gauzy-blue sash, this doll sums up those classic paintings to perfection, and was inspired by the work *The Dance Foyer at the Opera on the Rue Le Peletier*. Clea Bella has issued dolls in other costumes too; imaginary but beautiful outfits such as a Dragonfly and a Gypsy. Degas also provided inspiration for two very special Barbie dolls. Made from fine bisque porcelain, these two dancers, 'Lighter Than Air' and 'Classic Grace' could have stepped straight from a Degas painting. The first doll was dressed in a classic ballet gown with a corset-style bodice, delicate chiffon sleeves, and a multi-pleated tulle skirt, trimmed with flowers, while the second doll wore a delightful pink-and-orange multi-layered, pleated tulle skirt and a matching iridescent bodice embellished with tulle and taffeta.

The Tonner Doll Company has produced a large range of 16in-high ballet-themed dolls, dressed in costumes resembling those worn by the New York City Ballet in George Balanchine's production of *The Nutcracker*. The costumes, designed by Karinska, include 'Snowflake', 'Marie', 'Spanish Hot Chocolate', 'Cavalier', 'Candy Cane', 'Dance of the Lady Doll', 'Sugar Plum Fairy', 'Marzipan' and 'Arabian Coffee'. The attention to detail in the exquisite costumes is amazing – Marzipan's tutu is, surprisingly, trimmed with bunches of carrots! In 2006 Tonner issued a New York City Ballet 'Dance of the Lady Doll'

Degas, Clea Ballet.   Swanhilda, Robert Tonner.

depicting one of the dolls made by the toymaker Drosselmeyer. She wears the ballet ensemble of Columbine from *The Nutcracker*, with a pale-green bodice and ankle-length white skirt, trimmed with gold-and-black ribbon and gold pompoms.

The same company has also issued dolls from *Coppelia*, *L'Hiver* and *Spanish Rose*, as well as costumes for *Swan Lake* and *The Firebird*. Mattel has issued many Barbie dolls, including various collectors' editions, of popular ballets such as *Swan Lake* and *The Nutcracker*. They have also produced Barbie dolls in costumes to tie in with the various Barbie animated movies. Ten years ago Golden Bear produced a set of cloth dolls, some with hard plastic heads, which were created in conjunction with the Royal Ballet. These dolls, with soft, bendy bodies, were called the 'Lilya' collection and were dressed to resemble dancers from various well-known ballets. The dolls could also be obtained complete with a stage, which played ballet music as they revolved.

Of course, the classic ballet doll is from *Coppelia* or *The Girl With Enamel Eyes*, and she has been brought out in doll form by Robert Tonner and others. The story is that when doll maker Dr Coppelius makes a beautiful lifelike doll and puts her on his balcony a young man called Franz sees her and falls in love. Unfortunately, he already has a fiancée, Swanhilda, who becomes angry. When she and her friends find a key that opens the doll maker's door, they creep inside and discover that Coppelia is just a doll. Swanhilda decides to take her place and pretends to come alive when Dr Coppelius tries to put Franz's spirit in the doll. Another ballet with a doll, or puppet, storyline is *Petrushka*.

The Manhattan Toy Company issued a set of soft dolls from *Cirque du Soleil* dressed to resemble characters from the show, including a 'Little Dancer from O', while Mattel issued a series of Barbie dolls dressed as cabaret dancers. These were, according to the company, 'inspired by classic femme fatales from the Broadway stage'.

Surprisingly, there don't seem to be many dolls based on the musical theatre, though Mattel did produce a limited edition *Phantom of the Opera* Barbie and Ken gift set for FAO Schwarz. Peggy Nisbet made various doll lookalikes including Lily Langtry. Other characters you might encounter include the 'Gainsborough Lady' (a woman dressed in the style of portraits by Gainsborough, who became famous in the 1930s and 40s for posing and tilting her head to one side at the start of films made by Gainsborough Pictures). Several actresses played the Gainsbourgh Lady, the most famous being Glennis Lorimer. Various companies made 'Gainsborough Lady' dolls.

Some companies such as Clea Bella and Ashton-Drake (Gene) have produced ranges of dolls which represent imaginary characters dressed as actors, actresses or dancers in various roles; for instance, the Gene 'Bird of Paradise' doll. This 15½in doll depicts the Gene Marshall character as a showgirl, swathed in pale-pink tulle. These dolls allow collectors to form a theatrical collection peopled with actors and dancers in elaborate costumes. The Clea Bella 'Dragonfly' and 'Gypsy' have been mentioned earlier. Other Clea Bella imaginary character ballet dolls include the 'Peacock' and the 'Time Bandit'. All the Clea Bella dolls are exquisitely dressed.

Sonja Henie, Reliable.

Innsbruck Winter Olympics.

Occasionally, personalities from the world of sport appear in doll form. Probably the most famous 'sports doll' is one which dates back to the 1930s, when an Olympic skater called Sonja Henie decided to break into the Hollywood movies. She became a phenomenal success, and being a determined lady who insisted on star billing, her ice shows were a sell-out with her fans wanting to see her in the flesh. The Alexander Doll Company made pretty Sonja Henie dolls from a hard composition, fully-jointed with mohair wigs, sleep eyes and open mouths with tiny teeth. They had dimples in their cheeks, just like the real Sonja Henie. Unfortunately they rarely crop up in the UK. Sadly, Sonja's fans were fickle. By the late 1940s she was no longer a box-office draw and the dolls were discontinued, although a plastic version did briefly put in an appearance in the early 1950s.

Slightly later than Sonja was a young Canadian ice-skater, Barbara Ann Scott, who won an Olympic gold medal in 1948 – even more of an achievement than usual as the rink was outdoors and the ice was rutted. On top of everything else, her musical accompaniment suddenly stopped, making it necessary for her to repeat her performance. The medal was just what Canada needed after the rigours of the war, the citizens were immensely proud of their young ice-skater, and the Reliable Toy Company of Toronto commissioned famed American doll designer Bernard Lipfert to design a doll portraying her. The composition doll in her skating outfit was produced from 1948-1954. She was 15in tall, but to find one today in good condition is very difficult as the composition was prone to crazing.

It is often possible to find dolls representing famous football players such as David Beckham, as footballers are produced as figures for sale to fans. Mattel brought out a Barbie 'Torville and Dean' set in 1998 for the Nagano Olympics, but this was really just Barbie and Ken dressed as ice-skaters, rather than an attempt to provide actual lookalike dolls. Other sports dolls available may not represent actual characters, but have been produced to tie in with the Olympics over the years, including a Hasbro Sindy dressed in a smart white, orange and green costume for the 1996 swimming event. Barbie entered the same games as a gymnast wearing a patriotic stretch suit. Even the Cabbage Patch Kids featured in a set of four 'Olympikids' in the 1996 Olympics, representing the US Olympics team and taking part in Track and Field, Weightlifting, Tennis and Gymnastics. These small, moulded plastic dolls were packaged in a colourful, commemorative box featuring the five Olympic rings logo. Mattel issued 'Paralympic Champion Becky' seated in a racing wheelchair to tie in with the 2000 Paralympic Games in Sydney.

Amongst other sporting dolls which you might come across are costume dolls. These include an attractive pair of cloth dolls representing Haakon and Kristin, two children from Norwegian folklore which were produced for the 1994 Lillehammer Winter games. Another delightful costume doll is one made for the Innsbruck Winter Olympics in Austria in 1976. At first glance she looks like an ordinary costume doll, but on her wrist is a label bearing the official Olympics logo. Various others turn up from time-to- time, and are worth looking out for, because they would have been on sale for a very short period, and consequently are a piece of our sporting history.

Chapter Eight

Dolls Representing Royal Characters

ROYAL DOLLS have long been a favourite, not only with collectors but with manufacturers, too, because it gives them the excuse to indulge in elaborate creations using velvet, silk, fur, satin and diamante. Some companies issue just one or two dolls, maybe to cash in on a royal event such as a wedding or Jubilee, or perhaps even just to indulge a whim. But other makers, notably Peggy Nisbet, produced dozens of royal dolls, not just representing dolls in the current Royal Family, but likenesses of kings, queens, princes, princesses and other nobles dating from over the centuries. Dean's, Alpha Farnell, Rosebud, Chad Valley, Franklin Mint and Pedigree are just a few of other makers who produce costume dolls featuring the current Royal Family.

Royal dolls appeal not just to collectors, but to those looking for souvenirs of an event, or of a place or castle with royal connections which they may have visited. During the 1930s the public became obsessed with the 'Little Princesses' – our future queen Princess Elizabeth and her sister Princess Margaret Rose, daughters of George VI and Queen Elizabeth – and several companies produced dolls in their likeness. At the time, cloth dolls were enormously popular and had exquisitely moulded, painted felt faces, and most were affordable by only the more wealthy families. The Chad Valley company issued a 17in Princess Elizabeth doll, dressed in silk and organdie, complete with a pearl necklace. Labelled 'England's Most Popular Princess', she was included in the popular 'Bambini' line, and today is treasured by collectors. Later, the company made delightful representations of both Princesses, wearing delicate party frocks or fitted coats and matching hats.

In a similar mode, the Dean's Rag Book Company produced a charming doll with a moulded felt face, called 'Lilibet', the name by which Princess Elizabeth was affectionately known. Lilibet was made from felt, had jointed arms and legs, was dressed in a classic A-line coat trimmed with a velvet collar and six tiny buttons, and sported a hat with a turned-up brim. This pretty doll came complete with a little dog on a lead, but sadly, when she was updated 11 years later, she didn't have her canine friend in attendance. Yet another cloth doll manufacturer who made Princess Elizabeth cloth dolls in the 1930s was the Alpha Farnell Toys Company. Their dolls had blonde mohair wigs, side-glancing painted blue eyes and velveteen jointed bodies. A beautiful bisque Princess Elizabeth doll was made in the 1930s by the German company Schoenau & Hoffmeister. This doll is particularly popular with collectors of

Princess Elizabeth, Chad Valley.

Edward VIII, Farnell.

Queen Elizabeth in State Robes, Peggy Nisbet.

older dolls, and is very distinctive, featuring a cheeky grin and a mass of blonde curls. At the same time, in America, Madame Alexander issued a charming composition doll which was marked 'Princess Elizabeth'. The company has continued to produce dolls featuring the British Royal Family ever since. Fifty years later, Peggy Nisbet produced a limited edition pair of large porcelain dolls representing the royal sisters as young girls, wearing their trademark smocked summer frocks.

When King Edward VIII was due to be crowned in 1936, a stunning likeness wearing full Highland dress was produced by the J. K. Farnell company. This 14in cloth doll came complete with kilt, brass-buttoned jacket and bearskin, and today is very collectable. As we know the coronation never took place, due to the King's abdication in favour of his younger brother. Consequently, Farnell issued another doll; this time representing George VI dressed in a blue uniform as a Marshall of the Royal Air Force.

The 1953 Coronation of Queen Elizabeth II was the signal for the production of a rash of dolls dressed in coronation robes, including many play dolls intended for children. However, the event also caused problems for the Peggy Nisbet Company, which would later become renowned for the thousands upon thousands of dolls made especially for collectors. When 'Coronation fever' gripped the nation in 1953, Peggy Nisbet, then a designer at Bristol Pottery, decided to model some porcelain figurines of the new Queen. Her novel idea was to create a bisque figurine in a long gown, and then to dress it in silk and velvet coronation regalia, thus making a cross between an ornament and a doll. Once Peggy's prototype was ready, she took it to Harrods, and was amazed to gain an order for 250 dolls. She was a little unprepared for the reaction, and so then followed a hasty search for an artist to paint the faces and for top-quality needlewomen to sew the dresses. Working from home, Peggy managed to get the dolls assembled and delivered to Harrods in time for the Coronation, but interestingly only a couple have ever turned up. Somewhere, they must be lurking in cabinets or cupboards, and today would be quite valuable if found in perfect condition.

The dolls were so well received that Peggy Nisbet developed a thriving doll company specialising in small costume dolls. Over its life of thirty-five years or so, the company produced dozens of likenesses of many members of the modern royal family, amongst them the Queen, Queen Mother, Prince Phillip, Prince Charles, Princess Anne, Princess Diana and various junior royals. Often these dolls were depicted in their ceremonial robes or wedding outfits. She also produced King Edward VIII together with Mrs Simpson, and even dolls from other royal houses, including Princess Grace of Monaco. Although often the facial resemblance was slim, the detailing on the dolls was excellent, with crowns, jewels and clothing all beautifully produced in miniature. The dolls and outfits were all made in Britain, mostly in Peggy Nisbet's small factory in Weston-Super-Mare, while skilled out-workers sewed the clothing.

Amongst the Coronation dolls made for youngsters in 1953 were those made by Pedigree, Mark Payne, Rosebud, Peter Darling and others. Some of the smaller dolls were obviously also intended as souvenirs of the great event, and were treasured, which is why so many still survive today. In addition, as this was not long after the war, people were so used to 'making do' that they bought small plastic or composition dolls to dress themselves at home. Magazines such as *Woman's Weekly* featured appropriate knitting patterns to turn the dolls into queens or courtiers.

Pedigree produced a pair of 7in twins dressed as a 'Peer' and 'Peeress', a 14in 'Peeress' described in its catalogue as 'in approved robes and cap of state', and a 19in 'Marchioness', 'beautifully robed, complete with jewelled tiara and coronet.' Additionally, Pedigree issued larger play dolls, based on the young Princess Anne and Prince Charles, which it called 'Little Princess' and 'Bonnie Charlie', presumably to tie in with the royal event. The 'Little Princess' wore a spotted organdie dress designed by Norman Hartnell, and patterns were available for further outfits. 'Bonnie Charlie' was dressed in a Scottish outfit of kilt and silk shirt. Pedigree also issued a doll called 'Elizabeth' in the Queen's honour, though she bore little likeness to the Queen, as she was basically a girl doll dressed in cotton frocks. A different range of character dolls comprised those made by companies such as Dean's and Chad Valley, which produced a range of celebratory dolls, such as 'Coronation Cuddlums' and 'Cora-nation'. These were a range of cuddly, soft-bodied, patriotic souvenirs, often with plush bodies, presumably intended for small children, and not meant to resemble members of the Royal Family,

Although nowadays we think of the 1950s as the era of the hard plastic doll, composition dolls were still around. In 1953, the Peter Darling and Mark Payne companies, both famed for their singing and speaking dolls, produced large, 26in composition dolls dressed as the Queen, though no attempt had been made at facial realism. These dolls sang, amongst other things, 'God Save The Queen' when the protruding handle, which activated a disc mechanism in her stomach, was turned. Although the resulting sound was scratchy, the dolls contained a wide repertoire of sayings and songs. The Mark Payne and Peter Darling dolls were dressed in white satin gowns, with fur-trimmed scarlet cloaks, blue sashes and golden crowns, and turn up for sale quite often, presumably as they were rather cumbersome for everyday play. Consequently, they are frequently still found in their original boxes, and, amazingly, it is obvious that many were entrusted to the postal services of the day, as sometimes the boxes bear postage stamps from around the time of the Coronation. Of course, in those days there was no bubble wrap, and the dolls were just tissue wrapped.

The next major royal event to inspire doll makers was the Queen's Silver Jubilee in 1977, though it didn't really have much of an impact on the market. Peggy Nisbet, of course, commemorated the occasion, but the strangest doll issued was made by Flair Toys, and designed by fashion queen Mary Quant. The doll was called 'Daisy', an 11½in teen doll wearing a dress which seemed to be made from the Union Jack with two shoulder straps attached, and which just draped over her. However, the box of this 'Britannia Daisy' was delightful, and depicted a patriotic design which included the Coronation coach, crown, Nelson's Column, the Houses of Parliament and a troop of Household Cavalry. It was obviously intended to appeal to tourists. At the same time Pedigree's

Sindy appeared in a much less over-the-top outfit called 'Royal Occasion', which consisted of a cream lace-trimmed gown, matching hat and parasol. This doll, too, was presented in a souvenir box depicting celebratory themes.

A few years later, we entered into Princess Diana fever when dolls were made not only of her in her bridal outfit, but also wearing various dresses she had worn at social functions. These dolls were made as collectors' items by, amongst others, Madame Alexander, Peggy Nisbet, Danbury Mint, Franklin Mint and Ashton-Drake, in both porcelain and vinyl, and were very elegant. But there were problems when Diana met her tragic death in 1997. This was marked by a series of porcelain replicas from Franklin Mint which became the subject of a court case when the Princess's Memorial Fund attempted to sue the company for using her likeness. This company and others went on to produce dozens of designs, amongst them a range of seated, large-eyed toddlers as an imaginary concept of what the Princess could possibly have looked like as a baby. Other dolls issued after the Princess's death included a well-detailed, 11in doll of the Princess by Manley Toy Quest, which was attractively packaged in an oval-fronted box, dressed in a cream, satin wedding gown with a long train, a glittery tiara and a net veil. The box bore the wording, 'From her golden blonde hair and dazzling outfits, to her endless time and involvement in children's charities, Diana was truly a princess.' As it was sold through toy stores, it is one that turns up on a regular basis.

When Diana joined the Royal Family, naturally Peggy Nisbet was one of the first makers to produce a doll, and over the years, Princess Diana became one of her more favourite royals, produced in various mediums, scenarios, outfits and heights. There were several of the standard, 8in-high, resin-type dolls, some of the Princess with her husband, Prince Charles, some of her alone and some of her (or both of them) and a baby. Additionally, Peggy Nisbet teamed up with Royal Doulton to create a series of Princess Diana porcelain dolls, as well as issuing a range of 16in-high vinyl Diana dolls. These beautiful dolls featured Diana in her bouffant wedding gown, and in outfits such as a pale-pink suit, a formal state dress and the famous deep-blue velvet dress she wore on her first visit to America in 1985. When Sarah Ferguson married Prince Andrew in 1986, a 16in doll, an excellent likeness in her wedding dress, was added to the set. The Peggy Nisbet 16in royal vinyl dolls are surprisingly difficult to find nowadays.

For a while in the 1980s, newspapers were filled with pictures of Sarah on the ski slopes, and the German company Gotz produced an attractive 20in play doll, dressed in a royal-blue padded ski-suit and white fur hat. She had a smiling freckled face, and her box was labelled 'Fergie', just in case there was doubt in anyone's mind as to who this doll with the flaming locks was meant to represent. Today, she is extremely collectable. Sarah Ferguson's wedding was commemorated by two of Hasbro Sindy's friends, 'Mark' and 'Marie'. Red-haired Marie's lace and satin full-skirted wedding dress was almost as spectacular as Sarah's, while Mark wore a splendid gold-braided naval outfit with a scarlet sash, similar to that of Prince Andrew's.

Another major royal event was the birth of Prince William, son of Prince Charles and Princess Diana, on 21 June 1982. Two years later he was followed

Queen Elizabeth Coronation Play Doll, Mark Payne.

Queen Elizabeth, Danbury Mint.

Princess Diana, Peggy Nisbet.

Prince William Toddler, Peggy Nisbet.

Princess Catherine, Arklu.   Charles I, Peggy Nisbet.

Henry VIII with Anne Boleyn, Catherine of Aragon and Anne of Cleves, Peggy Nisbet.

by Prince Henry (know as Harry). Once more, Peggy Nisbet was at the forefront, but other dolls included those made by the British company Alresford, founded in 1978 by Margaret Jones. Alresford pioneered porcelain doll-making in Britain and amongst the numerous dolls produced during the existence of this short-lived company were delightful representations of William and Harry as babies. Various companies, such as kit-doll supplier Ridings Craft, issued dolls that they named 'William' in celebration of the new baby prince. As most of these were issued around the time of the royal births, no attempts were made at likeness, as one new-born looks very much like another.

When Peggy Nisbet produced a series of large vinyl play dolls of the princes, collectors were unsure what to make of them. Too expensive for the average child, yet rather large to display, these dolls seemed to fit uncomfortably in the range of dolls produced by the company. These dolls were 18in tall, and were chunky, bent-legged babies or straight-legged toddlers, created in an excellent quality pale vinyl which gave the dolls the look of porcelain. The first vinyl Prince William as a baby doll was issued in 1984, and was available in two costume designs, 'Prince William Sunday Best at Buckingham Palace' and 'Prince William at Highgrove House.' Highgrove William wore a blue-and-white smocked romper suit with a matching beret-type hat, while the Buckingham Palace Prince William was obviously dressed for a very special occasion in a suit of royal-blue velvet, white frilly shirt, blue velvet hat and red velvet bow tie. The outfit was a red-white-and-blue patriotic tribute to his grandparents when he visited them at Buckingham Palace. In 1986, a slightly older version of Prince William was available – 'Prince William Sailor Suit', wearing a white and navy get-up, while the Prince Harry Sunsuit', in red and white, was also issued; an identical doll to the William ones. In the same series, Peggy Nisbet produced 'Prince Harry as a New Born Baby' dressed in a long white baby gown and a white bonnet based on the outfit worn in the first photographs taken by Lord Snowdon.

The most recent major royal 'happening', the marriage of Prince William to Catherine Middleton, has also been commemorated in doll form, but so far, fewer dolls have appeared than with the other major events. The first doll to appear depicted Catherine, or Kate, as she is familiarly known, in the sapphire-blue dress she wore to announce her engagement. Made by Bradford Exchange, she is 16 in tall, vinyl, and her likeness to Kate is exceptional. The wedding took place on 29 April 2011, and was viewed by millions across the globe. Danbury Mint was determined to be the first to issue a replica. Amazingly, it took just five hours for its designers to copy the bridal gown and put up a collectable doll for sale on the company's website on the actual wedding day. They managed it by arranging for a designer and seamstresses to sketch, create and sew Catherine's bridal gown and veil, fashion her tiara and reproduce her hairstyle, on a ready-sculpted doll, in order to create a prototype. By noon on the great day the bridal doll was complete and orders were already being taken.

Another company, Paradise Galleries, advertised not just Catherine in her wedding dress, but her groom, Prince William, in his uniform of the Irish Guards. These 17in-high dolls, modelled from vinyl, both had impressively accurate depictions of the costumes. Arklu Ltd produced a limited edition

Barbie-sized doll, entitled 'Princess Catherine', with rooted brown hair. She was dressed in a blue outfit with a bright-pink hat, and the box boasted that 'the doll has been dressed and accessorised by hand-picked British fashion and design leaders'. A portion of the proceeds were donated to the 'Help For Heroes' charity. The company also produced a 'Royal Wedding' doll.

Dolls depicting the current Royal Family continue to surface, not only in the UK, but also abroad, notably in the USA. Ginny, for instance, has appeared several times as 'a queen', while Madame Alexander has made a delightful set depicting Prince Charles and Princess Anne as toddlers. Some representations of the Royal Family are quirky, unusual or disrespectful, such as a series of royal caricatures based on puppets used in the television programme *Spitting Image*, in the 1980s. Amongst them were vinyl heads and even dog toys in the form of rubber dolls. Also sometimes seen are sets of wooden matryoshka (Russian nesting dolls) bearing likenesses of the Royal Family. When the engagement of Prince Charles to Lady Diana was announced, Sylvia Wilgoss of Dean's designed a set of rag dolls sold as a printed sheet to be made up at home. Unfortunately, due to the construction of the dolls, 'Diana', in her blue engagement suit, was distinctly podgy with enormously thick legs, and Charles did not fare much better.

It isn't just the current Royal Family that inspires doll manufacturers; the richness of royal costumes through the centuries cries out to be depicted in doll form. Once again, the undisputed designer of these historical royal dolls was Peggy Nisbet, who not only produced models of the tried and tested, such as Henry VIII and his wives, but also issued dolls representing much lesser-famed royals. For instance, amongst her repertoire were such dolls as Hengist King of the Angles, Richard III, Henry VI, James VI, William III and Richard I. The Tudors proved an extremely popular set and Henry VIII in his iconic pose is beloved by so many doll makers, as are his six wives. Apparently, when Peggy modelled the first Henry VIII doll, his stomach was so fat it kept sinking. She also found that his feet, when in the characteristic position, wouldn't support him, and eventually had to model his body in once piece down to the ankles and then attach the feet separately, so that they could be turned out.

The full-skirted gowns of the wives, with their rich brocades and trims, were not only attractive to Peggy, who made several versions over the years, but to a plethora of other makers. Companies such as Rexard, Shallowpool, the Little Gallery of Penzance, Regency Fine Arts, and Ann Parker, as well as countless smaller makers who often produce one-off dolls or limited handmade dolls for the tourist trade, all enjoyed modelling this period. Not only were the clothes appealing, but the Tudors were also very popular with collectors and as holiday souvenirs. Out of interest, makers of these dolls, especially the small, 8in-or-so, types, often had great difficulty sourcing the fabric. By their very nature, brocade and velvet are thick and heavy and, a few decades ago particularly, the ultra-fine versions now available were not around. Therefore, makers treasured any less-heavy versions of rich materials that they came across, and even small snippets were utilised in the dolls' costumes.

Shallowpool, a cottage industry based in Fowey, Cornwall, made several beautiful royal dolls. Completely handmade, with plaster heads and padded wire armature bodies, no two were alike. At first glance, their dolls are similar in style to Peggy Nisbet's creations, but they are not resin and on comparison the difference is obvious. Shallowpool made such characters as Charles II, Henry VIII and his wives, and Elizabeth I, and these can sometimes be found, but are nowhere near as plentiful as the Nisbet dolls, which is why they tend to sell for higher prices.

Historical dolls produced by the Rexard Company, based in Worthing, Sussex, were a common sight in the 1960s, 70s and 80s. They were made of a basic, hard, thin plastic, standing around 8in tall, all with similar faces, with painted eyes and their wigs coloured and styled to suit the character. Often they bore a tag which read 'Designed by Odette Arden. Made in the British Empire.' Their historical range covered many of the popular royal dolls, including a set of Henry VIII and his wives, and although the dolls were not of the quality of the Peggy Nisbet dolls, they were still very attractive. The dolls were packed in boxes which were usually triangular, but sometimes square, and were widely sold in newsagents, corner shops, confectioner's shops, and tourist outlets. They were a cheap way of adding a costume doll to a collection. As with the Peggy Nisbet dolls, they were not intended to be undressed, and so there are still thousands upon thousands of the dolls around, invariably in good condition, as in the main they were kept on display. Mattel included some royal dolls in its 1990s 'Great Eras' collection, amongst them 'Elizabethan Queen', representing Queen Elizabeth I, 'Egyptian Queen' (Cleopatra) and Chinese Empress Guo Zong, from the Qing Dynasty. All these dolls were, as with all Mattel collectors' dolls, stunningly dressed and sold in a special display box.

Another historical doll frequently seen is Mary, Queen of Scots. Most of the figures depict her in black velvet with a white ruff and a crucifix, so she is very distinctive. Coming a little more up to date, Queen Victoria is another popular subject. The gift shop at Windsor Castle has sold delightful soft cloth dolls depicting Victoria, as well as the Prince Regent, later George IV.

Over the years, dozens of manufacturers, both here and abroad, have created dolls to represent past and present members of the royal family. Events such as royal weddings, investitures and visits have all been commemorated too, and so there are plenty to look out for. Royal dolls make a fascinating collectable, and although we don't know what the next royal event will be, you can be sure that someone, somewhere, will produce a doll to commemorate it.

Elizabethan Queen, Mattel.

Chapter Nine

Topsy-Turvys and Face-Change Dolls

I T'S EXCITING when one doll suddenly becomes two – and it happens quite a lot in the doll world. One minute you are looking at a pretty, smiling doll, and then you move her skirt and find you are holding a grumpy, crying doll instead! Dolls that can be altered in appearance have been popular for decades, and as well as providing extra play-value they give novelty interest. Centuries ago in England, rag dolls with different faces on either side were used as a form of shop sign for rag merchants and called 'Moggy Dolls', so face-change dolls have a long history. It seems magical to children when a sad doll becomes happy, or a doll in tatters is transformed into a princess. Sometimes, a prince or a witch might be revealed with a quick wrist-flick, meaning that storytelling gains another dimension. Nowadays, numerous people are building up collections of 'transforming dolls', and for the most part they aren't expensive.

Dolls can be made to change their appearance in several ways, but probably the most commonly-found are topsy-turvy dolls, which consist of two half-dolls joined at the waist. Sometimes there is an extra doll attached at the back, or maybe a hat can be pushed aside to reveal an extra face. Other transformable kinds include dolls with interchangeable heads, two- or three-faced dolls, dolls with blank faces which can be redrawn again and again, and dolls whose expressions change because their rubber faces are moulded over a moveable wire armature.

Cloth topsy-turvy dolls are the easiest to find; frequently they have fabric, china, celluloid, composition or papier-mâché faces. They might even be knitted, as there are plenty of knitting patterns available, including a range by Jean Greenhowe who specialises in knitted dolls. Sometimes, topsy-turvy dolls tell a story; they may portray Cinderella in rags turning into the belle of the ball with a flick of her skirts, or perhaps Red Riding Hood who changes to grandma. The wolf could be incorporated too, maybe when grandma's hat is moved, to give even more value. All these topsy-turvy dolls work on the same principle; they wear long skirts, and hidden beneath them you'll find another head and body rather than a pair of legs. Another commonly found theme is a black doll turning to white. Topsy-turvy dolls are often found in tourist shops abroad, and the West Indies seem to have a particular penchant for them, selling all kinds of colourful creations.

These changeable dolls have been made by many manufacturers, amongst them Peggy Nisbet, Bruckner, Jellycat, North American Bear Company, Madame

Alexander, Roddy and Toy Works. The Peggy Nisbet dolls appeared during the 1980s and featured porcelain heads. One of the dolls was Cinderella, who turned from rags to riches, which is quite a popular theme amongst makers. The other doll was an unusual one representing 'My Fair Lady', changing from poor Eliza Doolittle to posh Eliza dressed for Ascot. In the 1930s the Madame Alexander Doll Company made a composition doll which consisted of a pair of dolls joined at the waist, one sprayed black, the other pink. The first doll had pigtails of black woolly hair, while the other doll's hair was moulded and painted. Dolls such as these have been found by several other makers too, and various legends abound, including one which states that black-and-white dolls came into being during the time of the slave trade. Little girls wanted black dolls like them, but the slave traders disapproved, so the doll had a white head under the skirt which the child could quickly flip up. Another story is that as white dolls were considered more special, the slaves' children were not allowed them, and so their dolls were made to be changed to black-headed ones when necessary.

At the beginning of the 1900s, Albert Bruckner produced a topsy-turvy doll with moulded, printed, stockinette face masks for Horsman Dolls in America. The doll bore the patent date 8 July 1901, and had a particularly attractive, gentle face, with the white doll having printed hair and the black doll having coarse, fibre hair. Plastic topsy-turvys include a Roddy girl doll from the 1960s, made up from two torsos joined at the waist. This was possibly a prototype, as not many are around. Fairly easily found today is a very pretty topsy-turvy doll made by Knickerbocker in the 1970s. This doll has two moulded soft vinyl heads. One is slightly smiling with open side-glance eyes and delightful blushed cheeks. The other has the eyes shut and a very cross face. The 'awake' doll wears a full-skirted blue and yellow braid-trimmed dress with floral bonnet, while the 'grumpy' head's skirt is blue, and her bodice and bonnet are spotted.

The British company Jellycat, maker of many quirky soft toys, produced cloth topsy-turvy dolls up until recently. Its dolls were particularly elaborately made and included exciting themes such the 'Frog Princess', 'Nursery Rhymes' and 'The Enchanted Garden', as well as the more usual Cinderella. One unusual Jellycat doll featured Alice in Wonderland, who changed from Alice into the Queen of Hearts. This innovative Alice was beautifully dressed in a blue, silky, full-skirted dress, which was appliquéd around the hem and had green trees and images of creatures such as the White Rabbit. Her apron was trimmed with red, and she held a blue-striped teapot containing the Dormouse. When she was turned upside down, she morphed into the Queen of Hearts in a long, red-and-yellow satin dress. Unfortunately, factory costs subsequently caused Jellycat to concentrate on their quirky toy animals.

A company called Taylors made another interesting doll, Snow White, with the seven dwarfs attached to her skirt. When the skirt was flipped, the scary witch, in the disguise of the old apple seller, was revealed. The North American Bear company has produced a large range of these delightful upside-down dolls, amongst them Dorothy from Wizard of Oz (who changes into her dog, Toto), Alice in Wonderland (changes to Queen of Hearts), Rapunzel (flips to a castle with the prince and witch), and a mermaid that flips to her alter ego with legs. The company also makes some triples – a Frog Princess with a prince who has a removable frog mask, Bo Peep with a 'lost sheep' and a 'found sheep' (including sound effects!), and the Nutcracker which reveals Clara, the Prince and the Nutcracker.

Other cloth topsy-turvy dolls often seen are colourful stockinette dolls from the West Indies, whose costumes change when they are reversed. Usually their skirts are embroidered with the place name, or it is printed onto the fabric, such as St Lucia or Barbados. Another form of costume doll has a moulded felt face with painted side-glance eyes, which turns from a Spanish senorita into a peasant girl. These dolls have a Lenci (a doll produced by designer Elena Scavini) appearance but their origin seems unknown. The black-to-white idea also appears in cloth. In order to promote racial harmony, an Australian company called Milly Molly brought out a rag doll that turned from white to black. The dolls' slogan was, 'We may look different but we feel the same', and the marketing theme was a 'reconciliation doll for world peace'. Another method of changing a doll's appearance is to make a cloth doll with two fronts. This method was used for an attractive doll, 'Bobby Snooks', made by American company Toy Works in the 1980s. On one side he is a smart schoolboy, but turn him over and you find a different boy, tattered and torn after a fight, complete with a plaster on his nose. (*See Chapter 3.*)

Manufacturers have for years puzzled about how to produce dolls which changed their expressions and have come up with plenty of innovative ideas. A maker called Dominico Checkeni took out a US patent for a four-faced doll in 1866. Curiously, the heads turned on a horizontal axis; the majority of the later rotational-headed dolls used a vertical axis. Antique china dolls sometimes had swivel-heads which could be changed with a twist of a knob. These dolls could have several faces, though usually two or three, and these were usually a smiling face, a sleeping one and a crying one, with a bonnet covering the spare faces so that at first glance the doll looked conventional. During the 1970s and 80s, this method was revived and a number of inexpensive multi-faced bisque china dolls appeared in the shops. These dolls are now becoming sought by collectors as the early ones cost so much. The same technique has been used with plastic dolls which were particularly popular during the 1950s and 60s in America. Companies such as Ideal issued a series of them such as a soft-bodied girl with a knob on her head hidden by a bonnet. Her three faces changed from sleep, to smile, to cry.

Various manufacturers have made vinyl face-change play dolls from time to time, and so the observant collector should keep a lookout as it is surprising what can be found, which is why any likely doll needs to be examined for twist knobs or handles. 'Toni Two', a toothy toddler wearing a red-striped dress, was sold in packaging which boasted, 'Turn my head and I'm mad, turn my head and I'm glad'. Another interesting doll was an unmarked 8in 'Hong Kong baby' dressed in a blue floral hooded suit, which featured a large knob on top of its head and, when turned, showed one of three expressions. Doll designer Marie Osmond has featured two-face dolls in her collector's range, including 'Missy', a beautifully dressed doll in a turquoise gingham frock and mob cap, whose expression could be changed from happy to sad. In the 1960s the American Toy and Doll Company issued an odd-looking, rather scary, three-faced caricature doll wearing a rubber

Spanish Topsy-Turvy.

Cinderella Topsy-Turvy, Peggy Nisbet.

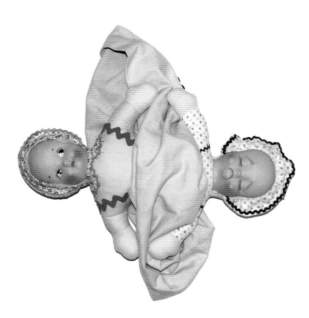

White to Black composition Topsy-Turvy.   Vinyl Topsy-Turvy, Knickerbocker.

Cheerful Tearful, Mattel.

Three Face Doll, unmarked.

West Indian Topsy-Turvy.

hat with a turn knob, in its 'Whimsie' dolls series. American company Falca Toys was responsible for one of the most delightful two-faced dolls of recent times. This sturdy, 22in-baby was made in the 1980s and two faces – one happy, one miserable – were beautifully and realistically moulded from quality vinyl. In addition, she featured a crying/laughing sound chip which, rather cleverly, would only operate when the correct face was forward. It would be extremely easy to overlook this doll by assuming she was just another well-made play doll, especially if she was wearing a bonnet so one face was hidden.

Manufacturers also developed a way of changing faces by modelling the doll's head on a wire frame, using thin, soft plastic for the 'skin', and this method was used by Mattel, such as in the case of its 1960 'Cheerful Tearful' or their later 'Saucy' doll. The expression of the Cheerful Tearful doll changed from a smile to a pout when her arm was raised, and she looked quite cute, but in contrast, Saucy was hilarious. She was operated in the same manner, but she grimaced, rolled her eyes, and made terrible faces, and it is quite likely she had a really bad influence on her little owners, as they were sure to have copied her! Famosa Toys later introduced 'Baby Expressions', a battery-operated face-change doll, available as either a boy or girl. These large baby dolls had a very thin plastic/latex over the wire armature, and although not particularly pretty, were very popular for a while.

Rarely, dolls are sold with spare heads, and this idea was patented by a French doll maker called Le Tort in 1884. The idea was soon copied. Decades later, a celluloid doll was produced using this method, and it came with three assorted girl heads, a boy head – and a cat! It must have seemed rather odd to have a cat-headed doll. During the 1960s, Telitoy made a teen doll called Brenda with three heads, each with different coloured hair. Today, the idea is particularly popular amongst some of the teen dolls made for collectors and allows the appearance to be slightly altered, even if the expression is not. Nowadays, plenty of dolls feature interchangeable wigs, while a clever 1974 doll known as 'Tiffany Taylor', had a scalp which could be twisted, thus changing easily from blonde to brunette. Dolls with 'hair-grow' mechanisms such as Tressy, Crissy and Goldilocks are another example of a doll changing its style to suit the owner's mood.

Possibly one of the most unusual ways of altering a doll's face was seen in Mattel's 'What's Her Face' dolls. These came with totally blank faces so the owner could design them as she liked, and they had spare wigs and funky outfits. They could be instantly given a new persona. Yet even that idea wasn't new; folk dolls, especially the straw types, sometimes come with blank faces. Dolls such as those made by the Amish people have blank faces because of their religious beliefs which forbid the depiction of the human face on any object. Sometimes manufacturers give play dolls bland or indistinct features to allow a child to stretch the imagination, often with just a couple of dots for eyes and a line for a mouth. The highly collectable Sasha dolls have neutral, moulded faces with little colouring, except for the eyes. The dolls can look happy, contented, sad, or dreamy according to the mood of the viewer, and so, although they are not 'face-change' dolls as such, they do allow for imaginative interpretation of expression.

Chapter Ten

Dolls in Advertising

A DVERTISING MEMORABILIA seems to be everywhere nowadays, yet it isn't a new phenomenon; ever since people made products, they have needed to advertise them. Sometimes, dolls are used for advertising promotions in which you can send away for a doll in exchange for a few tokens cut from a packet. Other promotional campaigns supply the doll free attached to the product, or allow you to buy the doll, probably at a reduced rate. These usually come with an advertising logo affixed. Over the years, dolls have been used to advertise a wide variety of products including soup, baby food, sweets, laundry, soap and hair products, comics and stock cubes.

Many doll collectors are attracted to one of the most famous of all promotional dolls, 'Betty Oxo'. Made by Dean's Rag Book Company, Betty appeared during the 1920s and 30s. According to Dean's Neil Miller, Betty was made in several versions, the first one known as 'Little Miss Oxo'. This pretty doll was filled with wood-wool and featured a 'Tru-to-Life' moulded face. She initially appeared in 1925, dressed in a navy-blue outfit, and her hair was short and fluffy. Promotional posters issued at the time stated, 'The dolls will be awarded to the 50,000 persons from whom the largest number of Oxo cube outside wrappers is received...' which conjures up an image of a small girl force feeding gravy to her father!

The 1930s version of Betty Oxo, wore a short velveteen dress, often with a fur-trimmed cape or collar, and a matching hat. Her hands were tucked inside a muff, and she had a sweet smile and side-glance eyes. Betty Oxo dolls in good condition fetch high prices with collectors today, but many that are found are very grubby and velveteen is extremely difficult to clean. Amazingly, to obtain one of these desirable dolls it was necessary to collect 480 Oxo wrappers, so stock cube gravy must have featured strongly on the menu in those days.

The Dean's Rag Book Company also manufactured advertising dolls for companies such as Boots the Chemist, though these don't seem to be as fondly remembered as the Oxo girls. Boots' dolls included a wounded soldier dating from 1915 which was sold to make money for injured troops, and a printed cotton 'Puss In Boots', but perhaps the most well-known of the dolls made for Boots by Dean's was 'Betty Boots'. This cute little girl, first issued in 1924, wore a checked romper suit and an enormous bow on her head. She was subsequently

Betty Oxo, Dean's.

Betty Boots, Dean's

Bisto Kids

Bertie Bassett, Diane Jones.

Ronald McDonald.

Jelly Babies, Trebor Bassett.

re-issued in 1991. Neil Miller states that these replica dolls were originally displayed in the baby departments of Boots stores but didn't sell well until they were switched to the gift section and sales soared.

Other promotional dolls produced by Dean's Rag Book Company included 'Miss Sue', dating from 1924. This rag doll wore an apron and chef's hat, and advertised Suet Flakes – 'Made from 100% pure fat'. A slogan like that used today would surely hold no appeal at all. One of the prettiest of Dean's promotional rag dolls was 'Mignonne', created by designer Pauline Guilbert in 1912. Mignonne stood 14in tall and was made from printed cotton. She wore a red-spotted dress with a green apron, and clutched a big-eared Dean's 'Puck' doll. Although she wasn't exactly an advertising doll, she was certainly an attractive promotional item. Mignonne was reissued in 1981 to mark the centenary of the Church of England Children's Society.

Many companies run such successful campaigns that their advertising characters become household names, and when reproduced in doll form, are instantly recognisable to consumers as well as collectors. Characters such as the Bisto Kids, the Milky Bar Kid, Bertie Bassett, Fred the Homepride Flour Grader, Sunny Jim, The Tetley Tea Folk, Darren and Lisa the Comfort dolls, Ronald McDonald, Jelly Babies and the Campbell Kids are just a few of the hundreds of advertising symbols that have been converted into doll form.

Cartoonist Will Owen created some advertising posters just after the First World War which featured a pair of scruffy urchins known as the 'Bisto Kids'. At the time, ragamuffins like these were a common sight, and this pair won hearts as they raised their noses in the air, sniffed and exclaimed, 'Aah, Bisto!' as they caught the delicious gravy aroma. It proved such a successful advertising campaign that we still recognise the Bisto Kids today, and the phrase itself is still regularly trotted out at many a mealtime. Various dolls and figurines have been made of the hungry Kids over the years including a composition-headed pair with soft fabric bodies, and a rare china cruet set made by Wade. In the late 1980s, a revamped design of the Bisto Kids was issued in the form of rag dolls, depicting them with modern clothes and less scrawny faces. These dolls were sold in aid of the NSPCC, and the message on their backs read, 'I helped raise £25,000 for the NSPCC Bisto Kids Fund 1989'.

A very well-known 'sweet' advertising character is the colourful Bertie Bassett, a man made from colourful liquorice allsorts, and carrying a liquorice stick cane. The 12in-high plush dolls were made by Welsh company Diane Jones International in the 1980s. Interestingly, the various liquorice allsorts sweets have names; the pink and yellow ones with black centres are 'coconut chips', the black cylindrical ones are 'plugs', while the round, pink-and-blue ones covered in tiny beads are 'buttons'. Another 'sweet' doll often found is a Jelly Baby, or to be exact, there are six of them, in various colours. Soft, plush versions of the babies can be found, as well as a vinyl range that dates from 1988, while, for chocolate lovers, a popular character who has appeared as a doll is the Milky Bar Kid. This young boy dressed as a cowboy first appeared advertising the chocolate in 1961 and various plush versions are often seen.

Tea drinkers will be familiar with the Tetley Tea Folk, amongst them Sidney, Maurice and the Gaffer, characters in an extensive television advertising campaign. These were made as attractive plush dolls during the 1990s, and later as plush money boxes, while the celebrated Robertson's gollies also appeared in doll form. Robertson's gollies had been linked to James Robertson and Sons (maker of preserves) since the early 1900s, when they adopted the golly as their mascot. Later, paper labels could be saved and exchanged for an enamel badge. In 2002 the company decided to drop the characters, to the dismay of golly lovers, and there was a scramble amongst fans to send off the last of their jam jar tokens for plush bride, bridegroom or ballerina gollies. Fred, also known as the 'Homepride Man', is a smart little man in a black suit and bowler hat, who has also been made as a soft bean-filled doll. One version bears his name embroidered on his foot.

Fast food chains have issued promotional dolls, notably Ronald McDonald, the brightly-coloured clown from McDonalds, and several versions have appeared over the years as soft toys. Ronald's jovial face and red-and-yellow outfit make him a firm favourite with youngsters. In the 1990s a vinyl girl play doll was issued, dressed in a blue romper suit with a 'Happy Meal Girl' bib. This cute doll came with her McDonald's burger, packet of fries and carton of drink, and, thanks to sound effects, not only did she slurp, but she burped as well. Hopefully, her young owner didn't copy her when they visited a fast food chain. In 1982 the company lent its logo to a Sindy doll, dressed in a smart, brown McDonald's trouser suit. This doll is quite difficult to find today. Barbie, too, has advertised McDonalds, amongst many other promotions. The Little Chef chain of food outlets features 'Charlie the Chef', a soft, bean-filled doll dressed in a chef's hat, white jacket and black-check trousers.

One of the most famous cloth dolls of all time owes his origins to an early 1900s breakfast cereal, Force wheat flakes, which ran a highly successful advertising campaign using a figure called 'Sunny Jim'. From the thirties onwards, Sunny Jim – an old-fashioned gentleman in an elongated periwig (a man's wig popular in the seventeenth and eighteenth centuries), and with a pointed nose and red jacket – was issued as a rag doll. The dolls were made for several decades and were obtainable through the Force cereal makers, A.C. Fincken & Co., based in Hertfordshire. Countless small boys called Jim gained the nickname 'Sunny Jim' when the advertising was at its peak. Posters bore slogans such as 'High oe'r the fence leaps Sunny Jim, Force is the food that raises him!' while an early rhyme ran:

'Vigour vim, perfect trim,
Force made him Sunny Jim.'

An unusual promotional doll from Unigate Dairies appeared during the early 1980s and depicted a beaming milkman dressed in a smart navy uniform trimmed with red and bearing the Unigate logo. This well-detailed toy came with a black PVC shoulder bag to hold his takings, but he didn't come with any

Unigate Milkman.

Cinzano Girl.

Lisa Weaver and Darren Denim, Comfort Dolls, Lever Faberge.

pintas. Another kind of drink was publicised by the Cinzano girl and boy. The girl wore a yellow, white and green harlequin-patterned dress and a black hat emblazoned with the Cinzano logo. Her shoes were white leather and she carried a large red suede-look bag, big enough to hold a small Cinzano bottle. The boy was dressed in similar colours. These well-made, attractive dolls were made in Slovakia and featured round padded-fabric faces and black bead eyes.

Coca-Cola has been linked to several doll promotions, including a set of Coca-Cola kids made by Ertl and issued in the 1990s. These small vinyl dolls wore various outfits all bearing the Coca-Cola logo, and they came with mini bottles of the drink as well as a toy such as skateboard or a scooter. Not long ago Madame Alexander produced a delightful Coca-Cola doll, just 10in tall and dressed as a 1920s 'Flapper' in a lacy dress.

A pair of dolls issued by Unilever's fabric-softening product Comfort, has enjoyed much popularity recently. Cloth dolls 'Lisa Weaver' and 'Darren Denim' have appeared in adverts produced by Aardman Animation which feature 'Clothworld', a world made from cloth. Fairy Soap also issued a doll based upon a towelling-nappy-clad toddler on its soap bars known as the 'Fairy Baby.' The soap was particularly popular during the 1940s and 50s, and subsequently, bendy-type dolls made from a type of foam rubber, complete with a painted-on quiff of hair, were produced. They were sold as 'Bendy Bubbas'. Also connected with soap was the famous little boy painted by Millais who was later used to advertise Pears soap, and various dolls featuring him in his green velvet suit have appeared over the years (*See Chapter 7*).

Many of the advertising dolls, though known in Britain, were much more famous in America, such as the 'Campbell Kids', designed by illustrator Grace

Gerber Baby.

Sindy Cabin Crew.

Wiederseim (later, Drayton). These cheeky, chubby toddlers advertised condensed soup, and featured side-glance eyes and curvy smiles. They first appeared on posters during the early 1900s, and because they proved so popular Horsman issued a selection of dolls with composition heads and fabric bodies in 1910. Composition Campbell Kids were made throughout the first half of the twentieth century, though they almost disappeared in the Depression. However, in the 1940s they bounced back to support the war effort by advertising 'Better Soups for Victory'. After the war the various types of vinyl Campbell Kids were made. In 1994 the dolls were sold packaged in soup cans to celebrate Campbell's 125th anniversary, and they are still very much collected today.

Another advertising doll particularly popular in America is the 'Gerber Baby', and many different types have been produced. Some of these babies are very sweet faced, though others have a more surly expression. These babies with their circular, open mouths first appeared during the 1930s, and were designed by an artist called Dorothy Hope, based on her neighbour's baby. At first, the dolls were fabric with silk-screened faces, but later, vinyl versions were made. Many of the dolls were only obtainable with tokens collected from jars of Gerber baby food. A porcelain-headed limited edition Gerber baby was produced in 1983, and Gerber baby dolls still appear from time to time. In America the Heinz Baby doll was issued; a squeaky, rubber tot wearing a bib, white pants and shoes. One of the US classics is the Pillsbury Dough Boy, also known as 'Poppin' Fresh', which doesn't seem very well-known in Britain. Created in 1965, this white, pudgy doll with bright-blue eyes and a chef's hat, chuckles when its tummy is pressed. In 1990 a 25th Birthday Special Edition was made,

Many companies have used small, hard plastic dolls to advertise their product, such as the British 'Colgate Fairy' and the American 'Colgate Princess' from the 1950s. The Colgate-Palmolive Fairy was a small Roddy doll who regularly turns up in Britain as it seems she was treasured alongside the Christmas decorations. Dressed in white with a silver trim, she was despatched when a small sum of money and some soap wrappers were sent to the company. The American doll, obtainable for 50 cents in 1951, wore a red-and-white-striped satin dress with a yellow braid trim at the bodice. Both the Colgate Roddy fairy doll and the Colgate Princess were approximately 8in high.

Various dolls bear a company's logo or tie in with a product even though they are not actually advertising characters in their own right, such as the 1952 Palitoy 'Pin-Up' doll to promote Pin-Up perms (permed hair was the in-thing at the time). The Pin-Up dolls had 'magic nylon hair which may be shampooed and play-waved with the Pin-Up Play Perm outfit supplied.' The same company issued the 'Girl' doll, a linkup with *Girl Comic* one of the leading comics of the day, who wore a logo-printed dress with a belt buckle in the shape of the comic's girl's head logo.

A growing trend is for companies such as airlines to sell souvenir teen dolls that are dressed in replicas of their uniforms. Other companies include holiday group Pontins whose doll was dressed as one of their famous Bluecoats. In the early 2000s Vivid Imaginations produced a Sindy doll wearing a Virgin Airlines red cabin crew outfit. More recently, Sindy was issued by British Airways in a 'retro' form. These retro Sindys represented 1960 and 1967, and showed the outfits worn by stewardesses at the time. The 1967 doll wore the pretty, flower-decorated 'paper dress' worn on flights between New York and the Caribbean, while the 1960s doll was dressed in the standard navy BOAC air stewardess uniform. Sindy was also involved in publicising mini Rolo chocolates during the 2000s when an extremely small number of the dolls were issued in Rolo T-shirts. These dolls are very rare. Barbie is often used in advertising by Bloomingdales, Hamleys, Disney, Warner Brothers, Toys R Us, McDonalds (as mentioned) and many other companies. So it always worthwhile to keep a look out as you go round the supermarket for special doll offers. Who knows? One day, they may become as valuable as Betty Oxo, who now sells for a three-figure sum, when originally, all she cost was a few-hundred stock cube wrappers!

There is one other advertising category – dolls representing people who have featured in advertisements. An interesting collection could be formed, though it probably wouldn't be very large. Models, actresses and other personalities are used in promotional work, many of which appear in doll form. For instance, Claudia Schiffer was the face of L'Oreal Elnett Hairspray in 2005, Naomi Campbell advertised Tesco (2005), Kylie Minogue appeared for Agent Provocateur in 2001 and in 2002 Victoria Beckham enjoyed Walkers crisps! Several Victoria Beckham dolls have been produced. (*See Chapter 11*). In 1995, Hasbro produced a Naomi Campbell doll, dressed in a pink and black stylised gown with a train while in the same series Claudia Schiffer wore a glamorous silver gown. Jakks Pacific Inc released two 12in versions of Kylie Minogue in 2004. One was based on the red Dolce & Gabbana performance costume that Kylie wore to the World Music Awards, and the other wore the 'Silvanemesis' outfit, also by Dolce & Gabbana.

Twiggy, (real name Lesley Hornby) began her career as a model in the 1960s and now features in adverts for Marks and Spencer. In 1966 Mattel issued an 11in Twiggy doll dressed in a striped mini dress and long yellow boots. Four decades later, in 2001, Franklin Mint produced a superb collectors' Twiggy doll, standing 16in high. She wore a psychedelic cat suit and dangly flower earrings. More outfits were available, as well as a large wardrobe trunk to store them. Twiggy dolls have also been made by other manufacturers. Additional dolls to include in this fun collection could be Emma Watson (Nestles Cheerios 2001), Keira Knightly (Chanel 2007) and Nicole Kidman (Chanel 2006 and Nintendo 2007), amongst others.

Chapter Eleven

Dolls in Music

THE LAST decade or two has seen a huge increase in the personality cult with programmes such as *Big Brother*, the *X-Factor* and *Britain's Got Talent* in which people can become celebrities overnight – but their downfall is often just as speedy. Exactly the same thing happens with a certain category of dolls. Dolls, often representing pop music personalities, flood the shops at inflated prices, but within a few months the star has fallen back to earth. Consequently, toyshops and end-of-line outlets have shelves stacked with dusty doll boxes, containing alter egos waiting to be sold off cheaply.

Boy George, Sharpegrade LJN.

Naturally, there are dolls representing major names from the musical world which usually, though not always, are consistent sellers. These include Elvis Presley, Frank Sinatra, Cher, ABBA, Michael Jackson, Kylie Minogue and the Beatles. Then there are others that were sold off cheaply at the time, but are now, for various reasons, in demand. Many of the 'classic' dolls are sold by Mattel in their Barbie ranges, including a 1999 set, 'Barbie Loves Frankie'. This depicted crooner Frank Sinatra, smart in his tan-plaid sports jacket and black slacks, together with Barbie in 1940s' get-up of pleated skirt and blue jacket, holding a 78 rpm record. A year later, Mattel brought out a Sinatra doll in a black suit and fedora hat, with microphone and music stand. Entitled 'The Recording Years', it appeared in the Timeless Treasures range. Particularly collectable is anything to do with the Beatles, such as the set of dolls issued in 1964 by Remco and which are now rare. These Beatles dolls were vinyl character-type creations featuring the group with moulded clothing, 'real' hair and overlarge nodding heads, and were ornamental. Paul, John and George came with an autographed guitar, while Ringo had a drum kit, and they were sold in Woolworths at 19/11 the set. With hindsight, they would have been a very wise investment – as would the ABBA dolls from the following decade.

The ABBA set represented the four group members Frida, Benny, Agnetha and Björn, and was issued by Matchbox in 1978. Each doll was around 9in tall, and today a complete mint and boxed set costs hundreds of pounds. Another set of dolls from around the same time was Sonny and Cher, though today's value is nothing like that of the ABBA dolls. Sonny and Cher were made by Mego, and were slightly taller at 12in. Many different outfits were available separately. Those designed for 'Cher' were by Bob Mackie. In recent years a Cher doll has been issued by Mattel in a fabulous series of collector's dolls with exciting and iconic costumes based on her stage outfits. Other classic singers from Mattel include Barbra Streisand and Diana Ross. Dolls such as these are created especially for the collector's market and are not intended as play dolls for children. This means that invariably, even on the second- or third-hand market, the dolls will still be in perfect condition. Therefore, although they should hold their value, they will probably not dramatically increase – unlike a play doll which can soar to the heights if still in mint condition.

Marie & Donny Osmond, Mattel.

Michael Jackson, Street Life.

Three of the Osmonds singing family – Donny, Marie and Jimmy – were issued by Mattel as 12in-dolls, again with various additional outfits. 'Marie' and 'Donny' came out in 1976, and 'Jimmy' ten years later. The basic dolls showed Donny and Marie in matching shades of purple and fuchsia; a jumpsuit with a silver belt for Donny and a very pretty tiered-dress for Maria. Many other outfits were available, including, for Marie, a long, white fur coat, a pink ice-skating costume, a blue, shimmery gown or a tiered-gown in vivid shades of blue, orange, pink, yellow and green. Outfits for Donny toned in with his sister's clothes. The later Jimmy doll was in a Lurex get-up, and is much harder to find than his two siblings. The facial likeness of these dolls was extremely good. Interestingly, Marie became a successful doll designer herself, creating beautiful dolls which are highly sought after – including Marie and Donny ones. Country and Western singer Dolly Parton has appeared in doll form many times. The version which crops up most often is a 12in poseable Goldberger 'Celebrity Doll' made in 1978 by Edge, and dressed in a glittery-red-and-silver jumpsuit.

Dolls depicting the late Michael Jackson first appeared in 1984 when LJN Toys featured a lookalike in a red sparkly jacket, black trousers and wearing his trademark single white glove. Other companies include Triumph International which created a 'Beat It' edition in 1995. This doll played a rendition of Michael Jackson singing 'Black or White'. Additional outfits were available for the doll, including a shiny-red jacket with lots of zips, and a colourful T-shirt. This company also produced various other Michael Jackson dolls. Other companies who have made Michael Jackson dolls include Street Life, Character Options and Spark Trading. Another interesting pop personality, Boy George, from the 'Glam Rock' era, was available as an unusual, soft-bodied doll complete with long beribboned locks, exotic eye make-up and stylish black hat. This very collectable doll stood 15in high, and was made by Sharpegrade LJN Toys in 1984.

Dating from the 1990s are a set of Take That dolls from Vivid Imaginations which featured Mark Owen, Gary Barlow, Jason Orange, Howard Donald, and, of course, Robbie Williams. The five boys were casually dressed in jackets, jeans and jerkins. The rise of Robbie Williams to mega-stardom made 'Robbie' dolls particularly popular. The likeness of his doll is especially good. Another boy band, Boyzone – Michael Graham, Ronan Keating, Shane Lynch, Steven Gately and Keith Duffy – were made a few years later by Vivid Imaginations as dolls wearing casual leather and denim styles. Steven Gately died in 2009. Unfortunately, Vivid Imaginations' 1997 version of singer Peter Andre doesn't seem in the least bit popular. It had a slight revival when Peter took part in the reality show *I'm A Celebrity, Get Me Out Of Here* in 2004 (he also appeared in the 2011 series), but now even mint boxed editions fetch little on the secondary market. Of course that's part of the fun of collecting these dolls; they reflect their doppelganger's career!

In the late 1990s through to the mid-2000s, a sudden influx of pop personality dolls flooded the shops, and long lengths of toyshop shelving were devoted to these flash-in-the-pan cult figures. The deluge began in 1998 with the Spice Girls dolls, which quickly made the news headlines because of the high cost, with each doll almost double the price of a regular 'pink box' Barbie or similar doll. Naturally, most children wanted the set of five dolls, and so it meant parents were faced with an unacceptable £100 expense. Despite this, initially the dolls were in great demand, with many being bought by collectors, but it wasn't long before 'Posh', 'Sporty', 'Scary', 'Ginger' and 'Baby' ended up in the bargain bins, as the group lost their popularity. Several sets of these dolls were made, some including Ginger Spice (Geri Halliwell), who later left the group, and others as sets of four. Probably the most iconic of the dolls is Geri in her Union Jack dress. The dolls were made by Galoob and Hasbro amongst others.

In 1999, a year after the initial Spice Girls dolls were released, came two other popular girl singers in doll form – Britney Spears and Christine Aguilera. The 'Britney' dolls were by Play Along Toys while Vivid Imaginations counteracted with 'Christine'. Both these singers were extremely popular with adolescent girls, and the makers cashed in on this by bringing out many differently dressed Britneys and Christines, many of them in their stage outfits. It was around this time that a major rush started, with groups such as S Club 7, B*witched, Steps, Five, Westlife and Hear'Say all appearing as dolls within a short period. Most of the dolls came from Vivid Imaginations, Character Options and Yaboom. As the average group had five or six dolls, the influx was staggering, and sales soon slumped as bewildered children (and collectors) faced with ranks of almost identical dolls, opted out of buying. Various gimmicks, such as sound chips, were installed on some of the dolls but it made little difference, and only the keenest fans bought them. Later, a few, such as the Westlife dolls, made a respectable recovery but most have little value, except to a collector of character dolls, of course.

Other interesting 'music' dolls including Justin Timberlake, came in a range of NSync dolls, marketed by Living Toyz. These were actually 9½in-high marionettes, and the modelling was excellent – Justin's face is instantly recognisable – and made for an attractive, denim-dressed doll. In 2006, actress and singer Miley Cyrus found fame as Miley Stewart and her alter ego Hanna Montana, in a television series, called *Hanna Montana*, which later appeared in movie form. Many of the singing and dancing characters from the programmes have been issued as dolls.

Dolls depicting singers Pussycat Dolls, Justin Bieber, Sugar Babes and JLS, amongst many others, have recently appeared; it seems that any new pop artist who catches the public imagination is soon immortalised in plastic. All these pop music dolls make an interesting field of collecting because the fickleness of the music industry means that stardom can be instantaneous. But at the same time, if the star falls from grace, or the next record is a flop, then the fans lose interest. Fame is ephemeral, which is why these personality dolls are never around for long. Therefore, a collection of these plastic icons provides a fascinating glimpse into the world of popular culture.

Robbie Williams, Take That, Vivid Imaginations.

Steve, Boyzone, Vivid Imaginations.

Christine Aguilera,
Vivid Imaginations.

Spice Girl Geri Halliwell, Galoob

Chapter Twelve

Historical Costume Dolls

THOUSANDS UPON THOUSANDS of dolls representing 'historical' characters have been created over the years and they are a particularly popular subject for collectors. Many of these dolls are small, around 7-12in tall, which means they will easily fit inside a cabinet. Here in Britain, the most famed maker of these costume dolls was Peggy Nisbet, but amongst the others are Pedigree, Rogark, Ashton-Drake, Sheena McLeod, Shallowpool and Regency Fine Arts, while American companies such as Madame Alexander also make representations of characters from history.

By far the most popular category of historical dolls is 'Royal Characters' (*See Chapter 8*). Additionally, they have been featured in Characters in the Arts (*Chapter 7*) and mentioned in other chapters. However, there are others which, though historical, don't fit into any specific category and it's these we will look at here. They include dolls depicting costumes from days gone by, especially

Sir Winston Churchill, Nisbet.

dolls in occupational or ceremonial outfits, or those dolls representing characters throughout history, such as Nell Gwynn, Lord Nelson, Sir Winston Churchill, President John Kennedy or Sir Walter Raleigh. Some manufacturers became very inventive, depicting little-known people from the history books in doll form as a change from the more popular figures.

In the late 1950s, three ladies living in Cornwall formed a cottage industry selling dolls to tourists. Their names were Joan Rickarby, Peggy Pryce and Muriel Fogarty, and their dolls became known as 'Shallowpool' dolls as they were created in the Shallowpool district near Fowey. These dolls stood 8in high, and had faces, hands and feet modelled from plaster of Paris cast in latex moulds created by Joan Rickarby. When the plaster was dry, the faces and limbs were hand painted and attached to wire armatures, padded with foam or cotton wool, and expertly styled hair was added. Peggy Pryce spent long hours researching in libraries and museums to design costumes for the dolls which reflect the history and culture of Britain's most mystic county of Cornwall. Later, she added famous names to the range, not just royalty but people who had made their mark in some way.

Of all the dolls produced by the trio over the twenty-five years or so when they were in production, the most enchanting must be those depicting the Cornish people – fishermen, smugglers, miners and sellers of various wares – yet, perversely, these are less sought after today than those depicting the more famed characters. Even though thousands of dolls must have been created over the years, and out-workers were employed, the business was, to all extents very much a small concern with everything done by hand. Some of the faces of the dolls featured exquisite painting, especially the male dolls, with plenty of delicately drawn lines and wrinkles.

As well as the smugglers, fishermen and miners mentioned above, there were characters such as ferrymen, cream maidens, apple sellers, pirate captains, primrose sellers, violet sellers, dairy maids, morris dancers, pig farmers, huntsmen and town criers. There were many more too. Particularly delightful are those dressed for the more obscure occupations such as tin miner, china clay worker, and bal maiden who used to break up the lumps of rock with her mallet. ('Bal' is Cornish for 'mining place'.) In the Shallowpool version, she carried her knitting in her apron pocket. The china clay worker wore a white suit – to show how his working clothes would soon look once he was covered in china clay – and carried candles. The tin miner held a tool for breaking up the rocks.

Judging by the number of them around, the most popular Shallowpool doll bought by tourists was the 'pasty maid', a young lady carrying a Cornish pasty on a plate. Just like several of the other dolls, she came with a poem:

'Pastry rolled out like a plate
Piled with "turmut, tates and mate"
Doubled up and baked like fate
That's a "Cornish Pasty".'

The pasty seller was typically Cornish, whilst some of the others, such as the dairy maid or the violet seller, could be from almost anywhere in Britain. The apple seller, a girl with long plaits and a basket full of rosy apples, also came with a verse.

'Ripe apples need picking when autumn is here,
For making the cider so golden and clear.'

The various morris dancers are fun; they came in assorted styles, including a 'traditional' white-costumed dancer with ribbons and bells, smart top-hatted figure from the Helston Furry Dance and an Isle of Wight version in a blue tabard. The smart red-coated huntsman, with his white moustache, held the brush of a fox, while the town crier had a 'brass' bell, a gold-braided traditional blue outfit and a tricorn hat.

One of the Shallowpool characters was a lady dressed in a riding costume as worn by a typical Daphne Du Maurier heroine. Author Du Maurier lived in Cornwall and many of her books were set amongst the moors and rugged coastlines. This doll version depicted a lady attired in a full-skirted outfit lined with cream satin over a cambric petticoat, and the skirt was looped with a peach ribbon to enable it to be lifted clear of mud. Around her shoulders was a lace-trimmed cream collar and her tall black hat was surmounted with a feather. She carried a fur muff.

Also looking as though they stepped from the pages of a Du Maurier novel were the handsome pirate captain and the fierce smuggler. The captain cut a dashing figure in his gold-buttoned, blue or red corduroy satin-lined coat, white shirt, coloured breeches and a jaunty black tricorn hat. His shoes had silver buckles and he wore an ornate-handled sword thrust into a scabbard. The smuggler sported a wooden leg, and was colourfully dressed in a striped shirt, trousers and a long, knitted cap. Usually, he had an eye patch and carried his barrel of rum on his shoulder, though he often had a jug of rum, or maybe a lobster pot and lobster. Many places were famed for their 'wreckers' – those who plundered stricken ships – so these were made too, carrying their lanterns. The Isle of Wight's Fanny Wheeler was reputed to have assisted her father to collect contraband and Shallowpool produced her as a doll, too. There were many other sea-related dolls with the 'standard' fisherman wearing a navy jersey and trousers, often with a place name such as 'Newquay' across his chest, and others in bright-yellow oilskins. There was also a shark fisher, in a fisherman's smock, who came with an enormous plaster of Paris shark! The ferryman had a leather moneybag.

Of all of the Shallowpool dolls, the most iconic and unusual were those which portrayed notable Cornish personages. One of these was Jenny Johns, a coal-heaver, renowned for carrying two-hundredweight of coal in a basket on her head supported by a leather band across her forehead, or Dolly Pentreath from Mousehole who lived to 102. Dolly's poem reads:

'Old Doll Pentreath, one hundred ag'd and two,
Deceased and buried in Paul parish too.
Not in the church with people great and high,
But in the church-yard doth old Dolly lie.'

Another interesting Cornish character by Shallowpool was Mary Kelynack, a Newlyn fishwife. Apparently, when this lady was 80 years old, she walked to London and presented Queen Victoria with half-a-pound of tea. Shallowpool portrayed her as a white-haired old woman holding a stick, dressed in a black-and-white dress, usually gingham or stripes, and with a basket on her back. Also

Tin and Clay Workers, Shallowpool.

Morris Dancer, Town Crier, Helston Dancer, Huntsman, Letter Carrier, Fanny Wheeler, Shallowpool.

Shallowpool group, Dolly Pentreath, Jenny Johns, Mary Kelynack.

Crofter by Sheena Macleod.   Rob Roy, Nisbet.

notable was William Cookworthy, born in Devon in 1705, who discovered china clay in Cornwall and devised how it could be used to make porcelain which was previously imported from China.

Sometimes the dolls carried accessories, often moulded from plaster of Paris: rosy apples, a pasty on a plate, fish, a dish of cream, a pail of milk, a barrel, and, most impressive of all, a large, pink pig which was carried by the farmer doll. This typical Victorian farmer wore a rugged knitted jersey and cotton trousers. Over them he sported a traditional cream cotton overall with smock-type sleeves. He had a squashy, brown felt hat, black boots, and carried the pig tucked under one arm. Other accessories often seen with the Shallowpool character dolls included small wicker baskets and creels to hold the apples, fish and other goods, mallets and hammers (found on the bal maiden and woman clay worker), candles for the miners and lanterns. The coal-heaver's basket contained a few tiny pieces of real coal wrapped in tissue to stop it turning everything black. Although the fabrics often have rather large patterns because the Shallowpool ladies bought much of their fabric from the local market, the details of the costumes were surprisingly authentic. From the dairy maid in her tucked-up blue gown over a striped petticoat with long drawers underneath, to the tin miner dressed in his corduroy waistcoat with all the buttons and button-holes defined, these dolls are a delight, and well worthy of the name 'Character dolls'.

Shallowpool also covered royal characters such as Elizabeth I, Charles I, Charles II, Henry VIII and his six wives, and miniature Nursery Rhyme dolls (*See appropriate chapters.*) There were also historical dolls including famous names such as Sir Francis Drake, Nell Gwynn, Sir Walter Raleigh, a 'Gainsborough Lady' and Lord Nelson.

Similar to the Shallowpool characters are a series of dolls depicting Scottish Highland characters at their trades, made by Sheena MacLeod in the 1970s and 1980s. These exceptionally well-crafted dolls have plaster faces, hands and feet (later, resin), mounted on a wire armature. A similar technique to Shallowpool was used but the hands and feet were much more detailed. The dolls depict people from various areas of the Highlands and Islands, such as a woman from Skye with her basket of heather, and a fishwife from the Western Isles. Others include such people as a crofter sitting at her spinning wheel, or an old man weaving a wicker basket. All the fabrics used are authentic Scottish wool or plaids. Highland Character Dolls were selected for the Design Centre in London in the 1970s, but are becoming quite difficult to find nowadays, as compared to Shallowpool, far fewer were made.

However, the most well-known of the small character dolls are those made by Peggy Nisbet during the 1960s, 70s and 80s. The majority of these dolls measured 7-8in tall – though size varied according to range – and each had hand-painted features and wore a detailed costume. The fabric patterns on the Nisbet dolls were usually of a much smaller scale than those of the Shallowpool types. Peggy Nisbet dolls could be broadly arranged by categories; 'Historical', 'Portrait', 'National', 'Shakespeare', 'British Traditional' and 'Happy Dolls' (*mentioned in applicable chapters*). As well as the small resin dolls, there were limited edition porcelain dolls, large vinyl dolls and cloth dolls, and for around thirty years, Peggy Nisbet reigned supreme as a designer of costume dolls. She presided over a huge concern and had factories and workshops in Weston-super-Mare and Scotland. Comparable in a way to the Shallowpool apple and flower sellers were the 'Cries of London', a series of dolls dressed as eighteenth-century street sellers. Their costumes were based on paintings by artist Frederick Wheatley. (*See Chapter 7.*)

When Peggy Nisbet first started making dolls in the 1950s she used small, hard plastic Rosebud dolls made by Nene Plastics, which depicted such characters as a 'Peeress of the Court' and an 'Elizabethan Lady'. The costumes were exquisitely detailed. As the dolls were unlabelled, they are very difficult to attribute today. The dolls had child faces, and Peggy wasn't satisfied because she really needed a more grown-up look, so she set about contacting various companies to see if they could help. One of the companies she approached was Dean's, makers of rag-dolls and soft toys, which developed a range of latex dolls to try. Another manufacturer made her a batch of resin dolls, but there were problems with the mix, and a chemical reaction discoloured the dolls' dresses and caused their arms to fall off. Eventually, experimentation provided exactly what Peggy needed – a solid high-impact polystyrene mix, cast all in one piece to make a heavy doll. The weight was vital because velvets and brocades would not hang correctly on a lightweight figure. Although made from plastic, they have an earlier, composition-look about them, and their hand-painted features add to the illusion.

The Happy Dolls range was a cheaper line of Peggy Nisbet dolls, slightly shorter at 6ins, and with less elaborate clothing. In her autobiography, Peggy Nisbet talks about the making of these dolls, explaining, 'New out-workers started with the Happy Dolls, and as they became more expert, they were put onto the more detailed and intricate 7in dolls.' These dolls consisted of various characters, and many of them had their right leg extended to one side, with the foot pointed. Amongst the Happy Dolls were historical personages including Robert Burns, an 'Elizabethan Sea Captain', 'Morris Man', 'Scottish Fishwife', 'Old English Costume', 'Cornish Fishwife', 'Victorian Girl', Robin Hood, 'Regency Man', 'Regency Woman' and 'Pilgrim'.

The actual Historical Characters and Portrait ranges were immense, and though many of the dolls listed in it were 'Royalty' or 'Literary' (*see separate chapters*), there were many other famous people replicated as dolls. Amongst them were Admiral Horatio Lord Nelson, Betsy Ross (credited with making the first American flag), 'Crinoline Lady,' Mary Fleming (a Scottish noblewoman and childhood companion of Mary, Queen of Scots), Regency dandy Beau Brummel, George Washington, Amy Robsart (first wife of Lord Robert Dudley, favourite of Elizabeth I), Joan of Arc, Abraham Lincoln, Sir Winston Churchill, John Kennedy, Sir Francis Drake, Napoleon, Duke of Wellington, King Tutankhamen and Queen Nefertiti. The Tutankhamen and Nefertiti dolls presented problems, as Peggy couldn't at first decide how to produce the famous headdresses. Eventually, she arranged for them to be cast in metal. In

Nefertiti, Peggy Nisbet.

Victorian Lady, Peggy Nisbet.

Bishop and Judge, Pedigree.

Pearly King & Queen, Chiltern.

the case of Tutankhamen, this meant using gold metal and painting it to represent the lapis lazuli, quartz, turquoise and cornelian of the headdress and collar. When all was complete, the doll was taken to the British Museum who could find no fault. There are far too many historical Nisbet dolls to describe in detail, but, as with Shallowpool, a tremendous amount of thought and planning went into each outfit, with plenty of attention to the smallest detail. Even buttons, epaulettes, necklaces and regalia were faithfully replicated, while hats were works of art in miniature.

Although most of the dolls were made in England, Peggy Nisbet's husband was Scottish, and so as well as a house at Weston-super-Mare, they owned a cottage at Coldstream, north of the border. Peggy discovered that tourists to Scotland understandably wanted dolls that had been made locally and it wasn't long before she set up a small production unit in the cottage to assemble the Scottish dolls. Skilled Scottish seamstresses sewed the outfits for historical characters such as Rob Roy (Scotland's 'Robin Hood'), Jacobite heroine Flora MacDonald and Lord Darnley (second husband of Mary, Queen of Scots), and the miniature tartans were woven in Scotland. Each Scottish doll had a label reading 'Made in Scotland'. During the mid-seventies the company's name changed to the House of Nisbet, and gradually teddy bears took precedence over dolls. In 1989, the doll moulds were acquired by Diane Jones. Diane was a teddy bear maker from Wales, who had already worked on many of the Nisbet bears. She continued to produce dolls to the specifications of Peggy Nisbet until 1999.

Sometimes dolls similar to Peggy Nisbet and Shallowpool turn up which depict country people and peasants, but are made from a heavier clay material. These dolls often turn out to be Santon de Provence dolls, which have been made in the Provence area of France for several centuries. These traditional dolls represent real people from the various villages and have a religious significance as they are on their way to pay homage to the Holy Family. Often they are displayed in churches alongside a nativity scene.

Like Shallowpool, Sheena MacLeod and Peggy Nisbet, Santon dolls depict various local occupations but these French versions include the important people such as the mayor and the parish priest. Then there are the craftsmen and the tradespeople – a butcher, baker, fromager (cheese vendor), potter, grocer, basket-maker, florist, needlewoman, vigneron (winegrower), dressmaker and hat-maker, as well as dancers and musicians. These dolls are often around 8ins high, and the clay is moulded over a wire framework. They are well-dressed and full of character.

Other dolls which feature historical or trade costumes include an unusual range from Pedigree, which appeared in the 1960s. Amongst them was a solemn judge in his red robes and moulded plastic wig. There was also a bishop with his mitre and crozier and a Knight of the Garter with insignia and sword. Each doll was 6in high, and the series was known as 'Cavalcade Dolls'. Many of the companies who sold hard plastic dolls in the 1950s and 60s, including Pedigree, Rogark and Chiltern, made Pearly Kings and Queens. Dressed in black, covered with pearl buttons and wearing pearl-strewn caps or feathery hats, these dolls were popular with tourists. (*See also Chapter 13.*)

Chapter Thirteen

Costume Dolls, Festive and Commemorative Dolls

FOR SOME reason, many doll collectors look down on 'national costume dolls'. Although these are produced in their thousands to satisfy the worldwide tourist and souvenir market, it doesn't mean that they should be ignored, and, apart from the fact that a collection of national dolls makes a colourful spectacle, many of them are beautifully and carefully dressed in accurate representations of the country's national dress.

Sadly, it is the fate of many of these souvenir costume dolls to end up gathering dust in charity shops or heaped on a stall at a boot sale, yet once, people spent ages choosing these dolls as a special memento of a happy holiday. Maybe they decided to spend their last handful of dollars on a patriotic majorette from a swish New York department store, found a frilly-skirted senorita on a Spanish market stall or bought a doll they had watched being dressed in a Welsh craft shop. Once back home though, the dolls were just another souvenir to be enjoyed for a few months before being dumped. In fact, costume dolls are one of the easier types of doll to display, as most are small and fit neatly onto a shelf.

There are several different types of costume dolls, and best of all are those which are made, often by hand, in the country concerned, and then clothed locally. Often these dolls are made from materials such as wood, papier-mâché or raffia, as opposed to plastic. These truly are souvenir costume dolls because they cannot be purchased anywhere else. Sometimes dolls are bought unclothed from large manufacturers by shops and companies in various countries, ready to be locally dressed in the appropriate costumes. Small play dolls were bought from British companies such as Roddy, Rosebud, Sarold, Pedigree and Tudor Rose. Rogark and Airfix also supplied small dolls for dressing in regional costumes, whilst a company called Rexard specialised in arraying hard plastic dolls in regional and historical costumes of the world.

The Rexard dolls all had similar faces, but were dressed in a wide variety of outfits. They were distributed from the company's main premises in Worthing, Sussex, and packed in display boxes. As these dolls were sold at pocket money prices, they particularly appealed to children, not to play with, but to collect. This is why there are still so many of them around, invariably in good condition; they weren't intended to be undressed and tended to stay in their boxes or on a display shelf. Dolls made by Rexard were usually of a hard, thin plastic and stood 7½in or 8½in high, depending on the model. Their wigs came in various styles and colours, and their eyes were painted, and as stated in a previous chapter, they normally bore a tag which read 'Designed by Odette Arden. Made in the British Empire.' This company distributed other ranges including a series of smaller dolls with sleep eyes and rounder faces, dressed as soldiers, policemen and guardsmen, while later, softer plastic types appeared.

During the 1950s and 80s, various hard plastic dolls were sold in Britain through companies such as Almar, Linda or Cowan de Groot (trade name Codeg), often as boxed sets of dolls from several lands. Woolworths stores sold a popular range of 8in hard plastic sleep-eyed dolls dressed as Native Americans, Eskimos and Indians. In 1967 Chiltern advertised a range of 'National Character Dolls', and amongst the colourful, well-detailed costumes on these hard plastic dolls, were those depicting 'Young Holland', 'Young Poland', 'Young France', 'Young Japan', and 'Young Switzerland'. Nowadays, vast proportions of costume dolls are mass-produced, plastic types originating in Taiwan, and are often dressed there too. Nevertheless, even amongst the plastics there are treasures to be found, with some of them being beautifully and intricately dressed.

Unfortunately, unlike Scotland, Wales and Ireland, England does not have its own national costume, so English souvenir dolls tend to wear uniforms such as 'policeman', 'Beefeater' or 'guardsman'. Sometimes, they are dressed as a London Pearly King or Queen, morris dancer, flower-seller, or in various occupational costumes. (*See Chapter Twelve.*) Another way round it is to dress souvenir British dolls in the Union Jack flag or in red, white and blue, as described in the patriotic dolls' section at the end of this chapter.

As already mentioned, Peggy Nisbet began selling small costume dolls made from a very hard vinyl in the 1950s, and amongst them was a range of national dolls dressed in costumes of the world. Apparently, Nisbet was shocked after returning from a French holiday to see all the shoddy soldier and Beefeater dolls available in Britain at the time. She realised the costume dolls sold in France were truly beautiful and wanted to emulate them. She also produced a set called 'Cries of London', which was based on a series of paintings by eighteenth-century artist Frederick Wheatley, and showed young ladies selling baskets of their various wares. (*See Chapter 7.*) With England having no national costume, these dolls made excellent souvenirs for foreign tourists. Cornish Shallowpool dolls depicted similar subjects. (*See Chapter 12.*) In some areas of Britain, many shops still sell dolls made from old wooden bobbins or reels, while craft workers use old-fashioned clothes-pegs to make peg dolls. Hand-crafted dolls are well worth adding to a collection, and in Britain are often dressed as country maidens, or as Welsh or Scottish girls.

Attractive handmade dolls can be found in Africa and India. African dolls are often of a 'primitive' style cloth-and-wire figure with stick limbs, dressed in raffia skirts and ornate headdresses. Frequently, the Indian dolls have plaster faces, and are very graceful with long limbs and shaped bodies. They are

Welsh doll, Norah Wellings.

Guardsman, Unmarked.

Indian Dancing Doll.

Wooden Polish Doll.

Japanese Lady.   Chinese Girl.

dressed in colourful saris, arrayed with jewellery, and have kohl-accented eyes. Many countries make cloth souvenir character dolls including Turkey's colourful multi-patterned dolls decorated with sequins and featuring hand-painted silk faces, and Spain's 'topsy-turvy' dolls with their stiffened faces and side-glance eyes. Jamaica, Barbados and other parts of the West Indies are known for ethnically dressed topsy-turvy dolls. (*See Chapter 9.*)

Wooden dolls are found in many countries. Traditional wooden, stacking Russian Matryoshka dolls are frequently seen in gift shops in Britain, as well as in their homeland. Many have been skillfully hand-painted, often bearing the artist's signature on the base, while others are very basic. Some show scenes from fairy tales, the ballet or fantasy landscapes, while others depict people. The brightly-coloured wooden hand-decorated Kokeshi dolls from Japan are also very collectable, (*see below*).

Similar to the wooden 'bobbin' dolls are the handmade wooden ball-headed dolls from Poland. Often, the faces on these dolls are very basic, with simple dots for eyes, but they are brightly dressed in woollen clothing. They wear impressive, elaborate, floral headdresses made from coloured ribbon and wire. Another medium often used for handmade dolls is cornhusk. Cornhusk dolls are simple, too, but very graceful, with the wide sheath of the head of corn forming a skirt. These dolls often come from countries such as Romania, Mexico, Africa and America. Sometimes, you come across dolls made from lavender stems, reeds, raffia, or woven from thin cane.

Also made from corn are the traditional 'corn dollies', which, though not strictly 'dolls' as we know them, are often made in a doll shape. Corn dollies have their origins way back into pagan times, and were a traditional fertility symbol. It was believed that the spirit of the harvest would be made homeless when the final sheaf of corn was gathered, and so the men working in the fields would plait and weave corn dollies from the last sheaf of the harvest. These dollies were regarded as a means of giving thanks to the goddesses of the earth and of fertility, and would be taken home into the warmth in order to safeguard the harvest for the following year. The spirit was kept alive inside the corn dolly ready for the next year's crop. Sometimes the corn dolly was hung up in the farmhouse, but often in the barn or local church. The corn dolly custom is found in many countries, and each country has its own legends and designs.

Non-plastic dolls usually seem to have more character, and it's especially worth looking out for dolls such as the dainty celluloid types from France, which have finely moulded features and pretty silk and satin regional outfits. France is divided into many regions, each with its own distinct costume, and so it is possible to build up an interesting and beautiful collection of dolls from this one country. Many other countries also use celluloid. Some of the German and Austrian ones are exquisite. These dolls are often hand-dressed in the finest of fabrics and with delicate detailing as many countries take pride in selling beautiful dolls which have been made and dressed by their own workers. Collectors soon learn to distinguish between the genuine and the mass-produced. During the early decades of the twentieth century many of the costume dolls were made from bisque china, and occasionally these turn up amongst a job lot of souvenir dolls, a real find, especially if they bear markings of well-known makers such as Simon & Halbig or Armand Marseille.

Various other substances are used for costume dolls; composition is popular, as is a resin-type plastic, which is very hard and shiny. There are some delightful Chinese and Japanese dolls to be found with composition or papier-mâché faces, whist many Japanese dolls have faces made or painted with gofun – a powdered seashell or eggshell. Sometimes washi, a thin paper, is used in the construction, and these dolls are very delicate. Many Japanese dolls are moulded on a basic wire or wood frame, with the costume (or pieces of silk) draped around, and often, even the faces are of silk with painted features. Kokeshi are traditional wooden folk dolls resembling skittles and bearing stylised decoration. Japanese culture embraces a long history of doll making and doll festivals, mounting special doll displays in the home on celebration days.

During the 1960s through to the early 1980s, a series of beautiful Chinese dolls exquisitely dressed in coloured silks, were often sold in gift shops in Britain. Both boy and girl dolls were available. The earlier ones were made from composition with hand-painted features, while the later dolls came in a waxy form of plastic. Sometimes found are small, colourful, silk-faced costume dolls, dressed as children playing. The delightful figures, handmade in China, are a joy in their bright costumes of cerise, turquoise and yellow. Over the last few decades there has been a spate of Japanese and Chinese dolls in gift shops; these are of varying quality, but some are very attractive and their gorgeous costumes make them well worth including in a doll collection. Occasionally Chinese

Huishan `Wuxi` clay figurines can be found in specialist shops, and though these clay people are not really dolls as such, they are delightful, and usually attractively painted. Most frequently seen is a pair in the shape of jolly plump babies, each holding a lion.

Many other countries used composition, especially Switzerland, Austria, Russia, Germany and Czechoslovakia. Some of the dolls are beautiful, such as a series of Swiss girls with glass eyes and human hair wigs, intricate detail on their dresses and metal trims and fine chains ornamenting their bodices – probably depicting the costume from the Berne region. Unusual dolls include a delightful Peruvian flute-playing boy with an animated face made from composition, dressed in brightly coloured garments and knitted hat, and accompanied by a fluffy llama.

However, a comprehensive collection of national costume dolls also needs to include the more commonly found tourist types; Lederhosen-wearing Germans, leather-clad American Indians, Maltese straw-hatted girls, white-skirted Greek male dancers, ubiquitous dancing Spanish senoritas and, of course, red-cloaked Welsh ladies.

There are many other types of costume doll. In Chapter 12 we looked at the historic costumes, but there are plenty of others, all of which can be used to form a themed collection – for example, fairy dolls, nuns, 'fancy dress', fairy tales, festive and patriotic. During the 1950s and 60s, the Pedigree company produced a range of small, hard plastic dolls with unusual splayed-fingered hands, known to collectors as 'starfish hands'. Often these dolls were sold dressed as various characters, such as pirates, cowboys, policemen or fairies. Other companies, including Rosebud, sold small dolls similarly dressed which appealed to the tourist market as well as to children. In the previous chapter, dolls dressed as judges, bishops and other occupations are mentioned. Particularly unusual was a range of dolls dressed as 'Bunny Girls', based on the waitress girls from the Playboy nightclubs. Made by Chiltern in the late 1960s, they were in hard plastic, jointed at the shoulders and hips, and were 7in high. According to a catalogue of the time the dolls sold at 8/9 (43p) each, had glued-on wigs, were dressed in swimsuits and wore 'white plastic cuffs and collar, fluffy bustle and plastic bunny ears.' Today, there would probably be an outcry if such dolls were sold to young children. More easily found are the myriad of dolls which were dressed as cowboys, cowgirls and 'Red Indians' (now referred to as Native Americans), dating from the 1950s and 60s, when 'westerns' were so popular on television.

Nowadays, dolls can be found dressed as practically anything as manufacturers of teen dolls vie with one another. Barbies, Sindys, Bratz and numerous other brands appear as punks, pirates, doctors, witches, nurses, dentists, cooks, vets, astronauts and even animals. As mentioned in Chapter 10, a few years ago, British Airways dressed a range of 'retro' Sindy dolls in replicas of various aircraft cabin crew uniforms from several eras, including the attractive 'paper dress' worn in 1967 and a 1960s BOAC air stewardess uniform.

Swiss Girl from Berne.

Fairy Doll, Armand Marseille.

Silver Jubilee Daisy designed by Mary Quant, Flair.

Patriotic Celluloid Mascot Doll.

Fairies form a collecting field all on their own, especially the fairy dolls dating from the first few decades of the 1900s. Though popular for years as Christmas tree 'toppers', by the 1970s fairy dolls had virtually disappeared, to be replaced by angels. Early fairies were usually made from wax or porcelain, such as a range of bisque 1920s and 30s dolls manufactured by the German company Armand Marseille. These dolls often had spun glass wings and were dressed in white, silver-tinsel-trimmed muslin dresses. By the 1950s and 60s, fairies were usually made from composition or from hard plastic, and were sold in their thousands every Christmas in stores such as Woolworths. The dolls were made by many companies, amongst them Rosebud, Roddy, Airfix and Pedigree. Another collecting field are dolls dressed in festive outfits – these still appear each year from many manufacturers, and tend to be dressed in green and red, so make for a colourful display.

Finally, dolls loosely labelled 'patriotic' can form an interesting group. Once again, these are usually created with the tourist in mind, though they also appear at special events and frequently, but by no means always, at royal happenings. Especially delightful are the small celluloid mascot dolls dating from the 1930s to the 1950s and dressed as soldiers or draped in red, white and blue ribbon, while soft-bodied play dolls were created by Dean's, Chad Valley and other companies to celebrate coronations. Slightly different are those dolls dressed as 'mods' or 'punks' which appear from time to time wearing dresses based on, or featuring, the Union Jack, such as a range of Bratz 'Punk' dolls. Designer Mary Quant issued a 'Daisy' doll draped in a Union Jack flag dress to commemorate the 1977 Jubilee and Geri Halliwell wore a mini based on the flag when the Spice Girls performed 'Who Do You Think You Are' at the 1997 Brit Awards music event. This outfit later adorned a doll by Galoob.

Dolls dressed in costume cover such a wide field, and the only way to form a manageable collection is to pick a theme that particularly appeals.

Chapter Fourteen

Dolls on Greetings Cards

SOME characters make their appearance on stationery, greetings cards or wrapping paper before making their way into the world of dolls, whilst others may have been originally been dolls but didn't find fame until they appeared as greetings cards. Many of these dolls have become household names, and amongst them are Holly Hobbie, Sarah Kay, Victoria Plum, Betsey Clark, Strawberry Shortcake, Rainbow Brite and Diddums.

Although the majority of the character dolls inspired by greetings card designs tend to date from the 1970s onwards – peaking during the character doll overload of the 1980s – there were many earlier dolls that also began their life as cards or stationery. In Britain, during the first few decades of the twentieth century, Mabel Lucie Attwell (born 1879) was a much-loved illustrator of books, postcards and greetings cards, and she was such a prolific artist that she drew over a thousand postcard designs. Apparently, at first she wasn't happy with the idea of putting her designs onto postcards because there was a certain snobbery about the idea – artists didn't feel it was quite the done thing. However, she let herself be persuaded, which was just as well as her cards proved extremely popular. Attwell worked for several companies, but her greatest triumphs were those hundreds upon hundreds of cards drawn for Valentine and Sons of Dundee, with whom she stayed for 50 years.

Many of her designs featured chubby, rosy-cheeked toddlers with adult-inspired comments underneath; babies howling because they weren't allowed to play in the coal scuttle, little girls knitting socks for soldiers, and beaming small boys driving toy pedal cars. They appealed to the sentiments of the time and her style spawned many imitators. Sometimes, a small cluster of pixie folk called 'Boo Boos' appeared alongside the toddlers.

Almost certainly Mabel's most famous character was 'Diddums', a roly-poly tot with a solemn face, and Mabel used Plasticine to make a model of the little boy which was then used by the Cascelloid/Palitoy company to create a plaster cast. From this, the company was able to manufacture thousands of celluloid dolls, and a surprisingly high number of these fragile toys have survived. Celluloid is a very combustible mix of camphor, alcohol and nitrocellulose, and it is also prone to denting and cracking, so the survival of these featherlight, hollow, paper-thin small dolls, shows how carefully they were played with in the past. Instantly recognisable, these bald Diddums toddlers were marked on their backs 'Palitoy Reg.Des: 819486/7 Made in England' and the head, body and legs were moulded all in one, with the arms attached separately on an elastic cord. Other Mabel Lucie Attwell characters transformed into dolls included 'Snookums',' Girlie', 'Little Happy' and 'The Toddler', as well as an ultra-rare black version of Diddums. Diddums was also made as a little rubber doll. Rubber is another material that doesn't stand the test of time particularly well, so those rubber dolls still around today tend to be cracked, faded, crazed or lacking in paintwork. In 1939, a china version of one of Attwell's toddlers was advertised by the London company Cecil Coleman Ltd, together with an assurance that they had approached the artist for permission to produce a replica of her famous character.

Of all the Mabel Lucie Attwell dolls, surely the most exquisite were those made by Chad Valley Ltd in the late 1920s. These cheeky-faced girls and boys were completely designed by Attwell, and were made from velveteen with jointed limbs, side-glance eyes and smiling mouths. In all, there were 16 designs, just as loveable as the children in her drawings, and beautifully dressed in typical fashions of the day – leggings, cloche-type hats, buster suits, and enormous hair ribbons. Amongst the dolls were a dungaree-clad black boy, a soldier, and a boy wearing a tail-jacket, check trousers and top hat. They were sold in special 'Bed-Bye' boxes, and available in several sizes. Additionally, Chad Valley produced a small unjointed girl doll that was labelled 'Mabel Lucie 5100'. Nobody seems to know whether it was meant to represent the artist as a tot, though it is fun to think that it does.

Mabel Lucie Attwell was such a perfectionist, that when Chad Valley held an exhibition of their dolls at Harrods, she insisted on sending along her maid to the toy department to rearrange their hairstyles so they met with her approval. Today, the early dolls are in great demand, and reach high prices if they are in good condition. Sadly cloth-faced dolls were prone to discolour or to disintegrate due to too much loving, and so were often discarded. Other related dolls include 1930s felt-dressed pyjama-case Mabel Lucie Attwell dolls. In the 1940s and early 1950s was a range of composition dolls manufactured by Roddy and sold in boxes decorated with coloured pictures of Attwell children. Although these happy-faced, rosy-cheeked girls didn't feature the laughing eyes and the grins of the earlier dolls, they still had a definite Attwell look. Jointed at the neck, shoulders and hips, the dolls wore mohair wigs and were sold in several sizes. They were quite expensive for their time – 53/6d for the 21in size – a lot more than the average family could afford to spend on a doll during the wartime economy.

During the 1990s, the American company Enesco issued a range of Mabel Lucie Attwell china figurines, based on characters from the postcards. They were finely detailed in pastel colours with a matt finish, and often came complete with a facsimile Mabel Lucie Attwell booklet showing the illustration on which the ornament was based.

Diddums, Cascelloid.

Mabel Lucy Attwell Bambina, Chad Valley.

Boo Boo, Hornby.

Holly Hobbie, Knickerbocker.

In 1986 the Hornby company, more known for its model engines, decided to introduce a selection of 'Boo Boo' dolls, following on from its successful Flower Fairies range. These 4in dolls first appeared at the Earl's Court Toy Fair and were dressed in colourful, shiny nylon outfits with antennae sprouting from their heads, and had shoes and accessories that glowed in the dark. Each Boo Boo was jointed at the neck, hips and shoulders, had pointed ears and circular blue-painted eyes with white pupils, and came with a bright-green leaf-shaped stand. Amongst the characters were 'Tidy' (blue outfit), 'Watchful' (pink), 'Helpful' (yellow), 'Caring' (red), Playful (green) and 'Kindness' (turquoise). Other accessories included a bell, lantern, broom and a heart. 'Tuneful', a Boo Boo dressed in orange, held a concertina and had a gramophone record which really worked. Large plastic insects such as a grasshopper, wasp or fly, were available for the Boo Boos to ride on. Some little girl Boo Boo pixies were included later but are hard to find now, They were pretty, wore cotton dresses, and had names such as 'Kisses', 'Jolly', 'Sweetness', 'Cuddles', 'Neatness' and 'Happy'.

According to Hornby and the Mabel Lucie Attwell drawings, the main function of the Boo Boos was to care for newborn babies. An unmarked 13in-high vinyl baby doll was issued by the company and is now extremely difficult to identify. She was dressed in a white, lace-trimmed gown and her main distinguishing feature was her round bald head, obviously intended to resemble Mabel Lucie Attwell's postcards of chubby, bald-headed babies! This doll was named 'Baby Twinkle', and she fitted into a 'Crib House', a plastic cradle shaped like a log, with a house beneath – home to the Boo Boos. Hornby also made a large, white fluffy puppy wearing a red collar with a bell, called 'Mops'. This cheeky puppy featured in many of the drawings.

Dolls were a very popular subject for greetings cards and postcards during the first few decades of the twentieth century, but very often they were photographs of dolls already in existence rather than characters expressly designed to feature on a card. One doll which frequently featured on cards was known as a 'Fums Up'. The Fums Up dolls were originally good luck charms, made of bronze or other metal with a wooden head, and the raised thumbs touched the wood 'for luck'. These small dolls were often given as mascots to soldiers serving in the First World War. Later, small bisque versions appeared, but instead of plain wooden heads, they had bisque ones with pointed ears, cheeky faces and a sprig of lucky shamrock printed on their heads. As well as the dolls themselves, good luck postcards featuring the Fums Ups were sent in their thousands.

American Dolls such as 'Kewpies', 'Dolly Dingle' and others, occasionally appeared on cards in Britain, but it wasn't until the 1960s that dolls from the US really made much of an impact here. Perhaps the most famous is 'Holly Hobbie', who first entranced us on a range of greetings cards in the 1960s, dressed in an old-fashioned print frock and an over-large bonnet. This little girl invariably appeared sideways on, with her bonnet totally obstructing her face, giving her a mysterious quality. Holly was created by Denise Holly Ulinskas Hobbie, a watercolourist, who used her own children as inspiration for her paintings which were set amongst the rural background of New England. Her brother-in-law was so impressed with her illustrations that he encouraged her to submit some of her work to the American Greetings Corporation in Cleveland, Ohio. The company was so taken by the illustrations of little girls in patchwork dresses that it decided to use them on a range of greetings cards, stationery and other items. These cards proved to be such a success that it wasn't long before the public wanted to know more about the little girl featured in the designs, and in 1975, the Knickerbocker Toy Company introduced Holly Hobbie cloth dolls.

At the time, this was quite an innovation as cloth dolls had, for the most part, gone out of fashion; vinyl dolls were all the rage and the few cloth dolls on the market were mainly intended for babies and toddlers. The Holly Hobbie cloth dolls reflected a bygone, gentler age, and were perfect for a decade, which was becoming nostalgic for liberty prints and long flowing skirts for women and little girls. Although the dolls were particularly popular with small children who found them cuddly and soft, and with teens who enjoyed them as mascots to decorate their bedrooms, people of all ages soon fell under their spell. Since then, many different types of Holly Hobbie dolls have appeared, from the basic soft-body types to vinyl play dolls and expensive porcelain dolls issued for collectors.

Holly Hobbie creations vary in size; some are tiny pocket-fitting girls, and at the other end of the scale are almost toddler-sized editions. Even though there are many kinds, the majority have round faces, widely spaced eyes, hair styled into plaits, long, patchwork-print dresses and the trademark over-sized bonnets. The cloth versions tend to have printed facial features and wool hair, with Holly often dressed in blue as depicted on the most famous of the card images, though sometimes she is found in other colours. She had several friends, all cloth dolls by Knickerbocker, such as 'Amy' (usually dressed in green), 'Heather' (beige or pink), 'Carrie' (red) and 'Robbie' (navy dungarees and red shirt). Various types of doll appeared, but gradually, just as with all fads, the love affair faded and with it went Holly Hobbie – though you can't keep a strong character doll down for long. The most unusual Holly Hobbie doll dated from the early 1980s, and consisted of a 6in-high vinyl figure wearing an enormous patchwork skirt. Beneath the skirt was a secret house, consisting of a large, circular swivelling base, divided by plastic walls into three segments; bedroom, kitchen and dressing-room. There was plenty of furniture too, as well as spare clothes for Holly.

It was no surprise when Holly Hobbie was revived in 1989, thanks to Tomy who brought out a new range of extremely pretty Holly Hobbie cloth dolls dressed in various outfits, including the familiar, blue patchwork dress and hat. These 15½in-dolls had thick, blonde woollen hair and shy smiles, and their outfits were adorned with homilies such as 'A gift from the heart is the best gift of all'. These kind of sayings were a vital part of the Holly Hobbie branding and appeared on the early stationery and other giftware, too, and though maybe a little sentimental for the British market, they fitted in well with the nostalgia theme. Shortly afterwards, Knickerbocker relaunched Holly Hobbie as a vinyl-

With each gift Central Arkansas Library System will:

- Place a bookplate or similar acknowledgement for the gift.

- Acknowledge the gift to family of the honoree or the honoree.

- List the gift in the Friends of Central ArkansasLibraries (FOCAL) newsletter.

To make a donation visit:
www.cals.org/information/donation.html
or call
501-918-3086

For information on creating a permanent book fund call:
501-918-3037

Your donation is tax deductible under 170 (c) (1) of the Internal Revenue Code of 1986.

Your gift fits perfectly... on our shelves

A memorial or honorarium is an excellent tribute to a friend or loved one.

www.cals.org

headed doll with a soft body, so she was still as cuddly as the originals. Unlike previous versions of Holly Hobbie, which tended to have fairly small eyes and gentle smiles, this doll had large, oval eyes, a snub nose and a grin. However, she was dressed in the usual multi-coloured patchwork dress and big floppy bonnet. This doll didn't seem to be quite as popular as the earlier cloth types and was soon selling at discounted prices. Consequently, today they are hard to find, so one in mint condition would make an excellent addition to a Holly Hobbie collection.

During the 1990s, collectables company Ashton-Drake released a series of porcelain Holly Hobbie dolls aimed at doll collectors. These lovely dolls stood 15in tall, and there were four in the series; 'Spring', 'Summer', 'Autumn' and 'Winter'. Spring wore light green and carried a bunch of seasonal flowers, while Summer was patriotic, celebrating the Fourth of July in a red, white and blue dress and waving the Stars and Stripes flag. The doll representing Autumn was dressed in the classic blue patchwork dress and large bonnet and carried flowering twigs and colourful Winter wore red, and proudly held a plum pudding. These dolls were designed by well-known doll creator Dianna Effner, and, presumably due to copyright, the leaflet that came with these porcelain dolls was at pains to explain that they represented a little girl called Maggie who enjoyed dressing up as her favourite character Holly Hobbie. Holly Hobbie is one of the most famous 'character dolls' recognised by people worldwide.

Very reminiscent of Holly Hobbie were the dolls that featured in the 'World of Sarah Kay' series by Pedigree, and nowadays, Sarah Kay dolls are invariably mistaken for the former. The Sarah Kay character cards were produced by the Australian artist Sarah Kay in the 1970s and 1980s, and just as with Holly Hobbie, the images were soon developed into a series of cloth dolls as well as many other licensed products. It is extremely difficult to discover information about this artist as she shuns publicity, but it seems that at one time she worked as a designer for an adverting agency. Later, when her daughter was very ill, Kay painted pictures for her, based on memories of her own happy childhood days spent at her grandparents' house. These paintings depicted children in a gentler, kindly age, the kind of world Sarah Kay would like her children to grow up in. Later, she offered the pictures to Valentine, a publisher of greetings cards, and 20 of them were subsequently produced as birthday cards and other stationery.

The main difference between the two ranges of drawings is that usually the Sarah Kay designs seem more wistful, gentle and delicate, often tending towards pastel colours, whereas Holly Hobbie wore deeper shades. In the late 1970s, Pedigree toys introduced a delightful range of soft, cuddly, cloth-bodied Sarah Kay dolls with vinyl faces. These dolls had a timeless look, not only because of their traditional-styled clothing of cotton print dresses, aprons and mob caps, but also because the vinyl used was very pale, with a porcelain appearance. The 1979 Pedigree catalogue proclaimed, 'The most beautiful rag dolls ever. High quality material. Detailed replicas of world famous greetings cards.' The features on these dolls were, according to the following year's

Holly Hobbie, Ashton–Drake.

Sarah Kay, Pedigree.

Pedigree catalogue, 'hand decorated', and they had rooted hair and bean-filled bodies. The bean filling made them posable as well as cuddly. The dolls' limbs contained foam, and the larger sizes had vinyl hands as opposed to the fabric hands of the 13in-high dolls.

There was also a range of Sarah Kay dolls that were completely made from cloth. These dolls had printed, rather solemn, faces, and long woollen hair which was often tied into bunches, and their eyes seemed to be spaced very far apart, giving them a somewhat wistful air. The hands of the cloth dolls, as well as those of the 13in vinyl dolls, were mitten-shaped, with no fingers; just a rounded hand with a thumb. They came in a surprisingly large range of sizes, from 6in to 24in. Presumably many of the larger dolls were intended as 'mascots' for teens and doll collectors, perfect for sitting on a bed or chair. All the dolls were dressed just like the artist's paintings, usually in pastel-coloured outfits, though occasionally red or sage green was featured. Instead of bearing thoughtful messages or uplifting sayings like the Holly Hobbie dolls, Sarah Kay dolls had names which reflected their nature; 'Tenderness', 'Sweet Thoughts', 'Gentleness', 'Sweetness' or 'Sweet Love'. At this time there also appeared a range of nightdress cases, initially marketed by Burbank, though later sold through Pedigree when Burbank was taken over. These nightdress cases contained a large plastic form to keep the doll in shape even when there was no nightdress inside, and to all intents and purposes resembled a normal doll.

Amongst the more unusual Sarah Kay dolls and figurines are the wooden sculptures, still made today. They are designed by Master Sculptor Ulrich Bernardi and produced by the House of Anri, which was founded and maintained by the Riffeser family over several generations. The pieces are hand carved from Alpine maple and are extremely popular. Several kinds of Sarah

Kay jointed wooden dolls have been made, including a 14in-high little girl, 'Martha', who was made in a limited edition of 750. Dressed in a typical Kay outfit of cotton frock and bonnet, Martha has the trademark freckles across her nose. Amongst the figurines is one of a Sarah Kay child with her doll in a highchair.

Betsey Clark, yet another character named after her designer, first appeared on Hallmark cards in the 1960s in a series called 'Whimsical Waifs'. This unmistakable little girl has a kind of elfin look with a pointed chin and unusual tear-drop-shaped eyes. Her distinctive, rather sad-looking face, wispy hair and raggedy clothes set her apart from most of the other dolls, though there is a slight similarity to the later Precious Moments dolls and figurines.

Artist/illustrator, Betsey Clark, lived in Texas and even as a young child knew that she wanted to draw 'waifs'. She likened her work to folk art; it was very detailed and depicted the world though faded pastel colours. Her little waifs designs were seen by Hallmark cards, who snapped her up as a designer in the early 1960s. By the end of the decade, 'Betsey Clark waifs' were featured on their own range of greetings cards.

Various Betsey Clark dolls appeared over the years, mainly during the 1970s and 80s. One of the nicest, and most collectable, is a 14in vinyl-headed soft-bodied doll, wearing either a pale-pink or blue outfit of patterned dress and striped, patched apron. The pastel colours complement the delicate hues seen in Betsey Clark's original illustrations, and the presentation of this doll was delightful. She was positioned behind a cardboard picket fence, and there was a verse on the back which read: '*Betsey's the very best kind of a friend, whenever you need her, she has time to spend. You can tell her your troubles when something goes wrong, and wherever you go, she likes going along! She can make you smile brightly*

Betsey Clark, Knickerbocker.   Precious Moments.

when you're feeling glum, when you tell her your secrets, she'll keep every one! She can make almost anything more fun to do, and she's coming to stay and have fun times with you.'

Knickerbocker also made a series of cloth Betsey Clark dolls as well as a range of 5- 6in vinyls, jointed at the shoulders and hips, and all perfectly resembling artist Betsey Clark's much-loved 'waifs' as she called them. Even the smallest wore patched dresses and overlarge shoes, and often had their wispy blonde hair tied with ribbon into a bunch on top of their head. Many of these smaller dolls came complete with delightful play sets. For example, the bath time set not only included a 5in Betsey Clark, but also a bath, a tiny baby doll and various related items, such as the all-important plastic duck. As well as Knickerbocker, over the decades, Betsey Clark dolls and figures have been made by such companies as Coleco, Hummel and Goebels. Betsey Clark died in 1987, but even today, collectors seek out the dolls and the charming, timeless illustrations.

Another doll with greetings cards links, Victoria Plum, was a character who later became linked to a celebrity. Broadcaster Angela Rippon was shown a series of greetings cards drawn by Roger Hutchings, a director of the W.N. Sharpe Company, and decided that the character was a fairy, later creating a background for Victoria Plum and writing a series of children's stories about her. The fairy soon appeared as a character doll. (*See Chapter 2.*)

Precious Moments can also be mentioned here. These sad-eyed characters were designed by Sam Butcher in the 1970s and later produced as greetings cards by a company he formed with a friend, known as Jonathan & David. Later, Sam was approached by the Enesco Corporation to develop a three-dimensional figurine based on his designs. Small vinyl dolls featuring Sam's sad-eyed children later appeared, amongst them a colourful figure with large teardrop-shaped eyes, dressed in a yellow mob cap, blue dress, red scarf and white apron. There is also a series of pretty cloth 'Precious Moments' dolls.

A major success of a greetings card character being transformed into a doll can be seen in the 'Strawberry Shortcake' range. This little girl and her cat, 'Custard', first appeared as a design by Muriel Fahrion in 1977 for the American Greetings Card Company. Muriel went on to develop 32 other characters. Her sister, Susan Trentel, crafted a Strawberry Shortcake doll which she based on the greetings card design. This made such a deep impression on the company owners, that within two years, Strawberry Shortcake evolved into a character appearing in books and on clothing, as well as a huge range of dolls and toys. The range was even given a new toy and licensing division, called Those Characters from Cleveland (TCFC).

By 1980 The World of Strawberry Shortcake and Her Friends had reached Britain and children's toy boxes suddenly started to smell delicious, because each doll was perfumed to match her name. The fruity scents of lemon, raspberry, blueberry, cherry, lime and strawberry were embedded into the vinyl of each doll, whatever its size. The most popular was a 5½in doll that was jointed at the hip, shoulder and neck, and was made from a hard vinyl. The dolls had large, rounded heads, slightly out of proportion to their bodies, cute faces with moulded snub noses and tiny eyes, while their mouths resembled the letter 'U'. Each doll had different coloured hair, and was marked 'American Greetings Corps 1979' on the back of its head. The dolls were made by Kenner and usually sold under the Palitoy name in Britain.

At first there were 12 dolls in the set; 'Strawberry Shortcake with Custard Kitten', 'Huckleberry Pie with Pupcake Puppy', 'Orange Blossom with Marmalade Butterfly', 'Cherry Cuddler with Gooseberry Goose', 'Lemon Meringue with Frappe Frog', 'Lime Chiffon with Parfait Parrot', 'Butter Cookie with Jelly Bear', 'Raspberry Tart with Rhubarb Monkey',' Blueberry Muffin with Cheesecake Mouse', 'Angel Cake with Souffle Skunk', 'Apple Dumpling with Tea Time Turtle' and 'Apricot with Hopsalot Bunny'. Each doll came with its own blow-moulded vinyl pet in a brightly decorated box and cost £4.75, which was quite expensive at the time and way above the average child's pocket money, so it took a long while to collect the dolls. There were also two slightly larger figures, meant to be 'friendly foes', the 'Purple Pieman with Berry Bird' and 'Sour Grapes with Dregs Snake'.

Of all the characters, Purple Pieman and Sour Grapes are the most difficult to recognise as members of Strawberry Shortcake's World. Both of these are tall (around 9in) and thin, with narrow faces – the complete antithesis of the round-faced Strawberry Shortcake children and toddlers. Purple Pieman has purple hair, eyebrows and trousers, all moulded from purple plastic, and a long, twirly, blue moustache. His fabric clothing consists of a turquoise top, white apron and floppy chef's hat. The Purple Pieman is cinnamon scented, his Berry Bird clips onto his arm and a yellow ladle hangs from his waist. Sour Grapes, the female friendly foe, has glamorous upswept rooted hair in shades of turquoise and purple, a long gown printed with bunches of grapes and a turquoise chiffon stole. Her purple boots and long green gloves are made from moulded plastic. Her pet snake, Dregs, hangs around her neck.

Later, more dolls arrived on the scene including 'Almond Tea with Marza Panda', 'Crepe Suzette with Eclair Poodle', 'Peach Blush with Melanie Belle Lamb', 'Mint Tulip with Marsh Mallard', 'Cafe Ole with Burrito Donkey', 'Plum Puddin' with Elderberry Owl', and the twins 'Lem and Ada with Sugar Woofer Dog'. There was also a peculiar pink and white dinosaur called 'Big Foot'.

All of the dolls were beautifully dressed, but it is quite difficult today to find them in perfect condition because the garments were so tiny that items soon became mislaid, especially socks, tights and shoes. In fact, around 1984 Kenner stopped including shoes with many of the dolls. Today, Strawberry Shortcake is the most commonly-found of the dolls, and is easy to recognise with her gingery-red hair and red frock topped with a white apron. As with many of the others, she also came with a floppy hat. Other hair colours include white curls for 'Angel Cake', bright purple for 'Almond Tea', yellow curls ('Lemon Meringue'), turquoise ('Blueberry Muffin') and dark blue ('Crepe Suzette'). The only boy doll is 'Huckleberry Pie', who wears an all-in-one light-blue shirt and blue dungarees. His hair is red-brown and he wears a yellow plastic straw hat. The babies are slightly smaller (4in), and include 'Cherry Cuddler' whose white

Strawberry Shortcake and Huckleberry Pie, Kenner.

Angel Cake, Raspberry Tart, Lime Chiffon, Kenner.

Rainbow Brite, Mattel.

dress is trimmed with cherries, 'Apricot' in an over-large apricot hat, 'Apple Dumpling' with a red apple motif on her yellow romper suit and yellow-haired 'Butter Cookie'.

Later, many of the dolls were issued wearing party outfits trimmed with lots of braid and frills, and in addition, a variety of outfits could be purchased separately. Strawberry Shortcake was also sold dressed as a ballet dancer in a strawberry-trimmed tutu, pink-and-white striped tights and her iconic hat. Dozens of accessories were available, too, including houses, creatures to ride on, shops and carry cases – for a while, the Strawberry Shortcake brand was invincible. Amongst the larger dolls in the series were various cloth creations, as well as a set of very pretty 14in 'Blow Kiss Babies', which were soft-bodied dolls with vinyl heads, arms and legs. They blew scented kisses when their middles were squeezed, and were extremely expensive for the time, costing £24 in 1984. In the early 1990s, Those Characters From Cleveland issued a totally updated 13in rag doll. The face had been altered and the clothing modernised, and somehow the range was turning into just another baby doll – the innocent charm had been lost. Other smaller dolls not mentioned so far include the 'Berry Babies', a range of small drink-and-wet dolls with feeding bottles, and also the highly popular 2in moulded vinyl figures, which children could just about afford to buy with their pocket money. Strawberry Shortcake editions still appear in the shops from time to time, but have lost that original charm.

The main rival of Strawberry Shortcake in the 1980s was 'Rainbow Brite', a colourful doll who began life as a character on Hallmark Greetings Cards in 1981. It seems that the concept was a pooling together of ideas, although the lion's share of the design seemed to fall on artist G. G. Santiago. Rainbow Brite had one special thing going for her, and that was colour! Multi-hued, dazzling – these dolls were completely different from the predominantly pastel-coloured dolls of the time – and the strong storyline, tied in with books and films, gave extra appeal. Further, unlike Strawberry Shortcake and other character lines, there weren't dozens of dolls to collect. After all, there were just seven colours in a rainbow, and even though a few extra characters appeared (plus a range of associated fluffy creatures and mascots) a set of dolls could soon be built up, especially of the moulded vinyl figures which were more affordable.

The marketing of the Rainbow Brite range seemed poorly thought out in Britain, and many of the American lines just didn't appear over here. There were few accessories and surprisingly, costume packs were very rarely available. Nowadays of course, this pleases the collectors as the dolls are more likely to be found still wearing their original outfits. Today, the doll that turns up most frequently at collector's markets is the 10in soft-bodied Rainbow Brite with a vinyl head and hands. Originally, she was sold boxed with a small, white, fluffy 'Sprite'. Rainbow Brite and her seven Colour Kids friends each had their own magic Sprite. Impossible to mistake for anything else, Rainbow Brite had wide-apart round painted eyes, a button nose, a sweet smile and a blue star on one cheek. Her hair was made from lengths of yellow wool styled into a ponytail and tied with a ribbon. Her arms and legs were made from a shiny nylon fabric striped in primary colours, and she wore a pretty, red and metallic-blue tunic with a rainbow logo across the bodice, and bright yellow shoes. Other sizes are sometimes found, including an attractive 18in version.

The Colour Kids were also issued as 10in vinyl-headed soft-bodied dolls, but some of them are very rare indeed, and it seems that not all the colours made it to Britain. 'Red Butler' in his red nylon jumpsuit with a star motif and yellow cape is fairly easy to find. His hair is made from red wool and he has orange and yellow fabric arms and legs. 'Patty O'Green' is recognisable instantly by her thick, green woollen plaits which stuck up straight on top of her head. She wore a tunic of Irish green. 'Indigo' was a pretty doll, with blue-streaked black hair and dressed in purple silk baggy trousers and a blue top with iridescent trim, while 'Canary Yellow' wore yellow shorts and leg-warmers and a top with iridescent pearl shoulder epaulettes. 'Buddy Blue' was attractive with blue woollen hair and a pale-blue outfit with a blue star motif on his belt, while 'Shy Violet' was a bespectacled girl in a violet outfit and 'La La Orange' had a long orange gown and a beret. Sometimes found are pink-haired 'Baby Brite', dressed in pink rompers over a striped top, and 'Tickled Pink', whose bright-pink hair was thick and fluffy. Tickled Pink was the rarest of the dolls and of course, she wore pink. The dolls had small strips of Velcro on their hands to enable them to hold a Sprite. Amongst the US range of dolls was a 15in Mattel Rainbow Brite soft-bodied vinyl-headed girl with short beige-blonde nylon hair rather than the familiar yellow. She bore a blue star on her cheek and was marked as being made in 1983, copyright Hallmark.

Other items that were available in Britain include the two villains, 'Murky Dismal' and ' Lurky'. Murky wore brown and fawn, had a pale- green face, black moustache and thick black eyebrows. Lurky was a large soft toy. There were various animals, notably 'Starlite', Rainbow Brite's white horse, and a puppy called 'Puppy Brite'. A turquoise plastic beach buggy was one of the few items intended for use with the 10in dolls, and is a nice item to find. Rainbow Brite has been revived a few times, but most of the new dolls look completely different and don't seem to be based on any particular story line.

Additional character dolls appear on greetings cards sometimes, but most will just have a tie-in doll or two rather than a complete range, as we've seen with Strawberry Shortcake, Rainbow Brite, Holly Hobbie and others.

Chapter Fifteen

In Search of Topsy

OFTEN MISTAKENLY referred to as 'topsy-turvys' (*See Chapter 9*), Topsy dolls definitely fall into a separate, special category. Topsy dolls are black dolls, distinguished by three pigtails on their heads; one on top and one at either side. The pigtails are frequently made from thick, black, plaited wool, and are normally tied with ribbon. There seems to have been a 'Topsy doll boom' in the 1930s, which explains why so many of these delightful dolls were made from composition, and a revival of interest in the 1950s, hence an influx of hard plastic versions.

Many British children liked to include a black doll in their collection if they could find one, and invariably the doll became called 'Topsy'. It was as though the name was passed down through generations as a good name for a black doll, and almost certainly the tradition can be traced to the classic novel, *Uncle Tom's Cabin* by Harriet Beecher Stowe, which featured a cheeky little black girl called Topsy. This novel was published in 1852, and in it there is a description of the child which read, 'She was one of the blackest of her race; and her round shining eyes, glittering as glass beads, moved with quick and restless glances over everything in the room. Her mouth, half open with astonishment at the wonders of the new Mas'r's parlor, displayed a white and brilliant set of teeth. Her woolly hair was braided in sundry little tails, which stuck out in every direction. The expression of her face was an odd mixture of shrewdness and cunning, over which was oddly drawn, like a kind of veil, an expression of the most doleful gravity and solemnity. She was dressed in a single filthy, ragged garment, made of bagging; and stood with her hands demurely folded before her. Altogether, there was something odd and goblin-like about her appearance.'

Gradually, the name 'Topsy' was used to describe a particular sort of black doll; one with three pigtails. The enchanting description of Topsy's woolly hair, 'braided in sundry little tails, which stuck out in every direction' describes the dolls' hair to perfection, and it would be very interesting to know which enterprising manufacturer was really the first to come up with the 'Topsy Doll'. Many of the composition types of Topsy dolls are unmarked, so it is difficult to attribute them to any particular maker. It is likely that the majority of them were made in America. Sometimes, a composition Topsy marked 'Reliable' will turn up – these were made by the Reliable Doll Company in Toronto, Canada, during the 1920s and 1930s.

According to *Uncle Tom's Cabin*, even Topsy herself doesn't know her maker! One of the most popular quotes concerns Topy's thoughts on creation, when questioned by Miss Ophelia:

'Do you know who made you?'
'Nobody, as I knows on,' said the child, with a short laugh. The idea appeared to amuse her considerably; for her eyes twinkled, and she added, 'I spect I grow'd. Don't think nobody never made me.'

The various composition Topsy dolls from different manufacturers, though similar, all seem to have their special quirks. Invariably they were originally dressed in one-piece romper suits, sometimes with little matching dresses over the top, and they all seem to be of the bent-limbed baby doll construction. They are normally made from a dark-brown matt finish composition, though sometimes shiny 'pot' finish dolls appear, and occasionally a waxy-finished composition type which tends to be a lighter brown. The dolls are usually jointed at the neck, hips and shoulders, though sometimes the neck is moulded in with the body so it doesn't turn. The limbs are often metal-sprung-jointed, or they may be elastic strung. Although the sizes of these composition Topsys vary, they tend to be around 9-14in. The dolls nearly always have painted side-glance eyes and the lips are painted red. Sometimes there is even a hint of cheek blushing, too. Often they wear bone or brass earrings, and the thick plaits emerge from holes drilled into the composition head. In addition, the heads are normally marked with moulded curls.

During the 1950s, black plastic dolls became exceedingly popular and were made by most of the British doll manufacturers. At the same time, several produced Topsy dolls, such as an 8in one from Roddy. This popular doll was a bent leg 'thumbs up' baby with a bead necklace, bead bracelet and a pair of brass hoop earrings. Her three topknots were made from mohair. Tudor Rose, another popular maker at the time, made a 7in Topsy, again with mohair plaits. This Topsy was a much darker brown than the Roddy doll, and was dressed in a raffia skirt, beads and plastic hoop earrings. Both dolls were made from shiny, hard plastic and featured amber sleep eyes.

When the Topsy craze was at its height in the 1920s & 30s, children would sing a song about a Topsy doll. It began:

I had a black dolly called Topsy,
Who didn't like sleeping alone,
'Cause Topsy's afraid of her shadow
Though in darkness I know there are none,

But Topsy is only a dolly
And doesn't know better you see
So I just put her under my pillow
I know she likes sleeping with me.

Topsy Dolls, Composition, Unmarked.

Topsy Dolls, Roddy & Tudor Rose.

And when I wake up in the morning
I sing till I think she's awake
Then I take her right down to the garden
And give her a bath in the lake…

I just hope that the little girls who sang that song didn't really try bathing their composition dolls in the lake, as they would have been ruined.

Chapter Sixteen

An In-Depth Look at Shirley Temple Dolls

IT SEEMS amazing that a doll, first issued in the 1930s, is still not only a major seller but appeals to people who never even experienced at first hand the phenomenal aura and hype that surrounded the young Shirley Temple. Today the doll, despite many different forms having appeared, is still instantly recognisable even to young doll collectors who presumably discovered the young starlet by watching DVDs and television reruns of those 1930s movies. Maybe, too, many people are attracted by the unmistakable 1930s little girl clothing of ribbons, ringlets, frilly dresses and bow-bedecked shoes. Rarely do small children dress like this today, and, if you are a fan of the movies, then it is fun to try to acquire dolls dressed in some of the costumes that are featured.

Shirley Temple was born in 1928 in California. Her mother, feeling that her little girl was 'special', enrolled her into a dance school while still a toddler. It is said that she amazed the teachers with her natural sense of rhythm and ability to follow routines at such a young age. One day, while Shirley was at the school, a film director called in to see the children, who were billed as 'Kute, Klever and Kunning' but unfortunately he was not particular impressed until he spotted the small girl crossly hiding under the piano, obviously sulking. In true Hollywood style, he said, 'We want her!' Whether this was true or not is a moot point, but certainly, aged just three, Shirley Temple appeared in a comedy 'short', called *Runt Page* in a rather debatable series know as 'Baby Burlesk'. In a way, the tots were exploited, being dressed in adult-styled costumes, but with nappies and giant safety-pins.

Even at such a tender age, Shirley's personality shone through, but of course she was growing, and soon looked silly wearing a nappy. It was obvious that a different kind of film had to be found for her. She was offered a few bit parts, but then a chance encounter with a Hollywood script writer earned Shirley a cameo role in *Stand Up and Cheer*. Her name was made – and the red-spotted, *Stand Up and Cheer* dress she wore when she sang *Baby, Take a Bow* quickly became the iconic Shirley Temple dress, appearing regularly on dolls. Another popular costume from the film was a very short, frilly full-skirted frock trimmed with flowers. Shirley Temple was a star – overnight, or so it seemed. This child with the cheeky smile and the ability to sing and dance was perfect for taking people's minds off the grey years of the Depression. For a few years films poured from the studio in a never-ending stream – it seemed that the directors were anxious to use Shirley as much as they could before her childish looks faded and turned to gawkiness. *Curly Top*, *The Littlest Rebel*, *Dimples*, *Little Miss Marker*, *Bright Eyes*, *Captain January*, *Rebecca Of Sunnybrook Farm*, *Stowaway*, *The Little Princess* and *Heidi* are just a few of the 60 or so movies she appeared in, all inspiring yet another doll's outfit.

By Christmas 1934 there was an official Shirley Temple doll in production. This scoop had been secured by the American Ideal Toy and Novelty Company when it masterminded an exclusive contract to produce a doll in her image. Doll designer Bernard Lipfert was given the task of creating a 'Shirley clone', and he later said he made 20 moulds before he was finally satisfied. Many years later, Abe Katz, the production manager at Ideal, explained much of the problem was due to the materials used to create the doll. The Shirley dolls were made from composition, using wood pulp, sawdust and glue. This would be compressed into shape, placed in a mould and baked under pressure, but sometimes the heat made the materials flow, consequently changing the doll's facial expression. Then the process would have to start over again. Nowadays, with modern plastics, the faces in a mould will come out identical time after time.

Shirley Temple, Stand Up and Cheer, Danbury Mint.

Shirley Temple 1930s, Composition, Ideal.

Despite the problems, the likeness to the little girl was excellent, managing to capture Shirley's sunny smile as well as her dimples. The doll was fitted with a wig arranged in a cluster of ringlets – even though they couldn't quite manage the 55 ringlets and a kiss curl which Shirley's mother painstakingly set in rags every night after supper. When Abe took the doll to show to the president of Ideal, he also showed it to a group of children he noticed in the street, and they immediately recognised the doll as Shirley, so he was satisfied the face was correct. Shirley's mother was very pleased with the doll's resemblance to her daughter. As for Shirley, she was thrilled with the doll created in her name, and Ideal ran an advert in the newspapers of the day which proclaimed in her childish, unpunctuated printing, 'I love my doll I play with it all the time it is just like me.' Alongside the advert was a telegram from Shirley's mother enthusiastically praising 'so beautiful a doll made in our Shirley's image.'

This first Ideal composition Shirley Temple doll stood 18in tall. To prove authenticity it was marked 'Shirley Temple' on the back of the neck. At $5 it was expensive for the time. It wore, of course, the white full-skirted dress with red polka dots from *Stand Up and Cheer*, together with a celluloid badge bearing a picture of Shirley and the words 'The World's Darling'. A whole range of dolls in various outfits followed: as new films were released, so dolls would be issued wearing featured costumes. Today, mint and boxed examples of these early dolls are very valuable. Additionally, many outfits were also available separately, and it wasn't long before other dolls, such as Shirley Temple babies with moulded hair appeared, and all kinds of related merchandise, including a delightful wicker pram with a photo of Shirley on the side.

Naturally, Ideal was quick to act on any breach of their copyright because many companies attempted to put their own versions of Shirley Temple on the market, but even so, some did escape detection. The more crafty manufacturers simply produced dolls with golden ringlets that might or might not be Shirley and left it to the public to decide – children at the time were desperate for a 'Shirley doll', and they didn't worry if it wasn't authentic as long as there was a resemblance. In 1936 a British company, Richards, Son and Allwin, makers of Allwin dolls, produced a range of 'unbreakable' dolls dressed in outfits based on Shirley Temple's screen roles and which even had badges depicting the child star. Unfortunately, the facial likeness wasn't particularly good despite the masses of Shirley-type ringlets.

All good things come to an end, and it looked as though Ideal's golden goose had laid its final egg when, in 1940, they decided to discontinue the dolls as they were no longer selling. The little Shirley had grown up, and as feared, had fallen out of favour with many of the audiences, especially with the children. It seemed the Shirley craze was over. However, never underestimate the ambitious Shirley, because in the late 1950s, now grown-up and shrewd, she contacted Ideal to say that she was once more dabbling in the entertainment world and suggested that perhaps the dolls could be re-issued. The idea appealed, but this time Ideal decided to make the dolls from vinyl, and they became popular all over again. Consequently, over the next few decades a range of vinyl versions of

Shirley Temple became available, including sets wearing the costumes from the films, just as in the past.

Many of the earlier vinyl Shirley Temple dolls were issued with silver script-name badges pinned to their bodice, a nod to the earlier celluloid badges found on the composition dolls of the 1930s. As before, outfits were available separately, and Ideal soon realised that collectors, as well as children, were buying the dolls and costumes. A set of 12 Shirley Temple dolls was available during the 1980s, dressed to represent some of her most popular roles. Amongst them were those from *Rebecca of Sunnybrook Farm, Dimples, Poor Little Rich Girl, Wee Willie Winkie, Heidi, Stowaway, The Little Colonel, and, of course, Stand Up and Cheer*. These vinyl dolls came in two sizes, 8in and 12in. In the 1980s there was a fad for using a very pale vinyl to resemble porcelain, and some of these film dolls were issued in this paler colour. In 1984 a special Collector's Series was produced which also used a porcelain-look pale vinyl, giving the face a translucent appearance. These attractive 16in-high dolls were sold in large blue boxes featuring a photograph of the young Shirley.

One of the largest Shirley Temple dolls must have been the 1960s' Ideal Play Pal Shirley, which stood 36in tall and could wear child-sized clothing. Unfortunately, this meant that nowadays they are difficult to find in their original outfits. In 1985 Ideal issued a special collector's limited edition 36in Shirley dressed in her red-spotted *Stand Up and Cheer* dress and commemorative badge.

Shirley Temple dolls continue to regularly appear, now aimed almost exclusively at collectors, and often made from porcelain. Danbury Mint issued a particularly attractive 1996 series designed by Elke Hutchens, which was based on Shirley as a toddler. The first doll in the series, 'Little Miss Shirley' had her in a seated pose with her legs folded under, and she wore a peach silk dress. Her face was lit by a mischievous smile and bore an outstanding resemblance to Shirley as she looked at the beginning of her career. Others in the series included 'Bathing Beauty', in which Shirley is standing, wearing a turquoise and navy bathing costume and holding a large ball, and 'Sunday Best', which has her dressed in a powder-blue fur-trimmed coat and matching hat, worn over a pink-striped dress. The same designer was also responsible for a series of 8in, all-porcelain dolls dressed in movie outfits such as the white, full-skirted pleated dress from *Baby Take a Bow*, maroon outfit from *Dimples*, tan costume from *Wee Willie Winkie* and the green travelling outfit from *Littlest Rebel*.

One of the most comprehensive sets of Shirley Temple outfits was produced by Danbury Mint in 1995, and known as the 'Dress Up Shirley Temple Fashion Doll'. It was made from vinyl and stood 17in high, and 25 separate outfits could be bought. Each outfit was beautifully designed and sewn, and came wrapped in 'Shirley Temple' print tissue paper in a white box, along with a special stand on which to display the outfit if you didn't want to put it on the doll. This varied collection included outfits from *The Littlest Rebel* (a floral full-skirted dress trimmed with lace), *Curly Top* (a green dress with white ducks appliqué), *Poor Little Rich Girl* (navy sailor dress), *The Little Princess* (white satin gown with gold-lined fur cloak), and *Stowaway* (yellow summer dress and hat). Many of the more unusual costumes were included, making it a special bonus for the dedicated Shirley Temple enthusiast.

No doubt Shirley Temple dolls will continue to be issued every so often as there still seems to be a demand. These pretty dolls evoke a long-lost childish innocence, and are charming and fun. Perhaps that is part of the magic of their continuing popularity. The strangest thing is that the majority of today's Shirley Temple doll collectors weren't even born when she was the darling of those 1930s movies.

Shirley Temple Early Vinyl, Ideal.

Suzanna Of The Mounties, Ideal.

Shirley Temple, Bathing Beauty, Danbury Mint.

Shirley Temple Toddler, Danbury Mint.

Chapter Seventeen

An In-Depth Look At Harry Potter Dolls

THERE CAN be few people in Britain who haven't heard of the boy wizard Harry Potter, together with friends Ron Weasley and Hermione Granger, and yet if author J. K. Rowling hadn't been so determined to find a publisher, the first novel might never have been printed. Rejected by many publishers, *Harry Potter and The Philosopher's Stone* was finally distributed in 1997 in a print run of just 500 copies by Bloomsbury Press. The title went on to win the Smarties Book Prize that same year. In the following two years *Harry Potter and the Chamber of Secrets* and *Harry Potter and the Prisoner of Azkaban* were published in quick succession. From the start, Ms Rowling knew that there was to be a series of seven books that followed Harry's progress through Hogwarts, the School of Witchcraft and Wizardry, and that the series would end with a climatic sequence of Harry facing his arch enemy, Voldemort.

Ever since the first Harry Potter film was proposed – *The Philosopher's Stone* was released in 2001 – dolls have been made as tie-ins with the films. As the cast were quite young children at the time, it has been fascinating to watch them grow and develop through the subsequent films, not just on screen but depicted in the dolls as well. The Harry Potter character was an absolute gift to toy and doll manufactures because Rowling had given him so many distinguishing features which could not be ignored, such as large, round glasses and a lightning-shaped scar on his forehead.

Some of the earliest dolls featuring Harry and his friends were a soft-bodied set made by Mattel in 2001 and called 'Gryffindor Friends'. These dolls were 12in high and had thick yarn hair. Each came with an appropriate metal charm – Harry had an owl, Ron a dragon, whilst Hermione had a sorting hat. Mattel has been responsible for several other Harry Potter ranges too, notably the 'Wizard Sweets' series, which featured 8in-high (young version) dolls packed in sweet shop illustrated boxes. The boxes included various sweet-themed items, and, as with the other Mattel dolls, these small dolls were probably brought by children rather than collectors and consequently played with, making them quite desirable nowadays if still mint and boxed.

Mattel also introduced sets of 5in dolls depicting the trio. In 'Hogwarts Heroes' (2001) the children were dressed in their school uniforms, complete with black robes with Hogwarts badges that could be 'magically' transformed into the Gryffindor shield. The 'Magical Powers' set (2001) featured various animated movements, such as Harry in his red Quidditch-seeker outfit, complete with accessories with which he could interact, and included Hedwig his snowy owl, the Sorting Hat and the mirror of Erised in which Harry's parents could appear. Hermione came with a magic trunk, a cauldron and light-up potion bottles, and although she was again dressed in her school uniform, she had a stripy Gryffindor scarf.

Other Mattel dolls included the Magical Mini range of 3in moulded figures which incorporated a far wider range of characters from the book than were usually available in the sets of larger dolls. Hagrid (the Hogwarts' ground keeper), Ginny Weasley (Ron's little sister) and Dumbledore (the wizard headmaster of Hogwarts) were all included, and each featured rooted hair, while Dumbledore had a long white beard as well. Each figure came with an accessory with which the doll could interact, for instance, Dumbledore had the mythical bird Fawkes and through magnets could make it move with his wand. There was even a model of the Hogwarts Express, all ready to leave from platform 9¾.

In 2002 the German Gotz company released a set of three excellent dolls based on the characters from the film, each in their school uniforms. Harry, Ron and Hermione were 18in high, and made completely from vinyl. The modelling was impressive, and the faces were slightly quirky, giving the dolls tremendous character. The costumes were very detailed and excellently constructed, and the accessories, which included a broom for Harry, books for Hermione and a rat for Ron, were well made. These dolls were limited editions, and expensive, costing around £100, but they didn't seem to sell as well as they should. However, their quality is sure to make them in demand for future collectors, not just Harry Potter enthusiasts but those who appreciate the Gotz range of quality dolls. Gund created a series of plush dolls a few years later which were skilfully modelled with detailed faces delicately painted on flocked heads. The dolls, which depicted Harry, Ron and Hermione, wore the familiar black robes over more casual dress of jeans and a coloured top. Gund also produced some of the more unusual characters including Hagrid, the burly half-giant, baby Norbert the dragon, Hedwig which was Harry's white owl, Fluffy the three-headed dog and Mrs Norris, Filch's cat, who was part Kneazle. All of these characters were created from soft plush or fabric. Gund also made a golden snitch with pearly fabric wings, all ready for a game of Quidditch, while Warner Brothers produced a 13in plush Harry with a vinyl head.

In 2005 prestigious American designer Robert Tonner announced that he intended to issue a line of Harry Potter dolls. Collectors were intrigued, as at the time, Robert was more famed for fashion dolls. Most of the dolls in the series stand around 17in tall, and are eminently posable with 17 points of articulation. The modelling is excellent, with each doll having an incredible likeness to the actor who played him or her, and the faces are all hand-painted. The first doll in the series was called 'Harry Potter at Hogwarts', and featured Harry in his school outfit of grey sweater, flannel trousers and black robe. Other Tonner versions of Harry have since appeared, amongst them 'The Yule Ball', which depicts a rather sinister Harry in a long black robe over a formal shirt, trousers, waistcoat and bow tie. The finishing touch can be added with a model of his owl, Hedwig, being perched on Harry's arm. The 'Quidditch Harry' features Harry dressed in a custom knit sweater over racing trousers, shin guards and wearing a red-and-yellow house robe with the Gryffindor crest. A magnificent Firebolt broomstick was available separately.

Ron Weasley and Hermione Granger dolls were also produced, and were equally stunning, especially the 'Yule Ball' versions in which Ron is dressed in his vintage tapestry robe. In the film, the robe is the subject of much mirth, and he wears it over a frilled formal shirt, trousers and velvet bow tie. The autumnal shades of the robe set off Ron's ginger hair to perfection. The Tonner version of Hermione at the Yule ball is stunning, depicting her in a gown of graduated shades of purple chiffon ruffles. Her upswept hair is styled in ringlets around her face.

Various other Tonner versions of the trio of friends exist, as well as other characters such as Cho Chang, Draco Malfoy, Professor Snape, and Voldemort. Cho Chang is elegant at the Yule Ball in an embroidered kimono-style dress, and there is also a school uniform version, while Draco Malfoy conveys not only a sense of smouldering evil, but also of smouldering good looks in his school uniform and in his Quidditch outfit. Other Harry Potter characters by Tonner include Dobby, Kreacher, Crookshanks, Fawkes and the Sorting Hat. A range of 12in dolls in the Harry Potter series, also by Robert Tonner, was released, amongst them Professor McGonagall, as well as the main characters. Robert Tonner dolls are intended for collectors, not as playthings, and the representation of characters from the film are superb.

The final Harry Potter film, *Harry Potter and the Deathly Hallows Part 2* was released in 2011, but it's almost certain that Harry will continue to weave his magic over doll collectors for years to come.

Hermione, Gotx.

Harry Potter, Gund.

Harry Potter Quidditch, Tonner.

Draco Malfoy, Tonner.

Chapter Eighteen

An In–Depth Look at Annie Dolls

L ITTLE ORPHAN ANNIE often seems to be confused with Raggedy Ann, but they are very much separate characters. In America, Raggedy Ann (a cloth doll based on the books by Johnny Gruell) is a doll which every child knows, rather like Little Noddy over here. Yet, in Britain, Raggedy Ann never made much of a mark. By contrast, Little Orphan Annie did create a stir, especially during the 1980s when the musical movie was released. Annie also, of course, became famed in America, but there still seems to be that hazy blurring of the two characters, not helped by both having red hair.

Unlike Raggedy Ann (*See Chapter 1*), Little Orphan Annie wasn't a doll, she was a little girl. She made her debut in a cartoon strip in the *Chicago Tribune* in 1924, the brainchild of artist Harold Gray. The cartoon told how the twelve-year-old girl survived by her wits as she made her way in the world, and it proved enormously popular, even more so when three years later she gained her 'official image'. This came about when, according to the cartoon strip, Annie was living with a kind lady called Mrs Pewter, who decided the little girl needed a new frock. She made her a red dress, with a white collar and cuffs, and that dress, together with Annie's mop of carrot-coloured curls made her instantly recognisable, just like Harry Potter's scar and glasses did for him. In the cartoons, Annie's eyes were drawn as two blank ovals, which was slightly disconcerting, but most of the dolls based on the stage musical and the film had normal eyes with pupils.

As the Little Orphan Annie cartoons were so popular, especially in America, Annie memorabilia was around long before the stage show and film were produced. In the 1930s and 40s various small red-dressed composition, wood or celluloid dolls were sold as Orphan Annies. Also in the 1930s, a replica of Sandy, Annie's faithful dog, was sold. This 8in toy was made from stuffed oilcloth and bore the names 'Sandy' and 'Gray' (Howard Gray, the artist), on his collar. Moving forwards to the 1960s, Remco Industries issued a 17in cloth doll with blank, expressionless eyes, just as seen in the cartoons, wearing the usual red dress, white collar and black belted outfit, and with hair made from yarn. This doll bore a 'kiss 'n' hug me' logo with hearts on her chest, and was marked 'Little Orphan Annie', Remco Industries Inc., by arrangement with Chicago Tribune 1967'.

When the musical *Annie* first hit the Victoria Palace Theatre, London, in 1978, following on from the Broadway production a year before, it was an instant success. Starring Sheila Hancock and Stratford Johns, with Andrea McArdle playing Annie, it ran for 1,485 performances. The show was followed by a movie version, and the memorabilia, including dolls, soon filled the shops. Both stage show and film told the story of how little orphan Annie was adopted by the benevolent millionaire Daddy Warbucks, but was cruelly tricked by scheming Miss Hannigan – who ran the orphanage – into believing that her parents were still alive. Filled with songs, such as 'It's The Hard-Knock Life', 'I Think I'm Gonna Like It Here', 'You're Never Fully Dressed Without A Smile' and, of course, 'Tomorrow' it had a feel-good factor with a 'happy ever after' finale. It was little wonder that many people wanted a doll as a souvenir.

One of the most appealing of the dolls was a cloth version made by Knickerbocker in the early 1980s. Standing 16in high, her ginger hair was sewn into dozens of tight wool curls, and her large eyes and happy smile were printed onto her face. Tucked inside the pocket of her red dress was a small, fluffy Sandy, the dog she adopted. Knickerbocker made other Annie dolls in various sizes. Cloth dolls were also made by Applause, and some of their versions had stiffened faces. The Applause dolls were interesting as the makers gave the dolls printed eyes which appeared to be gazing upwards, in an attempt to capture the blank-eyed expression of the original cartoon character. Their curls were looser and softer than the Knickerbocker dolls.

Knickerbocker proved exceedingly prolific with Annie dolls, making ranges of vinyl dolls too, including a charming one which stood 6in high, and was jointed at the neck, shoulders and hips. The doll wore the ubiquitous red Annie dress, and a child-sized 'gold' locket was included in the box – reference to the piece of jewellery which was a vital piece of evidence in the search for Annie's parents. Additional outfits were available, all of which were costumes seen in the film, and amongst them were a blue coat, a pink floral nightdress, a pale-yellow floral dress, a cream two-piece and a blue playsuit. All came with matching hats and shoes.

Other characters were issued in the same series, though they weren't as easy to find in Britain. They included many favourites, and Knickerbocker managed to achieve some excellent likenesses in these small dolls. Today, of course, these dolls are easy to source using the internet. Daddy Warbucks wore a black satin evening suit with a white shirt, black bow tie and red cummerbund, while the Indian, 'Punjab', looked smart in his white cotton suit and turban with a bright-red and black-striped sash tied around his waist. The scary 'Miss Hannigan' was dressed in a mauve two-piece, while little 'Molly', Annie's friend at the orphanage, wore a green pinafore over a floral long-sleeved blouse. Her brown hair was cut into a short bob with a fringe. The most impressive accessories made by Knickerbocker for these dolls were a 15in blue 1929 Model Duesenberg Limousine, complete with chauffeur, and an 'Annie Mansion' doll's house. This house was a kind of open play-set divided into rooms, and was based on Daddy Warbuck's mansion in the film, with a sweeping staircase leading to the top floor. The company also produced a particularly attractive 12in vinyl Annie. Called 'Movie Star', she was similar to the 6in version, with the same orange nylon curly hair, and though wearing her red dress in her display box, came with an additional yellow-flowered party frock.

The prolific Knickerbocker company also issued a set of plastic miniatures based on the characters from the film, each one carded in a bubble pack. These miniatures ranged in size from 1½in to 3in and incorporated some of the other characters, notably 'Pepper', 'Grace', 'Rooster', 'Lily', and 'Sandy', as well as those featured in the larger size. Three versions of 'Annie' were also included.

In 1999 Madame Alexander issued a delightful 8in vinyl version of Annie, complete with her dog Sandy. Annie wears her red outfit, trimmed with a while belt fastened with a gold buckle, and a gold locket. As with all Madame Alexander dolls, this creation is of the highest quality and is a very pretty doll. Her fluffy dog, Sandy, is, for some reason nearly as large as Annie herself. Effanbee, now owned by Tonner, produced a delightful series of Annie dolls and costumes in 2004, which used the original 1927 'Patsy' mould. The dolls were made from vinyl, and stood 14in high, with hand-detailed painted faces and rooted curly auburn saran hair. They were sold packaged either in undergarments or in the classic red dress, and perhaps one of the best outfits available was the orphanage rig of a floral dress, patched brown gingham pinafore, long bloomers, a cream 'kerchief and sturdy boots. The outfit came with a metal pail so that Annie could wash the floor as depicted in the 'It's The Hard-Knock Life' scene.

The quality of all these garments was amazing; everything was fully lined and beautifully finished with fancy trims and tiny buttons. 'Sweet Dreams' was a pair of pink pyjamas, together with slippers and a cuddly rabbit, while 'Daddy's Girl' was a stunning pale-blue coat with a matching hat, edged with soft white fur. This came with a pair of black gold-buckled shoes. Another outfit, 'Uptown' featured a smart fawn dress, matching coat and hat, with a faux leopard-fur trimming. Annie's friend Polly was also available in the same series, as was a wardrobe, or 'trunk' to store all the garments, decorated with images from the original cartoon drawings. Effanbee also issued a 9in version of Annie, in their Patsyette line, which came complete with a trunk of clothes, similar to the above. Even the 5in 'Wee Patsy' was issued in the red Annie dress. A few years before, in 1997, Robert Tonner produced a 14in Annie doll in his vinyl range. Wearing the classic red dress, this doll was distinguished by her unusual round eyes and her loose red curls tied with a ribbon.

Annie is such an iconic figure that there are dozens of different dolls to look out for, from the earliest creations made soon after the cartoons became popular to today's modern versions.

Annie, Cloth, Knickerbocker.

Annie Movie Star, Knickerbocker.

Daddy Warbucks, Knickerbocker.

Annie, Madame Alexander.

Annie, Effanbee.

Chapter Nineteen

An In-Depth Look at Alice in Wonderland Dolls

ALICE IN WONDERLAND must surely be one of the most-loved of all the characters in children's books, and certainly she has appeared hundreds of times in doll form and in all kinds of media to appeal to both children and to doll collectors. The book, *Alice in Wonderland*, was penned in 1865 by Oxford University professor Charles Dodgson, using the alias 'Lewis Carroll'. He was a teacher of mathematics, and was also extremely interested in photography, especially in taking pictures of small girls, which today might have raised suspicion. Six years later, in 1871, the sequel, *Through the Looking-Glass and What Alice Found There* was published.

The little girl of the title was Alice Pleasance Liddell, and Charles recounted his fantasy tale to her and her sisters (daughters of the Dean of Oxford from Christ Church College), during a boating trip on the River Thames on 4 July 1862. Charles was fond of all three girls, though 10-year-old Alice was his favourite. The girls enjoyed the story so much that he promised to write it out for them. He called it, 'Alice`s Adventures Under Ground', but on publication it had the more familiar title of *Alice in Wonderland*.

The 'classic' Alice image is of a young girl with long blonde hair wearing a blue dress, white apron and long socks, loosely based on the original illustrations by Sir John Tenniel, although often designers experiment with different hair or dress colour. Therefore, a collection of Alice dolls need not be a sea of pale blue! Nowadays, Alice is almost a cult figure and there are thousands of collectors worldwide who concentrate solely on accumulating Alice dolls. Designers regularly issue them, numerous types appear as play dolls for children in Disney stores and toy shops, while films, such as 2010's *Alice In Wonderland* starring Johnny Depp and Helen Bonham Carter, provoke new and exciting designs.

As Alice is such a popular character, dolls representing her have been made for decades, including a beautiful moulded painted stockinette range created by Martha Chase in the 1920s. Amongst this rare and delightful set were such characters as 'Alice', 'The Mad Hatter', the 'Duchess' and a 'Frog Footman'. In 1923, at the start of her career, Madame Alexander handmade many cloth Alice in Wonderland dolls, which she sold at around $14 per dozen to shops. Nowadays they would be worth a lot more. Other companies who made Alice in Wonderland dolls during the twentieth century included Arranbee, Ginny, Pedigree, Madame Alexander, Shallowpool, Palitoy and Nancy Ann (who made some bisque versions). Once the Walt Disney cartoon version of Alice in Wonderland was released in 1951, a wave of memorabilia was triggered. It is very difficult to select just a few representative Alice dolls of the many hundreds around, and so I've selected some which, for one reason or another stand out.

A Pedigree Sindy-type Alice in Wonderland doll was issued during the early 1970s as a Disney tie-in, with the doll featuring a Sindy body and a slightly remodelled head. The doll itself was simply dressed in the usual blue cotton frock and a white apron, but she was presented in a stunning box that was decorated with colourful graphics from the film. To find the doll today complete with box is a real bonus. As this doll is collected by both Sindy enthusiasts and Alice fans, it is in considerable demand.

When the television production *Alice in Wonderland* was made in 1972, starring Fiona Fullerton as Alice and directed by Josef Shaftel, it triggered a new wave of interest. To coincide with the programme Palitoy issued a 24in-tall, talking Alice in Wonderland doll. It came with three double-sided records of Fiona Fullerton telling the story of Alice and included songs from the film. The doll had beautiful blue eyes and wore the traditional light-blue frock. Her white apron was trimmed with pink braid and a pink sash, and she had white tights, black shoes and a blue hair band. Sadly a doll in mint condition complete with a working record mechanism is quite rare nowadays, as the spring was prone to breakage and the discs were often lost. Also, as the dolls were intended for children and so consequently played with, they tended to get redressed. Mint-in-box finds are treasured.

Plenty of official Disney tie-ins have been issued, many of them distributed through the Disney stores and at the various Disney theme parks. An attractive 1990s Disney/Mattel version was sold in Britain which featured a smiling-faced Alice with long wavy blonde hair, painted eyes, and a blue silky dress and apron. As with the Pedigree Sindy version, this doll too was packaged in an attractively decorated box, and contained cardboard cut outs of the Cheshire Cat and the White Rabbit.

Mattel has produced various Alice dolls, amongst them a rather unusual one that appeared in 2007 under its silver label range. Unlike a traditional Alice, this Barbie Alice wore a short, silky blue party dress, with layer upon layer of frills in various shades of blue. She had long auburn hair and came with a model of the Cheshire Cat. Her features were altered from the usual Barbie fashion doll look, changing her into a wide-eyed, pouty lipped beauty. At the same time, her boyfriend Ken was transformed into a Mad Hatter, and given a really zany costume. One of the most beautiful of the Mattel Alice dolls was the 'Queen of Hearts Barbie', stunning in a scarlet braided dress. Another 2007 doll, 'Queen Alice' was a brunette, all ready for a game of croquette, complete with her own flamingo.

If you intend to build up a collection of Alice in Wonderland dolls, then there are plenty to look out for, such as the 1970s 'Patsyette in Storyland' range made

Group of modern Alice in Wonderland Dolls, Moxie, Pullip, Ashton-Drake & Robert Tonner.

Alice, Pedigree.

Alice From the Television Production, Palitoy.

Storyland Alice, Effanbee.

Alice Through the Looking Glass, Robert Tonner.

Alice, Lee Middleton.

Nursery Alice, R John Wright.

by Effanbee. Patsyette is a classic face mould, and her solemn face, moulded hair and pretty costume made a very appealing Alice. The doll was further enhanced by the packaging which resembled a book with an illustrated cover. Inside was a tiny doll-sized version of the story. Amongst the other delightful Alice dolls that have appeared over the last twenty years or so are Madame Alexander's Wendy dressed as Alice, Vogue's Ginny as Alice, and the tiny Paulinette Alice by Pauline Bjorness-Jacobsen. This last-mentioned designer also issued larger sized Alice in Wonderland dolls, in both vinyl and porcelain. The porcelain doll, 14in high, came with a white rabbit and a large watch, while the 19in vinyl doll was dressed in a blue check dress with an apron embroidered with a design of flowers and the name 'Alice'.

The Amanda Jane Ltd doll company, founded in the 1950s and based in South Wales for decades, finally closed in 2007, but among its representations was a pretty sweet-faced 8in little girl. Her well-designed Alice costume was completely made in Britain, and consisted of a pink, broderie anglaise-trimmed apron over a blue dress. This Alice had short, bobbed blonde hair and, unusually, carried a tiny felt doll. If you like these small Alice dolls, then it is worth searching for the Heather Maciak limited edition dating from the early 2000s, which came with a white rabbit and was another little gem. However, if, on the other hand, you prefer larger dolls, then maybe you can find room for the 26in Alice in Wonderland made by the Lee Middleton company. Designed by Eva Helland, this doll wore a dark-blue full-skirted floral-print dress, white apron and red-striped stockings. Her White Rabbit wore a playing-card design tabard. Perhaps the most unusual Alice was a topsy-turvy doll (*See Chapter 9*) made by Jellycat. This cloth play doll wore an elaborate costume and transformed into the Red Queen.

Over the last few years there has been a spate of modern takes on the traditional Alice, and these usually have larger eyes, contemporary features, fashionable hairstyles and slightly quirky clothing. One example is the Pullip version. Pullip dolls are manufactured in Japan and bear a resemblance to the 1970s 'Blythe' dolls, on which they are based. They have ultra-large heads, pointed chins and changeable round eyes that are operated through levers at the back of the head. The Pullip 'Fantastic Alice' has vivid blue eyes, and is jointed at the wrists, elbows, knees and ankles, as well as the usual head, shoulders and hips. Her turquoise-blue dress is covered by a frilly apron. She also wears white stockings and black shoes, while her spectacle-wearing white rabbit has a smart check jacket. This Alice also comes with a small pack of cards and a tiny metal key, only ¼in long. Other interesting modern 'takes' are Robert Tonner's 'Hunting Rabbit' in the Kickit's series, Moxie Girlz's Alice and Ashton-Drake's Alice, which is in the same set as the 12in ball-jointed nursery rhyme dolls. (*See Chapter 3*) designed by Dianna Effner. This Ashton-Drake doll has a tumbling mass of white-blonde tight ringlets, and her blue dress and white apron are both trimmed with braid. She wears striped stockings and black shoes, and has a tiny 'Drink Me' bottle in her apron pocket. This is quite a young Alice. Her face is innocent and charming and full of wonder. Her white rabbit has enormously long ears and wears a pink bow. In contrast, the Robert Tonner Company's 8in vinyl Kickit's doll, 'Hunting Rabbit' has rather a knowing look. Tonner's Alice has long curly hair and wears a white cotton voile apron over a blue flowered dress. Her tights are striped, as are her lower sleeves, and she holds a limp-looking white rabbit!

The Moxie Girlz Alice in Wonderland, which is in the Fairytale series, was issued in 2011. Alice stands around 10in high and wears a light-blue silky puffed-sleeve frock, white lace-trimmed pinafore, black stripy footless stockings and black shoes. She has large transfer-printed eyes and a pointed chin and is another very pretty doll. Completely out of the ordinary is the Alice doll made by Robert Tonner as a 'special' for the American store Cherished Friends, as it depicts his interpretation of an Alice who has passed through the looking glass. This 12in doll shows an 'opposite' Alice, with black hair and a grey dress, to reflect the shadowy mirror world. Alice's dress is trimmed with wide black stripes on the sleeves, bodice and hem, and she wears a white apron, striped stockings and black shoes. Recently, the Nancy Ann Storybook company also made a 'Through the Looking Glass' doll. This delightful limited edition little girl wears the usual pale blue dress, but underneath has a pair of black checked drawers.

When the film *Alice in Wonderland* opened in 2010, it revealed a host of unusual costumes. The film told the story of a nineteen-year-old Alice who returns to the scene of her earlier adventures. Designer Robert Tonner, who seems to have found a niche producing character dolls from films, soon began issuing Johnny Depp as the Mad Hatter, Helena Bonham Carter as the Red Queen, Anne Hathaway as the White Queen and Mia Wasikowska as Alice. Alice, 16in high, is dressed in an organza gown with rabbit embroidery at the hem and decorated with tiny seed-bead buttons and lace trimmings at the collar. Her accessories include striped knit tights, striped mesh fingerless gloves, a soft cotton petticoat, black-and-white faux leather boots with tiny button details, and a gold chain necklace with a red 'jewel'.

According to Robert Tonner, his portrayal of Johnny Depp as the Mad Hatter features one of the most incredibly detailed costumes to date. This doll is 17in high and features the elaborate make-up with which many of the cast were painted. He wears a custom printed shirt with gold buttons, twill trousers with embroidery and lace trim, neck scarf and mismatched socks under faux leather lace-up boots. His amazing jacket is adorned with multi-coloured ribbon streamers, lace trimmings, lace-up draping and bird embroidery, while his bandolier (shoulder belt) is made of reels of thread with a fine chain. To finish it off, his top hat bears a wide flowing sash and jewelled hat pins. Just as spectacular is Robert Tonner's version of Helena Bonham Carter dressed for her role as the Red Queen.

Alice in Wonderland is one of the subjects which appear in the exquisite range of felt dolls modelled by R. John Wright, the American designer who specialises in felt dolls. Although his dolls are very expensive they are amazingly detailed, and are on at the very top of most character doll collectors' wish list. His 2004 limited edition of Alice – just 750 were made – was 17in tall, and showed her in a fine, blue felt dress, a silk-trimmed cotton apron and traditional blue-striped stockings. Her leather shoes were hand-cobbled. Around her waist was a red silk sash, and a brooch engraved with an 'A' was pinned at her collar. R. John Wright was also responsible for the 'Nursery Alice', depicting a slightly younger Alice, unusually dressed in a yellow pleated frock and white apron. She cradled a piglet. German doll artist Ruth Treffeisen produced a stunning set of Alice in Wonderland characters in 2006, which included not just Alice but also the Queen of Hearts, the Mad Hatter, the March Hare and Humpty Dumpty. Alice was 27in tall, and the group sets were limited to seven, worldwide, so were extremely exclusive.

There are so many different versions of Alice in Wonderland to look out for. She is a classic amongst doll designers, whether they are producing play dolls for children or special dolls aimed at collectors.

Alice, American Library.

Chapter Twenty

An In–Depth Look at Snow White Dolls

E VER SINCE the classic Walt Disney *Snow White* animated film was released in 1937, we tend to think of the archetypal Snow White doll as a black-haired young girl wearing a dress with a yellow skirt, blue bodice with puffed sleeves and a white, stand-up collar. However, as the story of the film was not something that Disney dreamt up – it was based on a legend dating from centuries ago – Snow White has been depicted in many ways and dress styles. One of the earliest written versions stems from 1634, long before the story was discovered by the Brothers Grimm, and it most certainly wasn't intended for small children, containing as it did such intrigues as an illegitimate baby, witchcraft, cannibalism, lots of blood, poisoning, murder and sexual awakening.

Snow White and the Seven Dwarfs, Chad Valley.

Perhaps it is unsurprising that when Walt Disney was searching for a suitable subject for his first full-length film, he chose the diluted Grimm version, which he made even more innocuous, but it still contains attempted murder, witchcraft, poisoned gifts and the rather dubious concept of a young woman living with seven unmarried men!

The Disney film was an enormous success, and the music and colourful cartoons enchanted both children and adults, even though some children were rather traumatised by the frightening scenes showing the witch. At one time the film was considered too scary for children, and so everyone under the age of 16 had to be accompanied by their parents. In 1939, *Snow White* received a special Academy Award that consisted of one full-size Oscar and seven little Oscars which were presented to Walt Disney by Shirley Temple. A young singer, Adriana Caselotti, had been chosen by Walt Disney as the voice of Snow White, and was so proud of her part in the film that even in her seventies she wore a 'Snow White' ribbon in her hair, and spoke in a babyish voice.

Many companies were quick to capitalise on the idea of media memorabilia, and amongst them was Chad Valley which produced sets of Snow White and the Seven Dwarfs. These sets are heavily sought after today, and can fetch vast sums if in good condition. Each beautifully modelled doll had a calico body and a moulded felt face with painted features. The sets were issued almost as soon as the film was released, and the Snow White doll stood 16in, while the dwarfs were 6in tall. Snow White wore a pink and blue rayon dress with white underwear and pink shoes, while the dwarfs had colourful outfits crafted from felt. The facial resemblances to the cartoon characters were excellent, and their hair and beards were all made from mohair. Occasionally, dolls are found bearing the original card swing tags, but all should still have embroidered Chad Valley labels sewn onto their bodies. Other early Snow White dolls occasionally come to light, such as a composition version made by the Madame Alexander Doll Company in 1938, wearing a yellow and brown dress, and one dating from the 1940s, dressed in pink. If you are interested in obtaining older dolls, then it is a good idea to visit auction sites and internet auctions, as they do sometimes turn up.

For most Snow White collectors a Chad Valley set is beyond financial reach, but there are still plenty of modern, but nonetheless attractive dolls, representing the ebony-haired girl and the comical dwarfs, available at affordable prices. Some are dressed as Disney portrayed them, while others wear outfits far removed from the cartoon version. Many of the Snow White dolls sold through the Disney stores from the 1970s onwards were made by Mattel, including a clever design of her in her famous blue and yellow gown with removable sleeves and skirt. When removed, she was revealed in a tattered dress all ready to scrub the doorstep. Usually, the Mattel Disney dolls incorporate a Barbie body, but have a specially modelled head to represent the character concerned and often, the likeness to the character is very impressive. In 1978 Pedigree issued a Snow White doll very similar to Sindy which is sought by collectors, not only to enhance their Sindy collections, but also because of the dazzling graphics from the film which decorate the box. In 1999, a very unusual 'Special Edition Snow White Barbie' from Mattel depicted her in the classic yellow and blue gown, but here Barbie has been given black hair and bright face paint, and the overall effect is stunning.

Another, fairly recent, Mattel Barbie, is the 'Holiday Princess Snow White, Special Edition'. This doll is dressed in a gown with a velvet bodice and a gold brocade skirt, with a gold and faux fur trim, all ready for winter. The doll came with a small rabbit. Although for many years Mattel produced play dolls to accompany various Disney films, they now also appear by other makers, including Vivid Imaginations and Simba. Disney stores and toy stores regularly bring out different versions of Snow White, both collectors' lines and play dolls. The play dolls often portray her in guises such as a child or a baby, or maybe dressed for ballet or even as a pop star. Vivid Imaginations made a set showing Snow White dressed, unusually, in pink, and it came with a rabbit, fawn, squirrel and several bluebirds, as featured in the classic scenes from the film.

Often, the Snow White dolls issued are general depictions of the character from the legend, rather than from the Disney film. Amongst the Snow White dolls aimed at collectors are several designed by Dianna Effner, who specialises in character dolls. She worked with the Edwin Knowles China Company to create a delightful version in its 1991 'Heroines From the Fairy Tale Forests' series, sold through Ashton-Drake. This Snow White, 14in tall, has a pretty, innocent face and wears a multi-striped skirt with a black bodice laced with red ribbons. Ribbons also decorate her lace-trimmed white blouse at the neck and cuffs. Her skirt is embellished with a flower and ribbon, and beneath her skirt she wears a white cotton petticoat and long drawers. She has black pumps with red ribbons and carries a shiny red apple. A smaller version, similarly dressed, was also made for a subsequent series.

Designer Robert Tonner produced a ball-jointed Snow White doll in 2009, which featured a brand new face sculpt. In a limited edition of 1,000 pieces, she was dressed in her iconic gown from the film – shades of red, blue, and yellow, with a matching satin cape. She also wore a ribbon headband, petticoat, tights, and bow-trimmed pumps. 2011 saw the release of an exclusive 11½in 'Disney Princess Designer Collection Doll Snow White', sold through the Disney Stores. This unusual and beautiful doll was inspired by the fashion illustrations of the 1950s and 1960s, and depicted Snow White as she might have appeared then, very glamorous with a high fashion edge while still capturing her classically unique look.

Other Snow White dolls to look out for include those by Madame Alexander, Effanbee and Vogue. Vogue's 2002 solemn-faced 'Ginny', an 8in replica, hard plastic doll from the 1950s, was dressed in a light blue silk and pale gold organza gathered ball gown trimmed with two flowers. Ginny, who had long rooted hair, held a red apple. Effanbee's 1970s sad-faced 'Patsyette in Storyland' range of character dolls included a Snow White doll with the packaging resembling a book with colourful cover. Madame Alexander's equally solemn-faced, 8in Wendy doll appeared as Snow White in the 'The Storyland Collection' in 2010.

Snow White, Pedigree.

Snow White Barbie, Mattel.

Snow White by Dianna Effner, Ashton-Drake.

Storyland Snow White, Effanbee.

Snow White, Moxie Girlz.

Wendy's side-parted black bob was accented by a red satin ribbon headband, and her dress featured a pale-yellow skirt with a metallic waistband and a blue-trimmed red satin bodice. The bodice was ornamented with floral braid and criss-crossed white ribbons, and she had a white taffeta petticoat and bloomers. Also from Madame Alexander was a 16in ball-jointed Snow White issued in the 'Disney Favourites' series, dressed in a blue and yellow gown with a black and red cape. Her face was hand-painted and she had black rooted hair. This doll was a limited edition of just 300.

If you prefer your Snow White to have a certain quirky look, then the 2011 Moxie Girlz Harlequin Snow White would be just perfect. This 10in-tall vinyl doll features large transfer-printed almond shaped eyes,

Snow White and the Seven Dwarfs, R. John Wright.

a shy half-smile and long black hair tied with a red ribbon. Her dress is loosely based on the traditional Disney cartoon version, though it is much, much shorter, ending just above her knees. The skirt is yellow, edged with red and the royal-blue bodice has red sleeves trimmed with yellow, yellow braid on the bodice, a red bow at the neck and a white frilled collar. Moxie's Snow White shoes are red. Another unusual take on Snow White is the recent 'Animator Doll' available through Disney Stores. According to the store, 'Disney's master animator Glen Keane re-imagines Princess Snow White as a little girl, who from the very beginning was always 'the fairest of them all'. This 16in vinyl doll depicts a very young Snow White with enormous eyes, wearing her iconic costume, and carrying a fluffy bluebird. In 2010 Ashton-Drake also issued a baby Snow White, but this doll, measuring 14in long, is still at the 'lying down' stage. She is a collector's doll, made from high- quality vinyl, and when a key is wound in her back, not only does a hidden music box play, *Some Day My Prince Will Come* but the doll wiggles as well!

Perhaps the most accurate and beautiful version of Snow White is the handcrafted doll by R. John Wright. Moulded in felt, perfectly painted, delicately shaded, and with a detailed costume also created from felt, this Snow White must be exactly how Disney first imagined his heroine. R. John Wright also modelled all the dwarfs, and they appear just as they were in the film. Other characters from the film sometimes appear, too, from various makers, notably the seven dwarfs and the Wicked Queen. Although Snow White might be the 'star' of the film, the unforgettable Queen must have given millions of children a fright over the years – she was evil personified, and Disney didn't soften her character to pander to the youngsters. Sometimes, collector's editions of the Wicked Queen are produced, such as a superb doll which appeared in the 1990s, in the 'Villains' series and sold through Disney Stores. Resplendent in a purple satin gown, red-lined black cloak, high white collar, gold crown and blood-red ruby at her throat, she was beautifully packaged in a sturdy display box.

During the 1990s, a part-work magazine published by De Agostini, was sold. Called *Disney Princess*, this innovative magazine featured a small porcelain doll attached to each issue; a perfect representation of a Disney character. Many of those featured were from Snow White, including Snow White herself, wearing her yellow dress, and another in a 'ragged costume', as well as the Prince, Queen and the seven dwarfs. These attractive small dolls still surface occasionally. The facial details are superb and a set would make a good addition to any Snow White or Disney collection of character dolls.

Sometimes, you can find delightful, small versions of Snow White, such as Mattel's 1990s 7in doll in its 'Dancing Princesses' series, which was mounted on a musical box. Small wheels under the music box enabled her to spin when the box was pushed along, and though tiny, she was finely dressed in her traditional yellow and blue clothing. There was also a 'Petite Holiday Princess' collection that contained a miniature Snow White with bells sewn into her skirt and a loop to hang her from a Christmas tree.

Naturally, you can't have Snow White without her equally important set of seven dwarfs. Sneezy, Happy, Doc, Grumpy, Bashful, Sleepy and Dopey played out the comic role to perfection, as well as adding to the pathos when they stood guard over her body. Plenty of sets of dwarfs have appeared since the film's release. As well as those in the Chad Valley set, mentioned earlier, a set was produced, also by Chad Valley, for Louis Vuitton in the late 1930s, and these are very rare today. A 1938 set was produced by Madame Alexander, consisting of the seven dwarfs made in hard rubber, and marked 'Seiberling Latex Products', each colourfully painted. They were accompanied by a 13in composition Snow White with a black mohair wig. An interesting one to look out for.

Coming more up to date, Mattel released a 1980s set of large vinyl dwarfs which performed various actions, such as Sleepy, who snored as his eyes closed, while a set of 1970s soft all-in-one moulded vinyl sets can also often be found. A Snow White was issued at the same time, but seems more difficult to come across. It's possible that these were intended as toys for very young children. The small size of these soft vinyl dwarfs means that they look good displayed next to the smaller Snow White dolls.

Mattel was also responsible for an ingenious Dopey and Sneezy set re-enacting a scene from the film when Dopey hid under Sneezy's long coat. This clever toy was composed of Dopey standing on Sneezy's shoulders, so appearing twice as tall, and wearing an over-size coat which completely covered Sneezy. Other Mattel dwarfs had colour-change functions, while Vivid Imaginations issued a set of all seven dwarfs wearing their night-shirts. Of course, the Prince has been depicted by various companies as well, including some innovative versions from Mattel, but without doubt the character doll display prize goes to the iconic raven-haired Snow White doll in the blue-and-yellow dress – one of Disney's most colourful creations.

Dictionary

This is a list of various famous dolls which have appeared over the years. It also includes some of the more successful of the thousands issued as replicas of famous people. There are so many character dolls now being produced, especially from the world of children's television and films, that it is impossible to include them all.

*Please note: Many of the entries here have fuller descriptions in the main chapters, so always check the index at the back of the book.

ABBA

ABBA was a highly successful Swedish pop group formed in 1972. It consisted of two married couples; Anni-Frid (Frida) Lyngstad and Bjorn Ulvaeus, and Benny Andersson and Agnetha Faltskog who used the initials of their first names to spell 'ABBA'. In 1974 they performed their song 'Waterloo' at the European Song Contest, and it was an enormous hit. After that, hits poured from the group, amongst them, 'Dancing Queen' , 'Money, Money, Money' , 'Mama Mia', 'SOS' and 'Knowing Me, Knowing You'. ABBA became one of the best-loved groups in the music world before giving their final public performance in 1982. However, there has been an enormous revival in ABBA music, with the *Mama Mia!* stage musical (in 1999 in London's West End and in 2001 on Broadway) and blockbuster film *Mama Mia!* in 2008. The Matchbox Company depicted the four singers at the peak of their fame in 1978 as small, 9½in-high vinyl, jointed dolls. These dolls show the performers dressed in their distinctive stage outfits. Anna and Frida wore short white minis and boots, Benny had a gold jacket and white satin flares and Bjorn sported a blue satin shirt under white dungarees. Extra ABBA outfits could be purchased separately. Today these dolls are very collectable.

Action Man, Palitoy.

Action Man

Palitoy made Action Man under licence from Hasbro in 1966. In the States Hasbro's version was referred to as 'GI Joe'. Palitoy also introduced a wide range of accessories, both military and civilian, leading to plenty of Action Man creative play. Action Man had a full range of outfits and vehicles and later became even more sophisticated with 'moving eagle eyes' and a speech mechanism. The early Action Man had painted, moulded hair, but in 1970 a fuzzy-haired type was introduced, some versions with beards. The doll was fully posable, and the first figures were a soldier, pilot and sailor, each dressed in a basic uniform complete with dog tags. For a while, Action Man was one of the top boy's toys (after initial parental concerns regarding 'boys with dolls' had been overcome), and they certainly had excellent play value. Unfortunately, in 1984 Palitoy closed down. In 1993 Action Man briefly reappeared, issued by Hasbro which later, in 1996, made him into an adventurer doll. Various collectors' versions have been brought out and in the late 1990s a series of James Bond Action Man was produced.

Aguilera, Christina

Vivid Imagination's Christina Aguilera dolls appeared in 2000, and were issued by Yaboom toys. The dolls were dressed in various outfits based on the singer's stage wear. Some of the dolls contained musical chips with extracts from her songs.

Alien

The *Toy Story* series of films featured a small green alien with three eyes and a cute, 'baby-sounding' voice. He wore a blue space suit. Several versions of the toy have been issued, in both vinyl and plush, by various companies. One of the first alien dolls was a talking version by Thinkway. It said 'The claw is my master', 'I have been chosen', and 'Ooooooooh'. This version was 12½in.

Amanda Jane (*See also* Jinx)

Amanda Jane was a 7½in-tall girl doll made by the Amanda Jane doll company from the 1960s through to 2009. She was the vinyl update of Jinx, and was introduced in 1964 after Jinx was discontinued due to a factory fire. The arms, legs, body and head were vinyl, and she had short rooted hair. Her eyes were originally a glassene type, and were rather large, but later Amanda Jane dolls featured painted eyes. Many outfits were available for her, all designed and sewn in Britain.

Amelia Jane

Amelia Jane, created by Enid Blyton, is a bossy doll who enjoys ordering all the toys around in the toy cupboard. She is a homemade doll, and Blyton stated that unlike shop-bought dolls, homemade types were never 'mannerly'. Invariably, the stories resolve with Amelia Jane becoming accepted, forgiven or penitent. She first appeared in 1939, in *Naughty Amelia Jane*, when she stole Nanny's scissors which she used not only to cut a handkerchief into tiny snippets, but also to chop off Pink Rabbit's tail. In the book the homemade doll wore a red frock, and was big, with long legs. She had black curls and was described as ugly.

Andy Pandy

Was Andy Pandy a boy, a doll or a clown? No one seems sure, but this little character in the striped all-in-one suit with the pompom-decorated hat was adored by thousands of toddlers in the late 1940s and early 1950s. Oddly, he lived in a hamper with Teddy and rag doll Looby Loo, so perhaps Andy Pandy was a toy as well. Of course, in the programme, children could see his strings and knew he was a puppet! One of the puppeteers was Audrey Atterbury and it was rumoured Andy Pandy was based on her little son, Paul (who grew up to be one of the stalwarts of the *Antique Roadshow*). Andy Pandy dolls have been made for quite a while by various companies, including Born To Play which issued a set consisting of the three partners in crime – Andy, Teddy and Looby Loo. Earlier versions include those by Golden Bear, while hard-headed versions date from the sixties. Andy also appeared as a bendy toy, a glove puppet from Chad Valley and as a string puppet from Pelham Puppets, together with Looby Loo.

Angela Goldenhair

This was the sweet little doll that appeared in Enid Blyton's *Noddy and His Car*. She lost her scarf, but for once, Noddy was innocent.

Angels

Dating from 1976, 'Angels' were a set of nurse dolls based on the BBC television series of the same name which delved into the lives of the staff at St Angela's Hospital. The dolls were made by the Denys Fisher company and wore lilac-striped uniforms. They were sold mounted on cards. A hospital ward playset was also available.

Annie

Annie started life as a cartoon character thought up by Harold Gray for the *Chicago Tribune* in 1924, which recounted the adventures of a 12-year-old orphan. She became extremely popular, and by the 1930s dolls were already appearing. However, the huge influx of Annie memorabilia really began when the musical film opened in the early 1980s, following the smash-hit stage productions in both New York and London. The iconic image is of a little girl with a head of red curls, wearing a red dress, which was brought out by many manufacturers, notably Knickerbocker and Effanbee.

Annette Himstedt

Annette Himstedt began making her porcelain dolls at her home in Delbrück, Westphalia, Germany, getting the moulds fired at a nearby porcelain factory. She finished 15 dolls for a craft fair in 1982, in Munich, where she sold her first one. She introduced her first vinyl collection in 1986, and her 'Barefoot Children' received enormous acclaim. She eventually opened the Annette Himstedt Doll Manufactory, and her dolls with their beautiful, serene faces and exquisite costumes, were in great demand. Sadly, as with many other manufacturers, the recession caused problems, especially as Annette was selling from Germany to America with discrepancies between the two currencies. Between 2003 and 2007 the company lost a vast amount, and ceased manufacturing in 2008.

Apple (*See also* Tottie)

Apple was a child doll who lived in the Doll's House in the book of the same name by Rumer Godden. In the later television series by Oliver Postgate and Peter Firmin, Apple was depicted as a curly-haired boy toddler dressed in a white short-sleeved shirt, red shorts and red shoes.

Archie Andrews

Archie Andrews was a ventriloquist's dummy, used by Peter Brough in a 1950s radio show *Educating Archie*. The show attracted 15 million listeners, and other cast members included Benny Hill, Beryl Reid, Tony Hancock, Max Bygraves and Julie Andrews. The concept of a dummy on a radio programme was strange, but no one seemed to bother, and it was soon released as a character doll/dummy, dressed in slacks and a blazer. Later, in the 1960s, the programme was transferred to BBC television. Archie Andrews dolls, dummies and glove puppets were made by Palitoy. The original mould, from which Archie Andrews was made in 1942, was destroyed in the Blitz.

Ashton-Drake

The Ashton-Drake company was formed in 1985 and concentrates on selling high-quality dolls to collectors, using many renowned doll artists. The dolls are mainly sold via mail order or the internet, and are made from porcelain, vinyl, resin or the company's patented 'Real Touch Vinyl'. Amongst the vast range are baby, toddler, girl and boy dolls in many sculpts. There are various special ranges including Celebrity and Royal dolls, Storybook, Ball-joint, American Indian and others. Ashton-Drake was also responsible for the initial range of 'Gene' dolls, and has produced replicas of several famous dolls including 'Blythe', 'Patty Playpal' and 'Chatty Cathy'. Amongst the many awards won by the company is the 2009 Industry's Choice Doll of the Year Award for its fashion doll 'Delilah Noir'.

Aunt Sally

Aunt Sally was the companion to the scarecrow Worzel Gummidge, a character in a series of children's books written by Barbara Euphan Todd. The first book, *Worzel Gummidge*, appeared in 1936. In the books, Aunt Sally was aunt to Worzel

Annie, Effanbee.

Betsy McCall, Tonner.

Blythe, Palitoy.

Buzz Lightyear, Toy Story, Disney.

Gummidge, but the writers of the 1979 television series obviously thought it would add more fun to the programme if she was his rather snobbish girlfriend instead. They depicted her as a wooden fairground doll series, played by actress Una Stubbs, alongside Jon Pertwee as Worzel Gummidge. (*See also* Worzel *Gummidge.*)

Aunt Sally (Game)
Aunt Sally is the name of a traditional British fairground or pub game, and originally consisted of a figurine of a woman, often with a clay pipe. The object of the game was to throw balls at the figure to knock the pipe. Later the figurine became replaced by a ball on a stick or plinth.

Baby Born (*See also* Zapf)
The classic Baby Born doll was launched by the German company Zapf in 1991. It was a 17in-high, bald-headed baby doll which drank from a bottle, wet and soiled its nappy and squeaked when its arm was pressed. The doll was so amazingly popular that Zapf cornered the doll market to such an extent that many other popular dolls of the time virtually disappeared. Since then, Zapf have released many other lines, but Baby Born remains a firm favourite. Not only is the doll of good quality, it is easy to dress, feed and bathe. There are a tremendous amount of accessories available, such as clothes, shoes, wardrobes, cots, prams, toys and changing-mats.

Baby Dear
Baby Dear was a doll designed by American author Eloise Wilkin and which appeared in her picture book *Baby Dear*. In 1960, the Vogue Doll Company introduced a vinyl and cloth baby doll with the same name, and bearing a strong resemblance to the doll in the book. The doll was 18in tall with a topknot of hair, and was intended to represent a young baby. She had a soft cloth floppy body, and her face hands and feet were modelled very realistically. A year later, she was given a full head of hair, and could be obtained in both 18in and 12in sizes. When Russian Premier Nikita Krushchev was visiting America in 1960, he saw the doll in the window of toy shop FAO Schwartz and purchased 13 to take back to the Soviet Union. Baby Dear dolls were produced until 1964. In all, Eloise Wilkin designed eight dolls for Vogue and Madame Alexander.

Baby Face
This rather spooky doll featured in the first *Toy Story* movie, and was basically a one-eyed doll's head with shorn hair, mounted on a spider-type body. He was the leader of the mutant toys and lived in the murk under Sid's bed, communicating with the other toys by tapping in Morse code on the metal bedstead with his claw. At first, Woody and Buzz were scared of him, but later they realised that Baby Face was friendly. Along with some of the other toys, he helped them to escape the clutches of the evil Sid. Issued in 1996 as a toy by Disney, this doll is becoming quite rare.

Babykins (1)
One of the best-loved of the hard plastic 1950s dolls, Babykins, made by British National Dolls, was issued in the early 1950s, with the majority of the dolls being distributed through branches of Marks and Spencers. BND had an arrangement at the time that the store would exclusively sell its dolls. Babykins (not to be confused with the much larger 1960s vinyl doll by Chiltern bearing the same name) was 10in tall, with chubby, bent legs and gracefully curved fingers. Each doll had moulded hair, sleep eyes and a slightly smiling mouth. Lashes were thick and fairly stiff. The moulded hair was a soft chestnut-brown, marked with tendrils at the front and in straighter lines at the back.

Babykins (2)
Confusingly, another very popular doll with today's collectors is also called 'Babykins', though whether intentionally or by coincidence, it's difficult to say. The vinyl doll was created in 1962 by H. G. Stone & Company which used the brand name 'Chiltern' on dolls and soft toys, and she came in two heights, 15in and 19in. She featured an impressive degree of modelling, especially of her hands, and her face was rather grumpy but attractive. Her hair was short, and roughly chopped. The smaller size seems more difficult to find today.

Ball-joint
Originally, in the doll collecting world, the term 'ball-jointed dolls' normally referred to the ball and socket joints found on the composition bodies of bisque dolls. The joints allowed plenty of movement, meaning that wrists, elbows and knees could be articulated, as well as the usual strung-elastic neck, hips and shoulders. More recently, the term has been applied to various fashion dolls, often referred to as 'BJDs' (ball-jointed dolls). These modern dolls are usually made from polyurethane resin and sold primarily in Japan, Korea and China, though there are now other sources, including some in the USA. The top quality BJDs are handmade and hand-painted, and strung with high-quality elastic. Companies include Volks, which created 'Super Dollfies' in 1998 and Luts who make Delfs. There are many others.

Barbie
Barbie, the world's most famous and iconic doll, was created in 1959 in America by Ruth Handler, based on a German doll 'Lilli'. In turn, Lilli was based on a cartoon of a 'good time girl' who featured in a cartoon strip in the German newspaper *Das Bild*. Ruth, wife of Elliot Handler, a co-director of Mattel, was visiting Switzerland when she came across Lilli dolls being sold in newsagents and tobacconist shops. They were intended to appeal to men as a novelty, and were often used as mascots in cars and trucks.

Barbie's full name is Barbara Millicent Roberts. She didn't really make her mark in Britain till the 1970s, though she was certainly imported in the 1960s. Her sophisticated looks, voluptuous figure, heavy make-up and glamorous clothes didn't really appeal to children in the UK, who at the time preferred the-girl-next-door charm of Sindy. However, once Barbie's features had been softened, and she was given a more casual range of clothes, sales took off. Barbie is 11in high and has appeared in numerous guises, from career women through to top fashion model. Although originally a play doll, nowadays many versions are intended for adult collectors, though naturally play versions still fill the toyshops.

Bartholomew Baby (*See also* Doll)
An early term for a doll which was sold at Bartholomew Fair, West Smithfield, London.

Beatles
British pop group The Beatles changed the course of popular music history with the release of their first single, *Love Me Do*, in 1962, which featured a new raw 'Liverpool sound'. Surprisingly, few dolls were made at the time, the most well known being a vinyl set made by Remco, featuring the group with moulded clothing, 'real' hair and overlarge nodding heads, which was sold at Woolworths at 19/11 the set (just under £1). Other similar sets later appeared, often by unknown manufacturers, while a Spanish company, Emirober, sold 3in plastic figurines in sets of four, packed in plastic bags with John, Paul, George or Ringo header cards. Rosebud Dolls issued a set of large-headed Beatles look-a-likes in the late 1960s, all-in-one models made from soft vinyl, and with odd-shaped open mouths. They had black silky hair, and the bodies were painted black with no attempt to mark clothing details. Pelham Puppets also produced Beatle clones. Other Beatle-type dolls available included polished wooden dolls with oval faces, thick string arms and black fur hair, known as 'gonks' or 'trolls'. Various other Beatles dolls/figurines have appeared over the years and latterly, had more realistic faces.

Bella Productions Doll Company
Clea Bella is a 15½in fashion doll designed in 2001 by Christina Bougas. Christina's love of theatre and dance inspired her to create a doll reflecting the grace, beauty and dignity of the performing arts, and since then, many theatre-based dolls have been made. The doll, 'Clea Bella' (short for Cleopatra Bellisimo), has a storyline which says that she can act, sing and dance, so consequently costumes are provided for all three performances. The dolls feature multiple points of articulation, and the ballet dolls have en pointe feet. The costumes are magnificent. Clea Bella vinyl dolls are produced at Christina's studio, Cobb Mountain Studios, California, to very high specifications and all the sculpts are created by Christina Bougas herself.

Beloved Belindy
Beloved Belindy was a black doll that featured in the Raggedy Ann series of books. She was made by various companies, including Knickerbocker, and is very collectable today.

Bendy Bubba (*See* Fairy Baby)

Bertie Bassett
These 12in high plush dolls were at one time made by renowned teddy bear and doll maker Diane Jones International, and resembled a man made from liquorice allsorts carrying a liquorice stick cane. Used as promotional items for Bassett's allsorts, the dolls proved very popular. Similar dolls are still produced today.

Betsy Mcall
Betsy McCall, a classic American girl doll, started her life as a paper doll in 1951 between the pages of the ladies magazine, *McCall's*. She was so popular that in 1952, Ideal acquired the rights to make a 14in Betsy McCall doll. Five years later, American Character followed up with an 8in doll. Other companies produced vintage versions of Betsy McCall, amongst them Horsman and Uneeda. Since the 1990s, Tonner Dolls, Inc. has been making Betsy McCall dolls. These modern dolls are made in 8in, 14in and 29in sizes, but some of the earlier, vintage versions were as large as 36in.

Betty Boop
Betty Boop, a popular cartoon character dating from the 1930s, has often appeared as a doll. The character actually began life as a dog when Grim Natwick, who worked for movie mogul Max Fleischer, was searching for inspiration for a new character. Grim had sheet music of a song sung by Helen Kane with a catchy 'boop-a-doop' chorus, and he doodled Helen's facial features and her distinctive black, spit-curled hair before giving her a curvy, Mae West figure, and a canine look. In 1930, the dog appeared in a film called *Dizzy Dishes*. Over the course of a few cartoons, the character morphed into a girl called Betty and was voiced by several actresses of the time, most notably Mae Questrel, also the voice of Popeye's squeaky-voiced girlfriend, Olive Oyl.

The Cameo Doll Company issued a jointed character doll of Betty in 1932, made from wood pulp. In the 1990s companies such as Mattel manufactured a range of Betty Boop vinyl dolls for collectors, while Madame Alexander made some lovely Betty Boop dolls, cleverly moulding the doll's face to make it pretty, rather than cartoonish, without losing the Betty look. Betty Boop dolls were also made by Marty Toys and Precious Kids, while various makers have produced soft-cloth versions. Most of the Betty Boop dolls feature Betty in her tightly fitting red dress, though some are more adventurous, using furs and colourful satins.

Betty Boots
Betty Boots was a cute toddler rag doll, with a printed checked romper suit and with a huge bow on her head. She was made by the Dean's Rag Book Company to promote Boots the Chemist, and was first issued in 1924. Much later, the company decided to re-issue her, and so in 1991 replica dolls appeared in the stores. Interestingly, Neil Miller from Dean's stated that at first these dolls were

displayed in Boots' baby departments but there was little interest. As soon as they were switched to the gift section, there was a dramatic increase in sales. Other dolls made by Dean's for Boots included a wounded soldier dating from 1915, sold to make money for injured troops and a printed cotton 'Puss In Boots'.

Betty Oxo
One of the most famous of the promotional dolls, 'Betty Oxo' was an attractive wood-wool filled-doll made by the Dean's Rag Book Company during the 1920s and 30s. The original doll was called Little Miss Oxo and first appeared in 1925. She featured a 'Tru-to-Life' moulded face, short hair and a navy frock. Promotional posters stated 'The dolls will be awarded to the 50,000 persons from whom the largest number of Oxo cube outside wrappers is received'. The later, and perhaps more well-known 1930s' Betty Oxo, was dressed in various-coloured velveteen, with side-glance eyes, a pillbox style hat, and with her hands in a muff. To obtain one of these desirable dolls, it was necessary to collect 480 Oxo wrappers, which might explain why the dolls are not particularly easy to find today.

Bewitched
The cult American TV comedy *Bewitched* was originally broadcast from 1964 to 1972, and starred Elizabeth Montgomery as Samantha, a suburban housewife who was also a witch. Often, she twitched her nose to perform a spell. Various doll tie-ins were made over the years, such an 11in range from the Ideal Toy Corp. dating from 1965, and a Madame Alexander 9½in doll from 1997. Assorted Mattel collectors' Barbie dolls, dressed as Samantha, have also appeared, while recently Tonner produced a collection of top of the range Samantha and Endora dolls.

Big Baby
'Big Baby' is a large baby doll that features in the animated film *Toy Story 3*. He has one eye half closed, carries a bottle around with him, and is adorned with childlike scribbling making him appear tattooed. In the film we learn that Big Baby once belonged to Daisy, but he, Lotso bear and Chuckles clown were left behind on an outing, and when Lotso finally made the trek home he was upset to discover he had been replaced. He lied to Big Baby, who was desperate to be reunited with her owner, that Daisy didn't want him anymore. Eventually the trio reached Sunnyside and Lotso took full control. Big Baby acted as his right-hand man and initially comes over as a rather scary character.

Eventually, Woody discovers that Daisy did still care about them all, and Big Baby is pleased and refers to her as 'Mama', which angers Lotso who prods him in the stomach with his walking stick causing Big Baby to cry out in pain. Suddenly, the tables are turned, and Big Baby grabs Lotso and throws him in to the rubbish bin, which allows Woody and his friends to escape Sunnyside. In the final credits we see that Big Baby is now having a happier time at Sunnyside, under the care of Barbie and Ken.

Bild Lilli (*See* Barbie)

Birdie (*See also* Tottie)
A character from *The Doll's House* by Rumer Godden, Birdie was a small and sweet wax doll. One day she ventured too close to a candle and shrivelled up, quite a traumatic experience for all those small girls viewing. Because of her death, the programme gained the reputation of featuring the first-ever murder on children's television.

Bisto Kids
The Bisto Kids – two ragamuffin children, a boy and a girl – first appeared in 1919, sniffing the air with delight as they said, 'Ahhh, Bisto!' They were designed by cartoonist Wilf Owen to advertise Bisto gravy powder, and when the adverts appeared in newspapers, both the children and the slogan captured the public's imagination. In the 1930s in Birmingham, a competition was held to name the urchins, and the winners – who came up with the names of 'Bill' and 'Maree' – were awarded a prize of a china doll. Around the same time, dolls representing the Bisto Kids were created, with character composition shoulderheads and finely modelled faces. These 12in dolls had cotton cloth bodies and were dressed in their usual ragamuffin style. Much later, in 1989, a pair of promotional 9in Bisto Kids cloth dolls, designed by Anne Wilkinson, was sold in their thousands to raise funds for the NSPCC, and bore slogans on their backs which read, 'I Helped Raise £25000 For The NSPCC Bisto Kids Fund 1989'. Bisto was originally invented by Messrs Roberts & Patterson, and the strange name was dreamt up because the product 'Browns, Seasons and Thickens in One'.

Blythe
Blythe was produced by Kenner in 1972 and distributed in Britain by Palitoy. She was a distinctive novelty doll with colour changing eyes, and today has become a cult doll with originals changing hands for four figure sums. Blythe is 12in high, and is instantly recognisable with her slender, twist waist, teen body and an over-large head. At the time she was only on sale for a year, as she was extremely unpopular both with children and parents, who deemed her ugly and scary. In 2000 photographer Gina Garan used the doll as a model in a book, and Blythe suddenly became a cult doll, especially in Japan where her looks resembled their tradition of anime art.

The eye-change feature was Blythe's most amazing accomplishment. It was operated by pulling a cord at the back of the head, and changed the large round eyes from green to pink, amber and blue. The blue and green eyes were side-glance; amber and pink looked straight ahead. Twelve ethnic type outfits were available, and the doll was obtainable with four hair colours – brunette, dark brown, blonde and auburn – and some had fringes, others a centre parting. Today, several companies have brought out replicas/lookalikes, including Ashton-Drake, Pullip, Takara and Mattel.

Blyton, Enid
Enid Blyton, one of the most well-known children's authors, featured dolls in several of her books, notably Noddy and Amelia Jane. (*See entries.*) Born in 1897, this very prolific writer was especially popular in the immediate pre-war and post-war eras, producing adventure, fantasy and fairytale type books to appeal to children of all ages. She died in 1968, but her books continue to sell worldwide, with over 600 million copies sold so far.

BND
Founded by E.Ainsley in London in 1928, the BND (British National Dolls) company was run by three brothers. Initially they produced china-headed and composition dolls, but after the war they switched to hard plastic, using moulds from America. The resourceful company not only made their own dolls' clothing but even constructed the boxes used to package the dolls. The majority of their dolls were sold through Marks and Spencer, which proved to be BND's downfall, because in the early 1960s Marks and Spencer decided not to stock dolls any more, but by then BND had lost all their other contracts. Consequently they were forced to close the business.

Bo-Peep
A popular nursery rhyme character who has been depicted by many manufacturers. Bo-Peep was portrayed as a feisty woman doll enamoured of Woody the Cowboy in the Toy Story series of films. Initially, Bo-Peep, was available in the US as a collector's doll, dressed in her pink-spotted white frock and pink bonnet, and she could also be found as a McDonald's promotional give-away.

Boudoir Dolls
During the 1920s and 30s long-legged, slim, sophisticated mascot dolls appeared, known as 'Boudoir Dolls'. Sometimes they were referred to as 'Vamps', 'Hooplas', 'Art Dolls',' Sofa Dolls', 'Bed Dolls' or 'Flapper Dolls'. The craze is believed to have begun with French couturier, Paul Poirot, when he advocated that fashion-conscious ladies should carry a doll as a chic accessory. The French dolls were expensive because they were costumed by designers such as Madame Lanvin and Pacquin, but soon other doll manufacturers began to include the dolls in their ranges. Makers such as Deans, Lenci and Chad Valley produced boudoir dolls in their thousands, whilst smaller factories often turned out cheap and cheerful, poorly-sewn copies. Soon, they became available to the ordinary young ladies of the time. Often the boudoir dolls' construction was flimsy, with padded wire or straw-filled cloth bodies, and these usually had bisque, silk or composition faces and limbs. Another common construction was a doll completely made of fabric. These often had faces made from stiffened silk or stockinette over papier-mâché. Occasionally, wax-headed boudoir dolls are found. Normally the lower legs and ankles of boudoir dolls were shapely, with moulded-on strappy shoes or fancy boots.

The sizes varied tremendously, from around 12in to 36in, and the majority were elegant and sophisticated, with flirty side-glance eyes and heavy make-up, especially rouge, eye-shadow and lipstick. Lashes were always long and luscious, and a cigarette was likely to be dangling from her lips or scarlet-tipped fingers. Clothing would be the height of fashion, using luxurious fabrics such as silk, fur, satin, brocade and velvet. Wigs were mohair or silk, with plenty of waves, curls and ringlets, though occasionally, hair would be painted directly onto a china head. The boudoir dolls' design was influenced by the film stars of the day, as this was the great movie age and dolls such as these brought a little glamour into the lives of the young ladies working in shops and factories.

Boyzone
A 1990s Irish 'boy band' which was captured in doll form by Vivid Imaginations in 1995. The group split in 2000, but reformed in 2007. The Boyzone set comprised band members Ronan Keating, Stephen Gately, Mikey Graham, Keith Duffy and Shane Lynch. Dressed in various casual wear, such as jackets, waistcoats and denim trousers, the jointed dolls were 11in high and made from vinyl. Following the sad death of Stephen Gately in 2009, the asking price of his particular doll soared.

Bratz
A range of large-headed, pouty-lipped teen dolls which came with up-to-the minute clothes, and feet that popped on and off when a change of footwear was needed. Bratz were produced by MGA Entertainments, and were so successful that they pushed Barbie of her perch, which led to a lawsuit launched by Mattel. The company claimed that design work for the Bratz doll range had been done in Mattel's time, and therefore it should be entitled to a share in Bratz. Several lawsuits have gone ahead, and various appeals are being heard. Consequently, Bratz still appear.

Buddy Lee
Buddy Lee was an advertising character used by the Lee Mercantile Company to promote their jeans. He first appeared in the 1920s, although Lee Mercantile had been founded much earlier, in 1889. The 12½in dolls were made from composition, and were first displayed in a large store in Minneapolis. Once the promotional displays were taken down, Lee encouraged participating stores to sell the dolls, and various characters were made including cowboys, Coca Cola delivery men, railroad workers and gas station attendants. The dolls became exceedingly popular, and didn't cease production till 1962. In 1998, the dolls reappeared in the Lee Dungarees advertisements.

Buzz Lightyear
A much-loved astronaut doll that first appeared in the *Toy Story* movie, created by Pixar Animation and distributed by Walt Disney in 1995. He also stars in *Toy Story* 2 and *Toy Story* 3. Queues formed outside Disney stores when the doll was

released, just before Christmas and the tremendous demand took both retailers and manufacturers by surprise. This first Buzz Lightyear doll was 12in tall, with chiselled features, prominent chin, broad shoulders and flip-out wings, and he looked just as he did in the film. He said all the famous lines from the film, including 'To Infinity and beyond'. Other versions included Intergalactic Buzz in a silver space suit, and Special Edition Holiday Hero Buzz. This latter doll, now hard to find, was festive in metallic green, red and silver. His helmet lit up, his spacesuit wings expanded, and he said Christmas phrases, which included 'To the North Pole and beyond', 'I wish you a Merry Christmas and a Happy Light Year', 'I protect Christmas presents from the threat of invasion' and 'This is Buzz Lightyear. Come in Rudolf'. Many other versions of Buzz Lightyear have appeared over the years and he has become one of the most recognisable and loved cartoon characters.

Bye-Lo Baby
This bisque baby doll was developed in America by Grace Storey Putnam and issued in1922, shortly before Armand Marseille introduced My Dream Baby. The 'Bye-Lo' baby had more realistic face-modelling and a crumpled look was achieved with the porcelain, while little creases were put into the composition limbs to resemble a newborn baby. Bye-Lo babies later became nicknamed the 'million dollar babies' because they were so much in demand (in America) and were made by various German companies, including Kestner. In Britain, it was the My Dream Baby which was more successful.

Cabbage Patch Kids
Cabbage Patch Kids were a tremendous success in the 1980s. The dolls were the brainchild of Xavier Roberts, who experimented by making distinctive character dolls from cloth, with a gimmick that the dolls were adopted. Soon, the dolls were commercially produced, initially by Coleco, and created such a demand that, especially in America, scuffles between customers broke out in shops as people fought to get their hands on a Cabbage Patch Kid of their own. Every doll came with a certificate, and their new owner had to recite (hand on heart in front of a witness) *'I love my Cabbage Patch Kid with all my heart. I promise to be a good and kind parent. I will always remember how special my Cabbage Patch Kid is to me '*. Later, the promise was changed to remind owners that 'being different is what makes us so special'.

  Amazingly, no two dolls were alike. By combining a variety of facial moulds with various eye colours, freckles, hair colours and styles, individuality was ensured. Each doll was also given its own double-barrelled name, and they were colourfully dressed in assorted styles; girls, boys and babies were available, and the dolls had hair made from thick yarn.

Cadby, Carine
Author of various books, mainly for children, written during the early decades of the twentieth century. Many of the titles were illustrated with photographs

taken by her husband Will Cadby. Her most renowned book was *The Dolls' Day*, published by Mills & Boon in 1915, and which told of the adventures of three dolls who escaped from their young owner to climb trees and paddle in streams. The dolls were depicted in black-and-white photographs.

Campbell Kids

The Campbell Kids were two round-faced chubby children, a boy and a girl, originally sketched by Philadelphia illustrator Grace Wiederseim (later, Drayton) to advertise Campbell's soup in 1904. Dressed as mini-chefs, with ladles and cooks' hats, these children soon became iconic dolls, produced by Horsman, American Character and others. Grace later admitted that she had based the dolls' features on her own round face, chubby cheeks and turned-up nose, and she referred to the Kids as 'Roly-Polys'. As well as dolls, the images appeared on numerous items of merchandise, including millions of postcards. Later, the designer was responsible for another favourite doll, 'Dolly Dingle'.

Carnival Dolls

This ambiguous term is often used when referring to cheap vintage dolls, especially celluloid or chalky composition. 'Carnival' or 'Fairground' dolls were, as the name suggests, given away as prizes at fairs. Often these would be small celluloid kewpie-type dolls with side-glance eyes, wearing colourful feathers, given as a reward for throwing a dart at a lucky ticket or rolling a ball into the correctly numbered hole. By contrast, especially in Britain, the name is also used for very large composition/plaster dolls gaudily dressed in rayon frocks and large floppy bonnets, often seen at 1950s fairgrounds. Later, these were replaced by equally large, thin plastic dolls, also brightly dressed. Yet another type of 'Carnival Doll' was the black 'Winky' doll of the 1960s/70s. The larger sizes were inflatable soft plastic, while the smaller size was moulded. These strange dolls had lenticular eyes which made them appear as though they were winking. They had large ears, often with brass earrings, and usually wore a plastic 'grass skirt' or frock. However, the Carnival/Fairground term can be applied to any doll given away free as a prize, such as the fabric all-in-one baby bunting dolls of the 1940s/50s with pointed hats and moulded buckram faces.

Chad Valley

At first the company was a lithographic and bookbinding business owned by Anthony Bunn Johnson, founded in 1823, but in 1915 they switched to making soft toys. The Chad Valley name was registered in 1919 after moving to new premises. Chad Valley became renowned for their beautiful dolls made from felt and cloth, with moulded faces. They produced many classics such as a set of Snow White and the Dwarfs, which collectors seek after today. Other dolls included Mabel Lucy Attwell characters and a Princess Elizabeth doll, dating from the 1920s/30s. In the 1970s, the company was sold to General Mills, and later Woolworths acquired the brand name.

Charlie's Angels
Charlie's Angels was a popular American television series that aired from 1976 to 1981 and was produced by Spelling Goldberg Production Company. It featured the adventures of three crime-fighting women, and they were soon issued as a set of dolls, complete with outfits and accessory packs. The dolls were sold by Palitoy in the UK and Hasbro in the USA. Each doll measured 8½ins and featured rooted hair and a twist waist. They were Sabrina (Kate Jackson) in a red jumpsuit, Kelly (Jaclyn Smith) in a yellow jumpsuit and Jill (Farrah Fawcett Majors) in a white jumpsuit. When Jill left, she was replaced by Kris (Cheryl Ladd), and depicted by Palitoy in a green jumpsuit. Farrah Fawcett is the easiest of the dolls to find today.

Cher (*See* Sonny & Cher)

Chiltern (*See* H.G Stone)

Chucky
'The World's Most Notorious Doll'. This scary, spooky doll featured in the various Chucky movies. The first, *Child's Play*, was released in 1999, and tells how a serial killer and voodoo practitioner hides himself in a box of 'Good Guy' dolls, managing to transfer his soul to one of them. Subsequently, he kills his way through a series of horror movies, somehow always managing to survive the horrific experiences which befall him at the end of each film.

   The face alone of a Chucky doll is enough to strike fear into the hearts of most doll lovers. Chucky, together with Tiffany his 'Bride of Chucky' and their son Glen and daughter Glenda have all been produced. The first doll, the original Chucky, was 15in tall and made by Sideshow, in vinyl with a soft body. It was dressed in a multicoloured striped jumper and blue patterned dungarees. Sideshow later produced a 'Bride of Chucky' and a 'Battle Scarred' version of Chucky, which depicted the facial slashings and stitches. Several other versions have been produced including talking dolls.

Clea Bella (*See* Bella Productions Doll Company)

Coca-Cola
Plenty of promotional dolls have appeared through Coca Cola over the decades, such as a range of small Coca-Cola kids, made by Ertl in the 1990s. Each doll bore the Coca-Cola logo on its outfit and came with mini bottles of the drink. Madame Alexander recently produced a 10in Coca-Cola 1920s Flapper doll in a lacy dress, and others by the same company include a 1950s-style Cissette. In 1999 Mattel issued a Collectors' Barbie doll wearing a 1950s-style outfit printed with Coca Cola graphics and they have also made various pink box Barbies advertising the drink. Collectors' companies such as Franklin Mint have produced dolls advertising the product including a delightful 15in porcelain girl called Betsy, attired in a red-striped swimsuit and holding a rubber ring with a Coca Cola logo.

Campbell Kids.

Cornhusk doll.

Ariel, The Little Mermaid, Disney.

Dolly, Toy Story 3, Thinkway Toys.

Comfort Dolls
Lisa Weaver and Darren Denim are cloth dolls who live in 'Clothworld' and advertise the Unilever laundry softening product, Comfort. The campaign first appeared in 2000, and the characters Lisa and Darren were produced by Aardman Animation. Other characters now appear in the adverts, though are not, as yet, in doll form. The Lisa and Darren dolls are 8in tall, and very distinctive. Lisa is pink, Darren is blue, and they both feature printed-on features to give the appearance of embroidery and various fabrics.

Coppelia
A famous doll from the world of ballet, Coppelia was made by dollmaker Dr Coppelius. She was a mechanical doll who looked just like a real person, and when he put the doll on the balcony of his house, a young man called Franz saw her and fell in love. Franz's fiancée Swanhilda was angry, and managed to break into the house and disguise herself as Coppelia. Manufactures such as Tonner, Robin Woods and Madame Alexander have made Coppelia dolls.

Corn Dolly
A corn dolly was formed by intricate plaiting and weaving of the stems from the last sheaf of corn to be cut. The making goes back thousands of years; it was originally a pagan tradition. Although called 'dollies', they can be many shapes, and were at one time supposed to be the home of the corn spirit, who would reside in the ornament or corn dolly until the following harvest.

Cornhusk Doll
These traditional dolls, made from the dried leaves or 'husk' of a corn cob, are made in America as a link to Native culture. The cornhusk dolls are also made in other countries, including Czechoslovakia and Romania. Many of the dolls don't have faces – legend says that the Spirit of Corn made a doll from husks for her children, but the doll was so beautiful she kept gazing at her reflection in a looking glass. Consequently, the doll spent less time with the children. Eventually, her face was taken away to cure her vanity.

Cup of Dolly
A name sometimes bestowed on a cup of tea. Possibly London or cockney origin.

Daisy
Daisy was a popular teen doll designed by Mary Quant in the 1970s and subsequently marketed by Flair, taking her name 'Daisy' from Mary Quant's flower trademark. The doll stood 9in tall and there were various versions, including 'Dizzy Daisy' and 'Dashing Daisy'. She had a dreamy face with painted side-glance eyes. Many different fashionable outfits, all designed by Mary Quant, were available as well as accessories such as a wardrobe, horse and cottage. Flair went out of business in 1980, but Daisy dolls appeared till 1983.

Very similar to Daisy was 'Havoc', a 'Super Agent' doll, from 1976, also marketed by Flair.

Darren (*See* Comfort Dolls)

Dean's
Dean's Rag Book company was launched in the early twentieth century. It was a subsidiary of the Dean & Son printing works. Production started in 1903 and introduced many cloth and composition dolls alongside its soft toy production. Three more factories were built in London between 1920 and 1940 as the company was so successful, but by the 1980s they were only left with one factory, at Pontypool. Amongst the dolls the company produced were such classics as 'Betty Oxo', 'Betty Boots',' Ronnie', 'Peggy and Teddie', 'Miss Muffet' and various elegant cloth fashion dolls.

Dennis the Menace
One of the most famous cartoon characters, Dennis the Menace first appeared in the *Beano* comic in 1951, drawn by David Law and published by D. C. Thomson, Dundee. In 1988 he appeared in doll form. Instantly recognisable with his black spiky hair, black-and-red sweater and black shorts, the Dennis doll is 10in tall and made completely from cloth. There is an American character also called Dennis the Menace, a blond-haired boy who appeared in comic books and on television, wearing a striped T-shirt and dungarees. Various dolls have been made of this character in the US.

Dionne Quints
In 1934 the world was stunned when five living babies were born to Oliva and Elzire Dionne, a couple living in Canada. They called the quintuplets Marie, Emilie, Cecile, Annette and Yvonne Dionne. Horrifyingly, the Dionne Quints were taken from their parents, and brought up by doctors and nurses in a specially designed nursery, which had observation windows so that the general public could peep in at the babies. The press and public clamoured to know all about them, and many sets of quintuplet dolls surfaced, amongst them a set by the Alexander Doll Company, each with her own different colour blanket and outfit. Lots of unauthorised sets were imported from Japan, often made in a chalky kind of composition.

Disney
The Walt Disney company has provided the inspiration for thousands of famous dolls over the years. Many of the dolls have been sold through its own chain of stores, or through the Disneyland theme parks, but most toyshops feature some type of Disney or Disney-influenced dolls. Probably the earliest of the Disney dolls were a set of Snow White and the Seven Dwarfs, made by Chad Valley, entirely from cloth, and first sold in 1937, when the movie was released. Today, these dolls are extremely collectable. Since the 1980s there has been a tremendous surge in Disney-related dolls. Many have been made by the Mattel

company, though other manufacturers such as Tyco, Mattel, Vivid Imaginations and, at the top end of the scale, Tonner and R. John Wright, have all produced them. Characters including Ariel, Cinderella, Snow White, Belle, Woody, Esmeralda, Mulan, Buzz Lightyear, Sleeping Beauty, Mary Poppins, Peter Pan, Jessie, Tinkerbelle and various others have appeared. Most of the dolls are teen vinyl types, but they also are made in paper, cloth and porcelain.

Doctor Who
This cult BBC television series was first broadcast in 1963 and recounted the adventures of a Time Lord Doctor who travelled the universe in a blue 1950s police box. Various models representing the cast have been released, such as a model of Tom Baker as the Doctor, complete with ultra-long scarf. The Denys Fisher company made this doll in the 1970s in collaboration with Mego. The same company also issued a Leela doll, Doctor Who's companion at the time and a Cyberman. In the 1980s/90s, Dapol produced action figures of Sylvester McCoy, Jon Pertwee, Bonnie Langford (Melanie Bush) and various other characters, while Character Options issued a Christopher Eccleston figure in his role as the ninth Doctor. They also released a Billie Piper (Rose Tyler) figure. Since then they have produced other figures including the current Doctor Who, Matt Smith, and his side-kick Amy Pond, portrayed by Karen Gillan. Recently, a stunning pair of dolls in the likeness of David Tennant (the tenth Doctor Who) and Freema Agyeman (Martha Jones) was issued by the Tonner Doll Company, and both likenesses were fully authorised by the BBC.

Doll (1)
According to *The Oxford Dictionary*, a doll is 'a small model of a human figure, especially baby or child, a child's toy, ventriloquist's dummy'.

Doll (2)
Originally dolls were called 'babies' or 'Dorothys', but during the 1700s the word 'doll' gradually became acceptable, probably as a diminutive of Dorothy. Maybe it gained popularity from a seller at London's Bartholomew fair crying 'Buy my pretty dolls'. A book entitled *Poor Robin's Almanack*, dated 1695, contains a reference to a 'Bartholomew baby trickt up with ribbons and knots' – at one time dolls were called 'Bartholomew babies.'

Doll (3)
Diminutive of the name Dorothy.

Doll (4)
A hit in a game of Aunt Sally.

Doll (5)
A pretty young woman.

Doll up, or to get dolled-up
To dress up or get ready for a big night out.

Dolls' eye indicators
These indicators were used on manual telephone switchboards to indicate to the operator whether or not a circuit was in use. They resembled old-fashioned metal open/close dolls' eyes, hence the name.

Dolly (1)
This is the name that a young child often bestows on a doll.

Dolly (2)
An easy catch in cricket.

Dolly (3)
A moveable platform for a cine camera.

Dolly (4)
A diminutive of the name Dorothy.

Dolly (5)
The ball used in a game of Aunt Sally.

Dolly (6)
The name given to an old-fashioned three-pronged wooden device for prodding washing.

Dolly (7)
The name of the cloth doll in *Toy Story 3*. Dolly is a cloth doll with purple hair and an orange dress, trimmed with three large buttons of various colours and shapes. She has large, round google plastic eyes. When *Toy Story 3* was released, Dolly was one of the tie-in dolls issued, and she was made by Thinkway Toys. She was a clever doll, the brains in Bonnie's toy collection, and helped Woody to find his friends. When Dolly learns Woody's name, she asks, 'You gonna stick with that?' In the end credits Dolly shows drawings to the toys that Bonnie has made for them, telling Chuckles the clown that she got his smile right, making the sad clown smile for the first time since he was abandoned.

Dolly Bag
A dolly bag, sometimes called a 'Dorothy bag', is a small fabric handbag, gathered at the top with a short, matching cord handle.

Dollybird
A 1960s word for a young girl with pale lips and lashings of black eye make-up who was usually dressed in a pastel mini dress with puffed sleeves.

Dollybird Dress
A mid-1960s pastel-coloured mini dress with puffed sleeves, rounded collar and a few tiny buttons on a lace-trimmed bodice.

Dolly Blue
A blue powder, with ingredients such as ultramarine and baking soda, once used to whiten linen and made by William Edge and Son in the early 1900s.

Dolly Castors
Dolly castors are small wheels attached in threes to a hollow cup, in which the legs of furniture are inserted for ease of movement.

Dolly Dingle
A much-loved American character who also became popular in Britain during the 1920s and 1930s, Dolly Dingle was a chubby little girl, similar to the style of Mabel Lucy Attwell. Dolly Dingle was created by Grace Drayton (Wiederseim), the same artist responsible for dreaming up the Campbell Kids, and indeed, there is a great similarity between Dolly Dingle and her friend Billy Bumps, and the Campbell Kids. The Dolly Dingle character first appeared in 1913, in a publication called *Pictorial Review*, and became so popular that Grace Drayton went on to create more than 200 paper dolls in the Dolly Dingle series. Dolly Dingle dolls were later made by companies such as Goebel.

Dollyflops
Granny bedroom slippers with pom-poms on the toes.

Dolly Knot
A dolly knot is a special knot used by English truckers to rope a load on to a trailer, and which works the same way as a pulley. It enables much more tension to be put onto the rope, and the tension can be multiplied if another dolly knot is tied into the pulling part.

Dolly Mixtures
An assortment of tiny fondant and jelly sweets in various colours sold for small children, probably dating back to the 1920s.

Dolly Parton
Popular Country and Western singer Dolly Parton was depicted as a 12in doll by Goldberger Eegee in 1970, wearing a red-and-silver jumpsuit. Since then she has appeared in various guises by other makers.

Dollypeg
A traditional carved wooden clothes peg with a slot to hold clothes firmly onto the clothes line. The top of the peg has a small knob, making the peg resemble a doll. Often still used today by crafts people to make peg dolls.

Dolly Shoes
Dolly shoes are a style of shoe particularly popular with teenage girls and have either closed toes or peep toes. They can be flat or heeled. They are usually made of a pretty printed fabric, satin or pastel leather. Dolly shoes with no heels are common amongst ballet dancers.

Dolly the Sheep
The first cloned sheep, born 1996. She lived for six years.

Dollywood
The name of an American theme park owned by Dolly Parton located in Pigeon Forge, Tennessee. As well as amusements and rides, it features traditional music and crafts from the Smoky Mountains area.

Dora the Explorer
Dora the Explorer is a distinctive small girl with short dark hair and brown eyes who features in an animated American cartoon in which she introduces Spanish words and phrases. The series began in 2000, accompanied by much merchandise including dolls. The dolls are very popular, especially with pre-schoolers. In 2010 a 'teen' version was introduced. Dora dolls are made by such companies as Fisher Price, Mattel and Ty, and there are many versions. Her short bobbed hair, large brown eyes and wide smile make her instantly recognisable, and she often comes complete with a backpack, an item that plays a prominent part in the animated films.

Doug James and Laura Meisner (*See* Willow and Daisy)

Durbin, Deanna
A major star of the 1930s and 1940s, Deanna Durbin was blessed with a sweet, melodic, classical voice. Unlike Shirley Temple, Deanne wasn't a young child star. She didn't make her debut until she was aged 14 when she appeared in a short MGM film, *Every Sunday*, in 1936, alongside another newcomer, Judy Garland. MGM decided to drop Deanna, and she was snapped up by Universal, going on to make 21 films in 12 years, before she retired, aged just 27. The Ideal Toy company issued a series of dolls from 1938 through to the 1940s, which are still sought after today.

Dusty
Dusty was a rather sporty doll made by Kenner in the mid 1970s, and sold under licence to Denys Fisher in Britain. She was sold as a British Airways stewardess, and advertised as travelling the world with various exotic outfits available. She was an 11½in fashion-type doll, but slightly out of the ordinary, with a bright smile and a slightly muscular look. Many of her outfits were sport orientated, such as tennis, swimming, volleyball and golf, but she wasn't a particular popular doll and was only on the market for a couple of years.

Edison Speaking Doll

A very rare speaking doll containing a Thomas Edison wax cylinder mechanism first sold in 1890, and only marketed for a few weeks. Less than 500 of the dolls were made. The American-made 22in doll had a German Simon and Halbig 719 bisque head, with large glass eyes, heavy eyebrows, pierced ears and an open, smiling mouth with teeth. The head was attached to a metal body. The limbs were wood and composition. Edison Talking Dolls were meant to recite nursery rhymes and phrases, which played on the miniature wax cylinder phonographs inside the doll's torso. Interestingly, these miniature phonographs were assembled in a separate room inside the factory, where 18 young girls sat, each in their own cubicle, reciting nursery rhymes into recording machines. However, the sound that played back through the dolls was muffled and Edison later admitted, 'the voices of the little monsters were exceedingly unpleasant to hear'. Even so, many people were horrified by the dolls' realism. A four-year-old girl maintained that she didn't like talking dolls, 'because the fixings in the stomach are not good for digestion'. Unfortunately the wax cylinders soon wore out and couldn't be replaced, while the handle mechanism was difficult for a child to operate correctly. Most of the dolls were returned by the purchasers, angry at paying vast sums for dolls which soon stopped speaking, and later, the remaining dolls in the factory were stripped of their phonographs and sold as 'ordinary' dolls.

Edith (The Lonely Doll)

Edith was a small 1920s' Lenci felt doll that starred in books by Dare Wright, including *Edith The Lonely Doll*. There were several other titles in the series. The first book was published in 1957 and there was very little text as Edith's adventures were depicted using photographs taken by the author. In 1958 an Edith doll was made by Madame Alexander and featured a typical sweet Alexander doll face rather than a Lenci-type doll as depicted in the books. Later, in 1997, White Balloon 'Kids At Heart' issued Edith in her pink gingham frock and white apron complete with a copy of the first book, *The Lonely Doll* as a 40th anniversary special. A similar boxed set contained *A Gift From the Lonely Doll*, together with a 9in Edith doll wearing her 'Let It Snow' outfit of blue coat, black velvet hat, fur muff and sturdy black lace-up shoes. Other dolls available included Edith in a white jumper and kilt ('Playtime'), pyjamas ('Tuck Me In'), white dress ('A Day In The Sun'), red coat and ice-skates ('Wintertime Fun'), green dress and pinafore ('Holiday Party') and jacket and skirt ('A Walk In The Park'). Ediths have also been produced by designers such as Haut Melton, who made a limited edition of 375 hand-crafted felt dolls, each accompanied by a Steiff Little Bear. These 'Winter Time Edith and Little Bear' dolls wore red felt coats, knitted stripy tights and carried ice-skates. In 2008 R. John Wright produced a felt version of a solemn-faced Edith in her pink-checked frock, white apron and black shoes. This was the first Edith doll to be manufactured at her correct, original height of 22in.

Dora The Explorer, Ty.

Edith, 'Gift From the Lonely Doll', White Balloon.

Daisy, Flower Fairy, Alberon.

Hermione from Harry Potter, Tonner.

Elizabeth

A doll created by Pedigree in 1953 called Elizabeth, presumably in honour of the Queen, whose coronation took place that year. This was a slim teen, standing 19in tall, with a fair, short, wavy mohair – later saran – wig. She was made from a smooth glossy hard plastic and featured a closed, slightly smiling mouth and sleep eyes. She originally cost 42/- (£2.10p) and was described in the 1953 Pedigree catalogue as having a 'Print Dress and Best Brushable Wig'.

Elizabeth's original outfit consisted of a cotton dress with a full skirt, and there was a choice of fabric patterns and colours. The dress had a very distinctive white Petersham collar and also a white belt. She came in a pink-and-white-striped box bearing an attractive drawing of Elizabeth with slogans such as 'With all you need to dress her like a queen'. Various patterns designed by Veronica Scott, the fashion editor of *Woman* magazine were available, amongst them beach wear, a duster coat, dresses, winter coat, underwear and nightdress, so that the doll could have a comprehensive wardrobe.

Eloise

Eloise was the six-year-old girl heroine in a series of books written by Kay Thompson and illustrated by Hilary Knight. She lived in the 'room on the tippy-top floor' of the Plaza Hotel in New York, with her Nanny, her pug dog Weenie and her turtle Skipperdee.

Ernestine

Ernestine, a doll from the story *The Most Wonderful Gift* ('Tales of Silent Lou') by Martha Haut Melton, had an older sister, Marien, and a favourite rag doll, Louise. The set of three dolls was issued in 1996 by White Balloon for 'Kids At Heart'. Ernestine and Marien were both 10in tall and made from vinyl. Blonde Ernestine wore a sky-blue cotton dress featuring an embroidered pansy and a darker blue collar with yellow embroidery, while brunette Marien had a cream dress edged in green with green embroidery. Louise, the little cloth doll, had red curly wool hair, a pink frilly dress and large green shoes.

Eve

Eve was a fashion doll that appeared in the 2000 Walt Disney television film *Life-Size*. Originally, she was the plaything of Casey, played by Linda Lohan, but she came to life and developed into a life-size doll played by Tyra Banks.

Fairy Baby

The 'Fairy Baby' became popular during the 1940s and 50s. She was the logo of Fairy Soap and pictures of the nappy-clad toddler appeared on the wrappings, as well as being imprinted into the actual soap bar. Foam-rubber bendy dolls, complete with painted-on quiff of hair, based on the Fairy Baby, were sold as 'Bendy Bubbas'.

Fairy Doll (1)

Fairy dolls are traditional small, net-clad dolls with wings and wands that for many years topped Christmas trees in Britain. They were at their most popular from the 1920s to the 1980s, but nowadays have been toppled by angels and American-style tree-toppers. The earlier dolls were made from wax or bisque china; later came celluloid, and then plastic. During the 1950s 'golden age' of hard plastic, thousands of plastic fairy dolls were made by such companies as Roddy, Rosebud, Pedigree, Airfix and Palitoy and sold through stores at Christmas. Often, rather than net skirts, the dolls would be dressed in crepe paper and tinsel. Many fairy dolls are treasured and passed down through the generations, to reappear each Christmas on top of the tree.

Fairy Doll (2)

The Fairy doll is a character from the book of the same name by Rumer Godden. She befriends a little girl called Elizabeth, who builds her a fairy home. The fairy helps Elizabeth learn to read, remember her times tables, and, most important of all, ride her new bike without falling off. Then the Fairy doll is lost and Elizabeth is bereft – until Christmas arrives and, mysteriously, so does the Fairy doll.

Farnell

Established in 1840 by John Kirby Farnell in Notting Hill, the J. K. Farnell company originally made such items as tea cosies and pin cushions, but following John Farnell's death in 1897, his son Henry and his daughter Agnes leased a house in Acton where they began producing soft toys. In 1921 a new factory, known as Alpha Works, was built alongside the Acton premises. Subsequently, Alpha was registered as a Farnell trademark. As well as teddy bears, the company produced some outstanding felt and fabric dolls, many intended for collectors as they depicted personalities such as George VI. In 1959, a second factory, Olympia Works, was established in Hastings, Sussex, and five years later all production moved there.

Flower Fairies

The classic collectable range of Flower Fairies, made by Hornby Hobbies, first appeared in 1984. It was based on illustrations from the Flower Fairies series of books written and illustrated by Cicely Mary Baker in the 1920s and 30s. The dolls proved very successful and eventually a complete fairyland world was created. The first fairies issued were 'Guelder Rose', 'Heliotrope', 'Almond Blossom', 'Sweet Pea', 'Narcissus' and 'Pink'. The pretty, dainty dolls were made from vinyl. They were jointed at the neck, shoulders, waist and hips, and stood 6½in high, with sweet faces, rooted hair and pointed ears. Many of the costumes were identical to the illustrations in the original books, and were very well-detailed. They were made of taffeta or polyester, and each resembled a flower. Fabric wings mounted on plastic armatures clipped onto the dolls' backs by means of a small peg, and additional costumes were available separately. Boy fairies – pixies – were also available, as well as a range of fairyland buildings, vehicles and furnishings. Flower Fairies were also made by Alberon and others.

Flowerpot Men
Perhaps not strictly dolls, these well-loved characters first appeared in the 1950s *Watch With Mother* television series. There were two Flowerpot men, Bill and Ben, who looked identical – identified only by their names on their backs. Constructed from assorted-sized flowerpots, these strange characters spoke in an odd language, and they were friends with a flower called 'Little Weed'. Actor Peter Hawkins was the inventor of the Flowerpot Men's 'flobbadob' language, and also provided their voices. Hawkins later voiced the Daleks in *Doctor Who*. Dolls and puppets of the Flowerpot Men figures first appeared in 1953. In the 2000s the series was revamped and once more dolls of the characters, both plush and plastic, were issued.

France and Marianne
In 1938 King George VI and Queen Elizabeth carried out a state visit to France. The visit was commemorated by a very special gift of two dolls commissioned by the Société Française de Fabrication de Bébés et Jouets, which was sent a few months later on behalf of the children of France to Princess Elizabeth and her sister Princess Margaret Rose. Made by French company Jumeau, the two bisque-headed dolls were called 'France' and 'Marianne' and included a spectacular trousseau of 350 items. France was honey blonde; Marianne was brunette, and they had jointed wooden composition bodies, exquisitely painted faces and lustrous eyes. The eyes were made by M. Peigne, a Parisian maker of artificial human eyes. Included in the trousseau were garments designed by top Parisian couturiers of the day, as well as tea-services, jewellery, perfume, prams, cots, wardrobes and even two doll-sized Citroens. Since 1992, the dolls and much of their trousseaux have been on display at Windsor Castle

Fred the Flourgrader (*See* Homepride)

Gaffer (*See* Tetley Tea Folk)

Galldora
Galldora is a pert rag doll who first appeared in 1953 on the BBC's *Children's Hour*, later becoming the subject of three books by Modwena Sedgwick. The doll was made by a sailor, Uncle Jack, for his niece Marybell, and he gave Galldora shiny shoe-button eyes, wool hair and a sewn-on mouth. Even Marybell realises that Galldora isn't pretty but comforts her by saying that as she isn't beautiful, she'll just have to be clever instead. The name 'Galldora' was dreamt up by Uncle Jack who rearranged the letters in 'A Rag Doll', and the three books tell of the everyday events that happen to Galldora, who has a habit of getting lost, and Marybell.

Gene
Gene Marshall is a 15½in fashion doll for collectors, introduced in 1995. She was designed by Mel Odom, and broke new ground, being one of the first, and

certainly the most successful, of adult-orientated fashion dolls. She inspired an outpouring of similar dolls from other companies, including Tonner's 'Tyler Wentworth' and 'Kitty Collier', Bella Productions' 'Clea Bella', Madame Alexander's 'Alexandra Fairchild Ford', and many others. For ten years, from 1995 to 2005, the Gene dolls were sold through Ashton-Drake, but are now produced by Jason Wu and sold through Integrity Toys. There are several other characters in the line including 'Trent Osborn' and 'Madra Lord'.

Gerber Baby
The Gerber Baby is particularly popular in America, where it is a well-known advertising doll. Many different types have been produced since they first appeared in the 1930s. Designed by artist Dorothy Hope, the dolls feature round open mouths, and the early dolls were made from fabric with silk-screened faces. Later, vinyl and porcelain versions of the dolls were made, often only obtainable with tokens collected from jars of baby food.

Ginny
Ginny is a long-time favourite American doll, reminiscent of Miss Rosebud, who was introduced in 1951 by the Vogue Doll Company. She was created by Jennie Graves, owner of the company, and is 8in tall with sleep eyes. Originally she was made from a shiny hard plastic, but is now made from a matt plastic. The doll has also been made by other companies, including Meritus, Tonka and Lesney Products, but in 1995 she reverted to Vogue, which still produces the doll today.

Girl Doll
The Palitoy 'Girl Doll' was produced in 1953, and was made to promote the popular *Girl* comic published by Hulton Press. She was made from a shiny hard plastic and stood 14in tall, with a slim body, solemn face, lavender eyes and a shoulder-length wig. The Girl doll 'walked', as she moved her head turned from side to side. Her outfit publicised the comic and consisted of a white taffeta dress printed with a red girl's head (the comic's logo) and matching knickers. The logo also appeared on the doll's hair ribbon, and as a fastening on her belt. Various patterns could be obtained for extra clothes for the doll through *Girl* comic.

Golly (*See also* Robertson's Golly)
No one is really quite sure who made the first golly doll, and there are many versions of the history of the golly which may or may not be true. Based on the 1895 book *The Adventures of Two Dutch Dolls and a Golliwogg* by Bertha Upton, golly dolls became exceedingly popular and were made by most of the major soft toy manufacturers, including Steiff, Dean's, Merrythought and Chad Valley. A typical golly was a flat-faced doll made from black stockinette or felt with tufts of black woollen hair. He would have round eyes and a smiling red mouth, and would be colourfully dressed in long trousers, a shirt and jacket. Gollies were adopted by James Robertson's and Sons (maker of preserves) as their mascot in the early 1900s.

Gone With the Wind
This iconic film was released in 1939, an American historical epic set in the American Civil War based on the 1936 novel by Margaret Mitchell. Amongst its stars were Clark Gable, Vivien Leigh, Leslie Howard and Olivia de Haviland. The film inspired many doll designers and companies, notably Madame Alexander, Robert Tonner and Mattel. In America, particularly, *Gone With the Wind* dolls are exceedingly collectable.

Gotz
The German manufacturer Gotz, or Goetz, was founded by Marianne and Franz Gotz in 1950. One of the company's great achievements was to work with doll artist Sasha Morgenthaler, creator of Sasha dolls, from 1965 onwards, so that her dolls could reach a wider audience. Amongst the dolls produced by Gotz over the years are hand-crafted dolls, artist edition dolls, play dolls and licensed dolls, all of which are of exceptional quality, with some of the artist dolls now changing hands for considerable sums. Gotz artists include such top names as Didy Jacobsen, Carin Lossnitzer, Sissel Skille and Sabine Esche. Gotz also produced an excellent range of Harry Potter dolls in 2002, and is today especially famed for their Sarah/Hannah series of play dolls.

Grease Dolls
Popular film and musical *Grease* has given rise to several dolls. The film first appeared in 1978, and 25 years later, in 2003, Mattel issued an Olivia Newton John doll, called 'Barbie as Sandy'. The doll was dressed in slinky black leather and her hair was a mass of curls, just as she appeared in the famous scene where she duetted with John Travolta in 'You're the One That I Want'. Franklin Mint also manufactured Olivia as Sandy in her leather outfit. Larger than the usual teen dolls, she stood 16in high, and additional outfits were available including the yellow skirt and top she wore on her first day at Rydell High. The doll came with a spare straight wig, so that both demure and vamp looks could be created. Mattel later followed this up with a series of the dolls, including Sandy, dressed in other outfits from the film. Amongst these were 'Cheerleader' and 'Prom Dance', as well as the characters Rizzo, Frenchy and Cha Cha.

Hamble
Hamble was a doll who regularly featured in the BBC children's television show *Playschool*. Usually, when a show needs a doll a special character is created, but in this instance Hamble was purchased from a local Woolworths and was one of their own Winfield label 'Little Beauty' dolls. She would have been purchased in the mid 1960s. The first Hamble was a soft-bodied doll with thick brown curly hair and a rather strange face with screwed up features. In the 1970s Hamble was replaced by an all-vinyl doll with straight hair, also called Hamble. In the mid-1980s her place was taken by 'Poppy', a doll with an 'ethnic' look. Hamble lookalikes do turn up from time to time, and interestingly, the hair of the brunette versions has a tendency to develop a green tinge. The original Hamble disappeared, and was later rumoured to be seen in a rubbish skip.

Other toys which appeared in *Playschool* included 'Humpty', a large round soft doll who looked a bit like a cushion. Humpty had big round eyes, a round nose and a smiling, U-shaped mouth. The top half was made from green velveteen and the lower half was check fabric, with a pink collar and pink buttons. His pink hands and feet were at the end of narrow, shapeless limbs. He had a tuft of dark yarn hair. There were also two bears, 'Big Ted' and 'Little Ted' and a rocking horse called 'Dapple'. Details of the other two dolls, 'Poppy' and 'Jemima', can be found under their own entries. Some of the toys can be seen at the National Media Museum in Bradford, West Yorkshire.

Harry Potter
When the first Harry Potter film *Harry Potter and the Philosopher's Stone* was published in 2001, it opened the floodgates for film tie-ins, many of which were dolls. Made by several companies, amongst them Mattel, Gund, Gotz and Tonner, the dolls reflect the growing up and character development of the children at Hogwarts through the seven films. The films are based on the books by J. K. Rowling.

Havoc (*See* Daisy)

Heidi
The children's book *Heidi* by Swiss author Johanna Spyri was published in 1880. It is one of those books that have inspired numerous doll makers to create costume dolls, and as the films and television adaptations came out – notably the Shirley Temple movie which was released in 1937 – dolls appeared. The most beautiful are probably the 1990s felt dolls crafted by R. John Wright, who also made a doll of Peter the Goatherd.

Heidi Plusczok
Heidi Plusczok made her first doll out of cernit (polymer clay) for her daughter in 1980 and a year later made her first porcelain dolls. She decided to specialise in portrait dolls, often basing her designs on local children. After a meeting at a toy fair with one of the owners of Zapf, she was inspired to create her own vinyl collection. Today, Heidi Plusczok dolls are available in many sizes, from 10in dolls, to large 32in creations, and all are beautiful. She works in both vinyl and porcelain, and each year chooses a special theme for her collection.

Helen Kish
Helen Kish began working with clay and porcelain in the mid-1970s, and from the late 1970s to the late 1980s she sculpted more than one hundred dolls. She called the dolls 'Helen Kish Originals', and sold them primarily at shows. She also worked as a freelance designer for many companies, amongst them Danbury Mint, Franklin Mint and The Hamilton Collection, and in 1991 launched Kish & Company. The company creates and produces fine collectable dolls, and Helen's distinctive designs are recognised worldwide.

Henie, Sonja
This popular 1930s ice-skating star soon became a popular movie star as well, and, just as with Shirley Temple, many dolls were produced in her likeness. Sonja Henie was born in Olso, Norway, in 1912, and became skilled at many sports. She was 11 when she took part in the 1924 Olympics and competed twice more before switching to a movie career in Hollywood. In 1939 the Madame Alexander Doll Company issued a Sonja Henie doll made from composition, with blonde wavy hair, brown sleep eyes and dimples. The dolls wore various skating costumes and came in various sizes, ranging from 14in to 20in, with the small sizes featuring a twist waist. Later, the face mould was also used on various other Madame Alexander dolls, so be aware that although a doll looks like Sonja Henie, it might not have originally represented her. Sonja Henie dolls were made by additional companies, too, notably Arranbee.

Hershey Kisses Dolls
In America, Hershey bars are a favourite make of chocolate, and Marie Osmond's company has made several pretty dolls advertising the chocolate, sold under its 'Charisma' doll brand. One popular doll was a 9in porcelain girl, made to celebrate one hundred years of Hershey Kisses. Marie Osmond's 'Kiss Someone' keepsake wore a chocolate- brown dress with silver net underlining with a 'Kisses' ribbon trim and silver shoes. She held a blue banner that read 'Kiss Someone'. Other Hershey dolls by Marie Osmond included 'Hershey Hugs Tiny Tot', a 5in seated porcelain doll dressed in a chocolate-brown and silver-striped lamé dress, made to resemble a Hershey bar wrapper.

Hildegarde Gunzel
Hildegard Gunzel was born in 1945 in Tauberbischofsheim, Germany, and attended the German School for Fashion Design in München. For a while she worked as a designer in the fashion and jewellery industry, before beginning to make dolls as a hobby in 1972. Since 1980 she has been making dolls out of porcelain, which is then coated with a layer of wax to obtain the perfect translucent image. She later also made dolls using a resin.

Hitty
Another of the true famous dolls, Hitty was a wooden doll who featured in the book *Hitty, Her First Hundred Years*, by Rachel Field. Written in 1929, this told the story of a wooden doll carved in the 1800s from a piece of mountain ash. The book was illustrated by artist Dorothy P. Lathrop, and the name 'Hitty' was short for Mehitable. The American wood-carver Robert Raikes has produced many Hitty dolls, and in 2001 he introduced an open edition. Hitty kits, Hitty clothing kits and Hitty outfits are all available to fit the doll, though she is seldom seen or heard of in Britain.

H.G Stone and Company
Toymaker Leon Rees inherited the Chiltern Toy works and formed the company L. Rees & Co., after his father-in-law died in 1919. The company produced

Holly Hobbie, Ashton–Drake.

Kewpie, unmarked.

Little Miss No Name, Hasbro.

Florence, Magic Roundabout, Pedigree.

various dolls, and later Leon went into partnership with Harry Stone, who was formerly with teddy manufacturers J. K. Farnell. Farnell was also renowned for its felt and fabric dolls. They developed H. G. Stone and Company, eventually opening a factory in north London to produce plush toys using the 'Chiltern' brand name. Not long after the end of the Second World War, L. Rees & Co. became concessionaires for small dolls made by Nene Plastics for Rosebud, eventually selling them under the Chiltern name. Chiltern went on to produce many attractive vinyl dolls, notably 'Babykins'.

Holly

Holly was a doll who appeared in Rumer Godden's children's book *The Story of Holly and Ivy* in 1958. Holly is in a toyshop, and knows that she has to be sold by Christmas Day, otherwise she will be packed away for a whole year. But today is Christmas Eve! Ivy is a little girl living in an orphanage, and though the other children have gone to stay with kind people for Christmas, no one invited her. Somehow she knows that Holly is meant for her – and Holly feels the same. Sadly, Ivy has no money, nowhere to go, and it is cold and snowing. Ivy needs warmth, food and a grandmother. Beautifully illustrated with sketches by Christian Birmingham.

Holly Hobbie

Created by Denise Holly Ulinskas Hobbie (born 1944) who grew up in Connecticut, the Holly Hobbie character became famed in the 1960s as a little girl in a patchwork frock and huge bonnet. This child featured on Hallmark greetings cards and stationery. Soon, dolls appeared, the majority of them made from cloth, and were particularly popular during the 1970s and 80s.

Homepride

Homepride Men, notably 'Fred' with his black suit and smart bowler hat, are flourgraders who have been used by the Homepride company since 1965 to advertise its flour. Their famous slogan is 'Graded grains make finer flour'. Fred has been issued as a soft doll, including plush and beanie types, with one version bearing his embroidered name on his foot.

Horrid Henry

Horrid Henry is the child featured in a series of books written by Francesca Simon and illustrated by Tony Ross. The first book was published in 1994, and since then another 20 titles have been issued. In 1n 2006 an animated television series of 52 episodes starring Horrid Henry was commissioned. The series proved so successful, that now there are over 150 episodes. In 2011 a live-action 3-D film was released. Various Little Henry dolls have appeared over the years as book and film tie-ins.

Humpty (*See* Hamble)

Jackson, Michael

Born in 1958, in Indiana, America, Michael Jackson was the seventh of nine children, five of whom later formed the Jackson Five with Michael as lead singer. When his album *Thriller* was released in 1982 and went on to become the world's largest selling album of all time, Jackson was a superstar. The iconic rock star inspired several equally iconic dolls, notably the LJN American Music Awards King of Pop doll, 12in high, which was issued in 1985. This Michael Jackson doll wore a red military-styled jacket trimmed with gold braid and navy trousers. He wore one 'magic' glove. The company issued another doll at the same time, in a blue-and gold-outfit, for the Grammy Awards. Many other Michael Jackson dolls have been produced over the years, by various companies.

Jan McLean

New Zealander Jan McLean began doll-making in the 1980s, at first concentrating on reproduction dolls, but when she met doll artist Hildegard Gunzel, Jan was inspired and decided to sculpt her own dolls, producing her first creations in 1987. After exhibiting at the New York Toy Fair in 1991, her dolls became in demand. In 1998 she diversified the business and made her dolls more accessible, calling them 'Jan McLean Designs'. Her large-eyed, leggy teens, in particular, were extremely distinctive, as were ranges such as the fashionable 20in-tall, porcelain 'Lollipop Girls' which were later also produced as vinyl play dolls in a smaller size, and her 'Floozie' series. She also produced stunning wide-eyed child dolls, which are very collectable today. The company ceased trading in 2009.

Jane (*See* Lucinda)

Janie

Janie is the small rag doll owned by the evil Sid's small sister, Hannah, in the film *Toy Story*. Hannah loves Janie very much, but one day Sid decides to do what he calls a 'double bypass brain transplant', by ripping off her head. He then takes the head off his toy pterodactyl and fastens it onto Janie's body. Later, the mutant toys tape back their heads on the correct bodies.

Jelly Babies Dolls

Jelly babies – colourful jelly sweets shaped as babies or dolls –were launched by Bassetts in 1918 as 'Peace Babies' to mark the end of the First World War, but production was suspended during the Second World War. In 1953 they were relaunched as 'Jelly Babies' and soon became a favourite.

At times, they have become a 'cult' sweet, for instance during the 1960s, the Beatles pop group announced how much they loved them and subsequently became bombarded with the sweets when they appeared on stage. Since the early 1990s, each colour of Jelly Baby has been given a different name and shape: 'Brilliant' (red – strawberry), 'Boofuls' (green – lime), 'Bigheart' (purple –

blackcurrant), 'Bubbles' (yellow – lemon), 'Baby Bonny' (pink – raspberry) and Bumper (orange). Dolls in the shape of the babies have been issued in various forms, including large plush types, beanie dolls and a series made from vinyl.

Jemima

Jemima the rag doll, a stalwart of the *Playschool* television series, seems to have been continually replaced. If you looked closely, her appearance regularly changed, presumably because she didn't last long with all the rough-and-tumble the toys received on the show. She had a face with embroidered features, round pink cheeks and long brown hair made from wool with a ribbon tied on top. She wore various outfits, and was often seen in a print frock and apron. One version of Jemima can be seen in the National Media Museum, Bradford, West Yorkshire.

Jessie

Jessie was the feisty cowgirl character in *Toy Story 2* and *Toy Story 3*, and starred with Woody in *Woody's Roundup*, the fictitious television serial invented for the movies. However, she also revealed her vulnerable side as she explained she was once the much-loved toy of a little girl called Emily, who gave her away when she grew up. Jessie dolls were issued by Mattel when *Toy Story 2* was released, and appeared in various outfits; not just the cowgirl clothes as seen in the film. She had green eyes, a smiling face and a snub nose. Over the years since the films were released, there have been many versions of Jessie, including various Disney beanies. When Jessie was initially released in doll form, the stores sold out almost instantaneously.

Jinx

Extremely popular with today's collectors, Jinx was a small, 8in-high, doll made from hard plastic and issued by the Amanda Jane Company in 1958. Cast from a 'Miss Rosebud' mould, by Wilkinson and Gross of London, Jinx was jointed at the shoulders, hips and neck and was marked 'England' on her back. A huge variety of clothes and other items were available for the doll; all made by Amanda Jane, which, at the time, was based in Petworth, Sussex. In the early 1960s there was a terrible fire at the factory and the remaining stocks of Jinx, as well as clothing and patterns, were destroyed.

Joe

Joe was the subject of a charming still-frame animation series called *Joe* which centered on a wide-eyed young boy. The stories, by Alison Prince, were aimed at the very young and appeared in the late 1960s as part of the *Watch With Mother* series. Joe was created as a 16in vinyl doll, and his outstanding feature was large brown eyes.

Käthe Kruse

Creator of exquisite cloth dolls, Käthe Kruse was born in Breslau, Germany in 1883, eventually marrying sculptor Max Kruse and raising seven children. She wasn't happy with the breakable dolls in the shops, and so began to make soft, cloth dolls for her children. Later, she began to exhibit her dolls, and founded her own company, leading to worldwide success. Her dolls had sweet faces and painted eyes. Today, dolls bearing the Käthe Kruse name are still made.

Kewpie
Kewpie dolls were the inspiration of American illustrator Rosie O'Neil. She worked for many popular magazines at the time and created the kewpies for the Christmas 1909 issue of *Ladies Home Journal*. The little cherub-like creatures sported a topknot and tiny wings, and the name, 'Kewpie' is a variation of the word cupid. They became exceedingly successful and graced many magazines, greetings cards and story books, becoming something of a phenomenon, especially in America. There was even a comic strip called 'Dotty Darling and the Kewpies'. In 1912 *Women's Home Companion* began to print 'Kewpie Kutouts' paper dolls in the pages of its magazine. These Kewpie Kutouts were unusual because they were printed on both sides (at that time, most paper dolls were blank on the reverse), and they are extremely collectable today owing to their fragility.

Rosie O'Neil decided to have kewpie dolls made, and she commissioned sculptor Joseph L. Kallas to turn her kewpie drawings into 3-D creations. When she saw the result, she was so pleased that she granted Kallas exclusive rights to the kewpie doll trademark, and in 1913 the first kewpie doll was manufactured by a toy company in Germany. The early Kewpie dolls were made of porcelain or bisque, but soon less expensive celluloid or composition kewpie dolls became available. In 1925 a soft-bodied version, known as the 'Kewpie Kuddle', was marketed, and hard plastic versions were around by the late 1940s. Cheap versions of kewpies were often used as carnival prizes, and were frequently referred to as 'Carnival Dolls'. In 1939 a kewpie doll was included in a time capsule at the American World's Fair. Kewpie dolls are still popular today; companies such as Pedigree made versions in 1970s and 80s, while designer R John Wright has produced a series of the dolls hand-crafted in felt.

Kleeware
Kleeware was a plastics company founded by the Kleeman family in 1938. It was originally based in Welwyn Garden City, Hertfordshire, but later moved to Aycliffe, Co. Durham. At first Kleeware concentrated on small domestic items such as combs and ashtrays, and during the war it made radio components for the Ministry of Defence. After the war, it made small toys and dolls as well as household sundries. Kleeware's most recognisable dolls are all-in-one hard plastic babies that came in various sizes, with painted eyes and mouths. They had moulded hair and each doll was modelled sucking its right index finger. They also produced rubbery-plastic sitting dolls with outstretched arms, which fitted inside doll's houses, and it wasn't long before they made sets of doll's house furniture too. In 1959, Kleeware was taken over by Rosedale Plastics, makers of Tudor Rose dolls.

Knitting Nancy
Bobbin-shaped dolls, often referred to as 'Knitting Nancys', are a toy sometimes used to help children to knit. Four small hoops or nails protrude from the head of the doll, and the wool is looped over each hoop in turn. Eventually a long, knitted rope emerges through the hollow body of the doll. At one time, wooden cotton reels with four nails hammered into the top made a Knitting Nancy, but nowadays most cotton reels are plastic, so a purpose-made Nancy needs to be purchased.

Lee Middleton
Lee Middleton sculpted her first dolls to look like her own two children and word of her talent soon spread. In 1989, she opened a manufacturing facility in Belpre, Ohio, Midwest America, which produced more baby dolls a year than did any other manufacturer in America. The company was soon producing award-winning dolls, but in 1997 Lee Middleton died of a heart attack. Fate led to a little-known Canadian doll artist, Reva Schick, joining the company and her work was perfect, leading it to new heights with dozens of different beautiful vinyl dolls being produced each year. In the mid-2000s, other doll artists joined the company. In 2010 it was purchased by The Alexander Doll Company.

Legs
Legs was one of the mutant toys in the first *Toy Story* film. She was a toy fishing rod attached to Barbie doll legs, and was extremely strong, managing to hold the combined weight of Baby Face and Ducky. When Woody devised a plan to save Buzz from Sid – Sid was about to send him into orbit on a firework – he asked Legs to partner Ducky, and she opened a vent grating to get to the front porch. Legs lowered Ducky so that he could swing towards the doorbell before catching a frog and being pulled up to safety once more. When the mutant toys advanced on Sid and began to terrorise him, Legs lowered Baby Face onto Sid's head, and he was very scared.

Lisa (*See* Comfort Dolls)

Lissy
In the movie *Matilda*, which is based on the story by Roald Dahl, Miss Honey's doll, a prized childhood gift from her mother, was named 'Lissy Doll'. Matilda managed to steal the doll from the evil Miss Turnbull by using her magic powers and returned her to Miss Honey. The Madame Alexander Company has issued a Lissy doll in its 'Matilda' range.

Little Miss No Name
The strange 'Little Miss No Name' doll was launched by Hasbro in 1965, but was only on sale for a short while. She was created by designer, Deet D'Andrade, who later would be responsible for 'Blythe'. It is said that Hasbro loosely based the doll on the paintings of the American artist Margaret Keane, who specialised

in large-eyed children. Little Miss No Name stood 15in tall, with an over-large head, and had enormous round eyes. One of her eyes had a removable, blue plastic teardrop underneath, and her fair hair was cut in a rough-and-ready chop. Little Miss No Name was dressed in a plain brown burlap (a kind of hessian) dress with two patches, and matching pants. Her right hand stretched out plaintively, palm open, as though she was begging, and each doll came with a copper coin. Her neck was marked 'C Hasbro 1965 R'.

Little Miss Oxo (*See* Betty Oxo)

Little Plum
A delightful children's book by Rumer Godden which tells the story of a doll, *Little Plum,*written in 1963 (a follow up to *Miss Happiness and Miss Flower*). The book tells how two children, Nona and Belinda, think that Gem, the new child next door, is stuck up and they vow to have nothing to do with her. However, a beautiful Japanese doll in her window soon attracts their attention and they name her 'Little Plum' because her clothes are decorated with plum blossom. Unlike Nona's own Japanese dolls, 'Miss Happiness' and 'Miss Flower', Little Plum seems unloved and uncared for. The three girls must become friends. Rumer Godden was awarded the OBE in 1993 and died in 1998, aged ninety

Little Princess
Issued by Pedigree around the time of the Coronation, the 'Little Princess' doll was presumed to be based on the toddler Princess Anne. This hard plastic 14in-tall smiling doll featured blonde curly hair just like that of the Princess, and came dressed in a full-skirted organza frock designed by royal dressmaker Norman Hartnell. She was sold in a box bearing a picture of Buckingham Palace. Today, mint and boxed dolls fetch a high premium.

Little Princess (2)
The Little Princess is a small girl who happens to be a princess, and is the main character in a series of books written and illustrated by Tony Ross. (Tony Ross is also the illustrator of the Horrid Henry series.) The first book, published in 1994, was I Want My Potty, and other titles followed, as well as short animated films for television. Little Princess dolls are made by Aurora World Ltd.

Little Red
The Little Red character was created by Sarah Ferguson, the Duchess of York, for a series of children's books. The first title in the series was *Little Red*, published 2004. 'Little Red' is a small girl who lives in Buttercup Cottage on the edge of Bluebell woods. She carries a magic sack of smiles, and is accompanied by playmates, including 'Little Blue', 'Gino the Dog' and 'Roany the Pony'. The inspiration for the book *Little Red* came from a doll designed for US charity 'Chances for Children', which Sara Ferguson carried on visits to children in hospital. Prior to the 9/11 attack, the charity offices were located in the World

Trade Centre, and shortly afterwards, a fire-fighter found one of the Little Red dolls in the 'Ground Zero' rubble. Sarah was inspired to write the book, because she saw the doll as a symbol of survival and courage. The Little Red doll, made by FAO Schwarz, is a soft-bodied doll wearing a red dress and with yarn hair.

Little Women

This much-loved classic has provided inspiration for many doll makers over the years. *Little Women* was written by American author Louisa May Alcott (1832–1888), and set in the Alcott family home, Orchard House, in Concord, Massachusetts. It was published in two volumes, in 1868 and 1869. The novel, which follows the lives of four sisters – Meg, Jo, Beth and Amy March – was loosely based on the author's own childhood experiences with her three sisters. Dolls, especially from the Madame Alexander Doll Company, began to appear in 1933, in conjunction with the release of the now-classic movie starring Katharine Hepburn. Each year since then, Madame Alexander has produced a new line of dolls based on the characters of Jo, Meg, Beth, and Amy, and the company never runs out of inspiration for new designs, thanks to the rich detail of the book.

Lonely Doll (*See* Edith)

Looby Loo

The rag doll companion of 1950s string puppet Andy Pandy, Looby Loo lived in the hamper with teddy. They appeared on children's television.

Louise (*See* Ernestine)

Lucinda

Lucinda and Jane were the names of two dolls that lived in a doll's house in Beatrix Potter's tale *Two Bad Mice*. Lucinda was a china doll and Jane, the cook, was a wooden peg or 'Dutch' doll.

Madame Alexander

Bertha (later, Beatrice) Alexander was born in Brooklyn, New York, in 1895, the daughter of Russian immigrants. Her father owned a doll hospital, and she often played with the dolls there. She later married Philip Behman and founded the Madame Alexander Doll Company in 1923, where she created beautifully handcrafted play dolls. During the 1930s she began producing licensed dolls from the world of film and other media, and over the decades her creations were often inspired by great works of literature, the arts and different cultures. The Alexander Doll Company was acquired in 1995 by the Kaizen Breakthrough Partnership LP, but her original vision is still upheld by the company. Today designers and costumers continue to create successful, award-winning dolls while maintaining Madame Alexander's high standards of workmanship.

Jane and Michael, Mary Poppins, Mattel.

Old Cottage Doll.

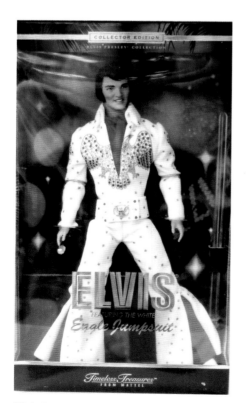

Elvis Presley, Mattel.

Buddy Blue, Hallmark.

Madeleine
Madeleine was the doll character in the 1970s classic children's television programme *Bagpuss* made by Peter Firmin and Oliver Postgate. She was a slim rag doll with curly wool hair and wore a striped dress. Madeleine always sat in a wicker chair, and didn't seem to move about at all. She enjoyed story-telling and singing, and was voiced by Sandra Kerr.

Madeline
Madeline is the youngest of the twelve pupils at a Parisienne school, featured in a series of books by Ludwig Bemelmans. Dolls representing many of the characters appeared in 1996, made by Eden Toys and, later, by Learning Curve. The Madame Alexander company has also produced a Madeline doll.

Madonna
When Madonna appeared in the film *Dick Tracy* in 1990, Applause created attractive soft-bodied dolls dressed in long, black velvet dresses to represent her. Madonna dolls are keenly sought by her army of fans. They also issued a Dick Tracy doll to go with her.

Magic Roundabout
This children's television programme, created in France by Serge Danot in 1964, was later produced by the BBC. *Magic Roundabout* appeared in Britain in 1965, and used the original stop motion animation but was dubbed in English by Eric Thompson. Although many of the characters, notably the popular Dougal the dog, were animals, there were a few 'humans' too, including Florence, Mr Rusty and Paul. These have appeared in doll form made by Pedigree, Link, Golden Bear, Pelham Puppets and others.

Marchpane (*See* Tottie)

Marie Antoinette
This was the nickname bestowed by Buzz Lightyear on a headless doll in *Toy Story 1* whom he was forced to join at a tea party by Sid's little sister, Hannah. There were actually two headless doll at the table, one was Barbie without her original legs (she had rag doll legs), and the other was a rag doll in a purple dress. The dolls had been 'tortured' by the evil Sid.

Marien (*See* Ernestine)

Mary Poppins
When the film *Mary Poppins*, based on the books by P. L. Travers, was released in 1964, it was the signal for a plethora of Mary Poppins dolls. Makers such as Peggy Nisbet, Effanbee, Horsman, Mattel and others have, over the years, produced many versions of the character. They have also depicted Bert and the two children, Jane and Michael. Julie Andrews played the part of Mary Poppins in the film, while Dick Van Dyke was Bert.

McDonald's Dolls

As well as their own Ronald McDonald clown dolls, the company logo is also often featured on promotional tie-ins. In the mid-nineties a plastic Happy Meal play doll was issued. The doll was dressed in a blue romper suit with a 'Happy Meal Girl' bib and came with her McDonald's burger, packet of fries and carton of drink. There were various slurping and burping sound effects. Sindy was used as a promotion in 1982 when the company advertised a Sindy doll, wearing a brown McDonald's trouser-suit. This Sindy is quite rare today. Barbie, too, has advertised McDonald's. McDonald's often gives away toys with its children's meals, and these have included small dolls such as Barbie. In America there have been several sets of Madame Alexander mini dolls dressed as various characters, all with the typical solemn 'Wendy-type' face.

Meg

Doll character in a series of books by Bertha and Florence Upton.

Memoirs of a London Doll

The classic book *Memoirs of a London Doll*, first published in 1852, tells of the adventures of a doll. It says, 'Edited by Mrs Fairstar', but was actually written by Richard Henry Horne. Told by the doll herself – a small wooden peg doll called Maria Poppet – it recounts a year of adventures with her various owners, and begins with the recollections of her own manufacture.

Mennyms

The Mennyms were a family of life-sized cloth dolls with blue faces that featured in a series of books by Sylvia Waugh. The dolls included 'Sir Magnus', 'Tulip', 'Joshua', 'Pilbara', 'Appleby',' Soubise', 'Vinita', 'Wimpey', 'Potpie', 'Miss Quigley' and baby, 'Googles'.

Midget

Doll character in a series of books by Bertha and Florence Upton.

Milky Bar Kid

The Milky Bar Kid character featured for many years in an advertising promotion for Nestlé's Milky Bar white chocolate bar. The boy was dressed as a cowboy with a large hat and spectacles, and the advert would invariably end with the cry, 'The Milky Bars are on me!' Promotional cloth and felt dolls of the cowboy were issued through Nestlé during the 1960s, 70s and 80s.

Minnie the Minx

Minnie the Minx is a much-loved character from the *Beano* comic. She was created by Leo Baxendale, and first appeared at Christmas 1953. From 1961 Minnie was drawn by Jim Petrie, who penned 2,000 of the comic strips. She is the third longest-running of the *Beano* characters, just beaten by Dennis the Menace and Roger the Dodger. She has appeared in plush doll form, notably a

2000s toy by 'Real Beano Gear', and also as plastic dolls given away free with children's meals at McDonald's and Burger King.

Miss Rosebud

Miss Rosebud was an extremely popular 8in hard plastic doll, dating from the 1950s. She had a solemn face, and featured sleep eyes and a mohair wig. The doll was jointed at the neck, hips and shoulders. Her back was engraved 'Miss Rosebud', and the mould was later used for Amanda Jane's 'Jinx' and Faerie Glen's 'Toni' and 'Sally'.

Miss Flower (*See* Miss Happiness)

Miss Happiness

Rumer Godden's classic story *Miss Happiness and Miss Flower* which tells of friendship and being part of a family, was originally published in 1961. It relates how Nona Fells had to leave India to move to England to live with her aunt's family, and how Belinda, her cousin, didn't like her at all. One day two dainty Japanese dolls arrive at Nona's doorstep, and everything begins to change, because, just like Nona, 'Miss Happiness' and 'Miss Flower' are lonely and homesick. They need their own traditional Japanese house and it is up to Nona to build it, but to do so she has to conquer her fears. A follow up story was written three years later, called *Little Plum*.

Moggy Dolls

Rag dolls with a different face each side were used centuries ago by rag merchants as shop sign advertisements, and were referred to as 'Moggy Dolls'.

Monroe, Marilyn

Legendary actress Marilyn Monroe starred in many films during the 1950s, and although she died in 1962, dolls are still being made to represent her as she was in her heyday. Companies such as Mattel and Ashton-Drake, and many others, make the dolls for collectors, often dressing them in outfits based on the classic costumes she wore in her best-loved films.

Mr Force (*see* Sunny Jim)

My Dream Baby

The doll known as 'My Dream Baby' was made by the German company Armand Marseille and was first issued in 1924. It was made from bisque, with either a closed mouth or an open mouth revealing two tiny teeth, and had a bald head with a low forehead. Usually a few curls were moulded onto the head. The eyes were set quite far apart, and there was a tiny snub nose which looked rather flat. The dolls were produced in many sizes. There was also a black version and an oriental version. Various types of My Dream Baby appeared on the market, with bodies of composition or cloth, while the hands might be composition, rubber or celluloid. They were marked on the back of the neck with the numbers '351' (open mouth) or '341' (closed mouth), and bore the name 'Armand Marseille', or the initials, 'AM'. The dolls came with either flange or socket heads (a flange neck is sewn onto a cloth body; a socket fits into a hard body). A letter 'K' on the neck indicates a socket head. Armand Marseille also sold the heads to several other companies, who marketed them under various names. Today, 'My Dream Baby' dolls are one of the easiest bisque dolls to find, and are normally comparatively inexpensive compared with other bisque dolls.

My Fair Lady
The musical film *My Fair Lady* was released in 1964; an adaptation of the slightly earlier stage musical. The film caused some controversy, as Julie Andrews, who had played the part of Eliza Doolittle in the stage production, was passed over in favour of Audrey Hepburn for the film. However, the film was a tremendous success, and various characters were issued, notably a 1995 Mattel series of 11in dolls wearing outfits from the film, including one of Richard Harrison who played the part of Professor Higgins. Dolls were also made by Eegee, Peggy Nisbet and others.

Noddy
Noddy, a little wooden nodding doll dressed in blue shorts, red shirt and a blue hat with a bell, first appeared in the 1949 book *Noddy Goes To Toyland* by Enid Blyton. Dolls featuring him soon followed as he was a very popular character, including a nicely dressed small rubber doll and a cloth version. Enid Blyton went on to write many more books about Noddy and his friends, especially Big Ears the Brownie. Noddy made his television debut in 1955 as a puppet. The early dolls were made by Merrythought, and today are produced by such companies as Play-By-Play and Golden Bear.

Norah Wellings
Norah Wellings started work in 1919 at Chad Valley, remaining there for seven years before leaving to start her own company with her brother Leonard. Her factory opened in 1926 and manufactured soft dolls and toys. She believed in quality, and the dolls were made from fabric, often velveteen. The heads were moulded from stockinette or felt over buckram (a stiff cotton). Many kinds of dolls were produced by Norah Wellings, including toddlers, babies, costume dolls and novelty dolls. She produced smiling grass-skirted native islander girls and souvenir sailor dolls which bore the name of various liners. The company was able to stay in production through the war years, but finally closed in 1959 after the death of Leonard.

Nursery Rhyme
Thousands of dolls dressed as nursery rhyme characters have appeared over the years. It is a favourite category amongst doll designers. The most popular characters are the girl dolls which look pretty in pseudo-peasant style pretty dresses, and which feature attractive props; Little Bo-Peep, Mary Mary, Mary

Had a Little Lamb and Little Miss Muffet, for example. The dolls have been made in many mediums, from cloth to porcelain and from vinyl to celluloid, and often are intended for adult collectors.

Old Cottage

The distinctive 'Old Cottage' dolls were created by the Fleischmann family who arrived in Britain in 1938 after fleeing Czechoslovakia. They settled at Rustington, near Littlehampton, West Sussex, but sadly, Margaret Fleischmann was soon widowed. She needed to earn a living and so decided to make dolls, registering the name 'Old Cottage Toys' in 1939. At first the dolls were all cloth but by the early 1950s they were made using a mix of PVA and latex rubber for the heads, which gave them a highly distinctive look. The hand-painted heads were attached to jointed cloth bodies. Margaret Fleischmann designed the costumes, and much of the sewing was executed by out-workers. Old Cottage Toys continued production up until 1980.

Osmond, Donny

Pop star Donny Osmond was issued as a doll by Mattel in 1978, dressed in purple and pink to match the outfit of his sister, Marie. Other outfits were obtainable separately. Donny has also appeared in doll form in the Marie Osmond range of collector's dolls, as well as in a porcelain edition by Knickerbocker in 1977.

Osmond, Jimmy

The Jimmy Osmond doll was produced by Mattel in 1978 as a small vinyl doll, and wore a silver jumpsuit with plum shirt. Jimmy is the rarest of the three Osmond dolls.

Osmond, Marie

Marie Osmond started out as a pop singer, sometimes singing with her brother Donny. A doll was made in her likeness by Mattel in 1978 with several outfits. The doll was sold in a graded lilac-and-pink dress, which echoed the outfit of Donny Osmond, sold at the same time. Other Osmond dolls have also appeared, including a porcelain set by Knickerbocker in 1977. Later, Marie switched track and began producing her own range of distinctive baby and toddler porcelain and vinyl dolls, amongst them dolls depicting her brother Donny.

Patsy Series

Patsy is one of the all-time American classic dolls, and she first appeared in 1928, based on an earlier, bisque little girl, 'Just Me'. Patsy is a sweet, 13in, solemn-faced girl with a moulded hairstyle, designed by Bernard Lipfert, a man responsible for many other classic dolls, and was manufactured by the Effanbee company. Originally she was made from composition, and was soon joined by 'sisters'. Each doll came with a golden heart charm bracelet and a gold paper heart-tag with her name; a tradition that still exists. In 1946, Effanbee was sold to Noma Electric and has changed hands several times since. Effanbee is now part of the Tonner Doll Company which acquired the company in 2002. Tonner also produced examples of other dolls from the Patsy series; amongst them 'Patsy Ann' (18in), 'Patsyette' (9in) and 'Wee Patsy' (5in), and they all retain the Effanbee name. Patsy and her sisters all feature the characteristic slightly bent right arm and straight left arm, and are created in a hard vinyl. They have moulded hair or short bobbed nylon wigs, with either sleep eyes or painted eyes.

Palitoy

Originally known as Cascelloid, the company was founded by Alfred Edward Pallett in Leicestershire in 1909, to produce celluloid household goods and small toys. It created its first doll in 1925; a small celluloid doll representing one of the Mabel Lucy Attwell children, 'Diddums', as depicted on her postcards. The company was bought by British Xylonite in 1931 and later began using the trade name Palitoy for its dolls and toys division. During the 1930s Cascelloid experimented with composition, producing a range of 'Plastex' dolls that were virtually unbreakable. After the War, the company began using plastics and vinyls. Palitoy was acquired by General Mills 1968, later passing to Hasbro and then, in 1984, to Tonka.

Pauline Dolls

These charming dolls designed by Pauline Bjonness-Jacobsen first came to prominence in the 1980s. Amongst her ranges were a late-1990s and early-2000s range of beautiful baby/toddler dolls. Later came the tiny Paulinette series. Amongst the Paulinettes are some delightful characters such as 'Bo Peep', 'Red Riding Hood', 'Mary, Mary' and 'Alice in Wonderland'. Pauline Bjonness-Jacobsen died in 2006 but the company continues, producing quality vinyl and porcelain dolls.

Peanuts Gang

Many of the Peanuts characters, designed by Charles M. Schulz, have been produced as vinyl, rubber, and cloth dolls. The Peanuts gang made their debut in 1950, and is probably one of the most famed newspaper strips, still featured in various publications today. Although Snoopy the dog is the main character, other gang members including Charlie Brown, Lucy and Linus have been issued by various companies.

Pedigree

In 1919 William, Arthur and Walter Lines formed Lines Brothers, and soon acquired premises in south London. Five years later, they registered their inventive brand name, Tri-ang Toys (three lines for Lines Brothers, forming a triangle). By 1931 they had over 1,000 staff and bought the famous London toy store, Hamleys. The company continued to grow, until by the 1960s they had taken over International Model Aircraft Ltd, Rovex plastics, Meccano Ltd, and various companies abroad. In 1962 it launched the Sindy doll – a rival to Barbie

– with a huge advertising campaign, and many other famous dolls were produced over the next few years. The company went into liquidation in 1971, and the Rovex Tri-ang complex was acquired by Dunbee Combex Marx. Lines Brothers/Pedigree eventually ceased production in 1986.

Peggy Nisbet Dolls

Peggy Nisbet entered the world of doll design in 1953 when she decided to commemorate the Coronation with a model of the Queen. She created a bisque figurine in a long gown, before dressing it in silk and velvet. It was a cross between an ornament and a doll. She took the prototype to Harrods and was surprised when she was given an order for 250 dolls. Later, she dressed plastic dolls, such as those from Rosebud, finally getting her own design produced in a solid, heavy matt-finish compound. Over the next 30 years, hundreds of designs poured forth from Peggy Nisbet's factories and workshops in Weston-Super-Mare and Scotland. The most frequently seen of the Nisbet collectors' dolls are the 7in and 8in dolls dressed as historical or royal personages. Others often found are in national costume, but many different ranges and sizes were made. The company joined forces with Royal Doulton in the early 1980s to produce various series of large porcelain dolls, and also made sets of vinyl dolls, including play-doll size models of Prince William and Prince Harry as toddlers. By the mid-1980s, doll production had slackened, as precedence was given to teddy bears. Eventually, the moulds were acquired by Welsh maker Diane Jones, who continued to produce dolls until 1999.

Perishers

This gang of streetwise children and a dog, who live in the fictional town of Croynge, were the subjects of a *Daily Mail* cartoon strip that first appeared in 1958, written by Maurice Dodd, and drawn by Dennis Collins. Wellington, the main character, was a resourceful boy who lived with a large English sheepdog called Boot. Other characters included Marlon, Maisie and Baby Grumpling. Pedigree made a set of dolls featuring the Perishers in the 1970s which were 15in tall and had soft bodies with vinyl heads and hands.

Philip Heath

Philip Heath was a talented designer and doll producer, whose range of ethnic children, often depicting them dirty, ragged and dusty, is instantly recognisable. All of his dolls were sculpted after real children. At one time he sculpted for Gotz, which produced his range in vinyl. Each year he would create a model based upon a real child he found in his travels and dress one as a 'lost' ragged child and another clothed after it was 'found'. Philip Heath left Gotz in 2000, and the next year opened his own company.

Pierrot

Although the Pierrot dates back to the sixteenth-century traditions of the Italian Commedia dell'arte, it was during the late 1800s that groups of performers,

Rosie & Jim, Golden Bear & Born To Play.

Santon Doll.

Scrump doll from Lilo and Stitch, Disney.

Princess Leia Slave Girl, Star Wars, Palitoy.

weeks. Lashes and, often, brows, are rooted too. Finger and toe nails are made to look like those of a baby. The bodies are normally soft, filled with fibre and pellets, and weighted to give the sensation of holding a real baby. Sometimes heat packs or heart beats are added too. Top 'Reborn' artists will charge hundreds or even thousands of pounds for one of their baby dolls; they may well have worked on it for months. In some quarters, especially the popular press, there has been controversy over these dolls amidst claims that women treat them as real babies, even taking them for walks in a pram. Occasionally this is a valid accusation, but mainly the dolls are bought by people who appreciate all the hard work that has gone into creating a realistic baby doll.

R. John Wright
R. John Wright, together with his wife Susan, established a company to create beautiful life-like felt dolls in 1976, and during the 1980s they turned their focus from adult characters to children. This move created a stir in the doll world, as the dolls resembled the creations from the 1920s and 30s when cloth doll making was at its peak. Since then, a bevy of classic dolls have poured from the R. John Wright studio, which has concentrated on depicting much-loved children's characters from literature, amongst them 'Alice in Wonderland', 'Snow White', 'Heidi and Peter', 'Christopher Robin' and 'Raggedy Ann and Andy'. The dolls are top of the range, extremely expensive, but the craftsmanship shines through.

Robert Tonner
In 1991 Robert Tonner launched Robert Tonner Doll Design (RTDD). It was renamed Tonner Doll Company, Inc. in 2000. The company is renowned for its high quality ranges of collectors' dolls, all of which come with exceptionally well-designed outfits featuring great attention to detail. Robert Tonner's fashion dolls include 'Tyler Wentworth', 'Antoinette' and 'Kitty Collier'. He has also built up a niche for the company specialising in character dolls from films such as *Harry Potter*, *Spiderman*, *Gone With the Wind*, *The Wizard of Oz*, *Alice in Wonderland* and many others. In 2006 Robert Tonner created the direct-marketing company, Wilde Imagination, forming a collectable fashion doll design business that markets direct to the consumer. Amongst the dolls available through Wilde Imagination are the quirky, exceedingly popular 'Ellowyne Wilde' range of teen dolls, as well as others including 'Evangeline Ghastly'. Robert Tonner also owns the Effanbee company, through which he has issued dolls such as 'Patsy' and 'Betsy May'.

Robertson's Golly (*See also* Golly)
The Robertson's company was founded in 1864 by James Robertson and originally produced marmalade before expanding into jam and mincemeat. In 1928 the company began a golly-brooch scheme, rewarding collectors of the paper golly labels on the jars with an enamelled brooch or badge featuring a large-eyed golly. The scheme continued right up till 2006. Plush Robertson's golly dolls were produced occasionally, but nowadays the golly has become

unpopular and is sometimes deemed racist. Robertson's retired their golly mascot in 2002.

Roddy

The Roddy company was founded by Daniel George Todd who went into partnership with J. Robinson in the 1930s, producing composition dolls and calling the company D.G.Todd. In the late 1940s they experimented with plastics and marketed their small 'Rodnoid' dolls before discovering that another manufacturer was using a similar name. They changed the name to 'Roddy', often selling through Cowan Dolls Ltd, and also frequently selling their dolls to other companies such as Faerie Glen. Roddy was one of the first manufacturers to embrace the new plastics medium. It made large quantities of plastic and vinyl dolls up until the mid-1970s, when the company was sold and became renamed Bluebell. In 1974 the Denys Fisher company took over, but Bluebell ceased trading in the 1980s.

Ronald McDonald

Ronald McDonald is the mascot of the McDonald's fast-food chain, and has been so since the mid-1960s. This clown character, dressed in a yellow suit with red-and-white-striped sleeves and socks, has bright red hair and features full clown make-up. Other McDonald's characters include 'Hamburglar' and 'Mayor McCheese'. Various cloth dolls and plush toys of the clown and his friends surface from time to time, including some recent dolls by Ty.

Rosebud

The Rosebud company was started by T. Eric Smith in the 1940s, when it was known as Nene Plastics and based in Northamptonshire. The 'Rosebud' name was registered in 1947. Originally dolls were made using a composition-type mix, before they later turned to plastics. The company was extremely productive; at its peak it turned out 10,000,000 dolls a year. In 1967 Mattel acquired Rosebud, with the company at first being known as Rosebud-Mattel, but the Rosebud name disappeared in the early 1970s. Later, the early Wellingborough factory became Rotary Plastics, and asked to use the Rosebud name, but Mattel refused, so they became Blossom Toys. Rosebud were responsible for a range of beautiful dolls, but probably the most collected and most loved today is the 8in 'Miss Rosebud' from the 1950s and 60s.

Rosie and Jim

Rosie and Jim, a pair of colourful rag dolls, were extremely popular in the 1990s. They starred on children's television in a series of *Rosie and Jim* shows produced by Ragdoll Productions. The storyline was that they lived aboard a canal barge called, appropriately enough, *Ragdoll* and had interesting adventures alongside the barge's owner, John Cunliffe (later replaced by Pat Coombes and then Neil Brewer). The joke was that John 'didn't realise that he was being followed by the cheeky dolls', and they were able to watch the interesting things he did. Several different play dolls representing the 'Rosie and Jim' characters in various sizes have been made over the years. Rosie and Jim dolls are instantly recognisable due to their colourful clothes and cheeky, good-humoured looks.

Roundy
'Roundy' was the toddler/baby doll who lived in a doll's house with his parents, brother Pip and sister Melia. The dolls featured in a 1950s series of small strip books by Enid Blyton, and were looked after by Mary Mouse.

Royal Dolls, Windsor (*See* France and Marianne

Rugrats
The animated television series *Rugrats* first appeared in 1991 and the name refers to the American slang name for toddlers. There were eight babies (and a dog) that featured in the series, and for a while the dolls were extremely popular. Made by Mattel and licensed by Nickleodeon, there were several soft-body plush types – some which featured wire armatures so that they could be posed. Gund also produced the dolls, as did Applause.

Sailor Moon
Sailor Moon dolls appeared in Britain in 2001, and their most distinctive feature was their overlarge, round eyes. The dolls were based on a popular Japanese cartoon and created in the Japanese 'Manga' style, often referred to as 'Anime'. The majority of the UK dolls were made by Irwin Toy. There were plastic and plush ranges in several types and sizes. The plastic dolls were 6in, 11½in and 17in, and all the sailor girls wore sailor-style dresses with short skirts and sailor-type collars trimmed with a large bow. Each doll was marked 'Irwin Toy 2000 NT/KTA Made in China'. The dolls' names included 'Sailor Moon', 'Sailor Venus', 'Sailor Mercury', 'Sailor Jupiter' and 'Sailor Mars'.

Sally
Sally, a small rag doll, was seen in *Toy Story 1* as Hannah's replacement doll for Janie. She was very similar to Janie, though Sally had brunette hair while Janie was blonde. When the toys finally decided to get their own back on the evil Sid who had been torturing them, he ran away in terror when he suddenly saw Sally. Hannah was intrigued by his behaviour but decided to capitalise on it, so she chased Sid upstairs and into his room, holding Sally as she tried to scare him even more.

Sally, Aunt (*See* Aunt Sally)

Santon Dolls
French Santon de Provence dolls are a traditional form of costume doll that have a religious significance as they depict local people off to pay homage to the Holy Family. They show various occupations, are usually around 8in high and made

from heavy clay over a wire armature. The dolls are well-dressed with expressive faces.

Sarah Jane
Doll character in a series of books by Bertha and Florence Upton.

Sarold
The Sarold Manufacturing Company was based in Liverpool, on the Kirkby Trading Estate, and registered its Sarold trademark in 1950. The hard shiny plastic that the company used seemed thinner than that of similar dolls of the time, with a tendency to crack. Sarold dolls came in many sizes; from 3in babies to huge 25in babies, but probably the most commonly found today are the 7in girls. They dolls were marked 'Sarold Made in England'. Sarold also supplied dolls to Woolworths stores, often undressed, ready to be dressed at home. The company was short-lived and closed down in the mid-fifties.

Sasha
Deservedly a classic, Sasha dolls were designed by Swedish artist-designer Sasha Morgenthaler and were first produced as very limited Studio dolls. In 1964, the Gotz company began manufacturing them and shortly afterwards John and Sara Doggart of the Frido company, later Trendon, of Stockport, England, were given the licence to produce the dolls too. Sasha dolls featured 'milk chocolate' coloured skin, and their features were barely defined, which meant that a child must use their imagination. The dolls were of exceptional quality, and today are very expensive collectors' items. Trendon ceased production in 1986.

Scarry, Patricia M.
American writer who collaborated with Eloise Wilkin in some of the Little Golden Books, such as *My Dolly and Me*. Patricia Scarry was married to author Richard Scarry.

Scootles
'Scootles' was a rather cheeky toddler doll designed by Rose O'Neill who is famed for her 'Kewpie 'creations. Originally, bisque versions were made in Germany, but later Cameo began producing composition versions, in sizes from 7½in to 20in. There was also a black version. Scootles, a chubby child, had moulded curly hair, painted side-glance eyes and a single line for a mouth. Some sleep eye versions are known. Later, plastic-and-vinyl versions were made by Cameo. Recently, a version of the doll was produced by the Lee Middleton company, and now Scootles is being made in felt by R. John Wright.

Scrump
'Scrump' is the strange-looking doll made by little Hawaiian girl Lilo in the Disney film *Lilo and Stitch*. According to Lilo, the reason that the doll's head was

so big was because a bug laid eggs in it after crawling into its ear. She added that it only has a few days to live. Lilo's friends were scared of the doll. Disney manufactured Scrump dolls, and also sold a Lilo doll holding a small Scrump.

Shallowpool Dolls
A series of small (approx 8in) costume dolls handmade in Fowey, Cornwall, in the 1960s –1980s by three women. The dolls were made on a wire armature, with plaster hands, feet and head. Many were dressed to resemble Cornish tradespeople or characters. Others were nursery figures or historical dolls. They were intended for collectors, not as children's playthings.

Sheena Macleod
Maker of dolls dressed as Scottish highlanders. The dolls were created from plaster over a wire armature, and are similar in style to the Shallowpool creations. However, the Sheena MacLeod dolls are much more realistic, and more care has been taken with clothing fabrics, using Scottish tweeds and weaves for authenticity. Many of the dolls feature 'props' such as a spinning wheel, basket or creel. In 1971 some of Sheena Macleod dolls were selected for the Design Centre in London – a prestigious accolade. Sheena Macleod died in a car accident.

Simpsons
This American animated satirical sitcom, *The Simpsons*, originally was broadcast as a short cartoon in 1987, making its main debut two years later. It revolves around the adventures of Bart Simpson, Homer, Marge, Lisa and Maggie. *The Simpsons* has won dozens of awards and has spawned plenty of associated memorabilia, including plush, vinyl and rubber dolls.

Sindy
Introduced in 1963 by Pedigree, Sindy was based on the US doll, Tammy, and she swiftly became a favourite doll for the next twenty-five years or so. Sindy was a teen doll with short bobbed hair, and when she was first introduced wore a patriotic outfit of a red-white-and-blue-striped long-sleeved top and blue jeans. The outfit was called 'Weekenders' and was designed by Foale and Tuffin, popular clothing designers at the time. Sindy was soon given a boyfriend, 'Paul', and a little sister, 'Patch', as well as a few other friends. There were lots of outfits to buy separately, as well as accessories such a house, furniture, car and assorted pets. In 1987 Hasbro took over the Sindy line, gradually altering the concept and the design of the doll. Later she passed to Vivid Imaginations and then to New Moons. The Sindy name is still owned by Pedigree.

Smallest Doll in the World
Several dolls have been marketed with this claim to fame, but perhaps the two that are most likely to be found by the collector are a Victorian wooden version and a 1950s hard plastic doll. The wooden doll is peg-jointed and is ½in high.

She fits inside a wooden acorn that unscrews into two halves. Sometimes these acorns are found inscribed 'The smallest doll in the world', but at other times they are plain, and it is believed they were made in Germany in the late 1800s to early 1900s. The 1950s doll is a ¾in plastic baby, moulded all-in-one. Made by Fairylite, she came with her own plastic bath and was sold in a tiny box marked 'The Smallest Doll In The World'. Often, tiny celluloid dolls are found, such as a 1940s 1in-baby sold in a matchbox complete with a bath, towel and dummy, while the original Polly Pocket doll could be a worthy contender to the title, too.

Sonny & Cher

Mego's 1970s Sonny & Cher dolls with Sonny sporting his trademark moustache and Cher with her long hair, are collectable dolls as a pair, though, later, it was Cher who was the star favoured by doll designers. One of the Cher dolls featured a 'growing hair' mechanism. Her showy gowns were designed by Bob Mackie using rich fabrics such as satin with fringing, net and feather trims. She has been depicted by several companies, notably by Mattel which has dressed her in her iconic outfits.

Spears, Britney

Britney Spears dolls appeared in 2000. Canny Britney set up her own company, Britney Brands, and the dolls were marketed by various concerns such as Character Options, Yaboom and Play Along. The dolls featured Britney in various outfits including her famous 'Schoolgirl' get-up, as well as white trousers and crop top, black top and trousers with green trim, or pink dress topped with a fur cape.

Spice Girls

The Spice Girls were a popular group of five girls, Victoria Beckham (née Adams), Emma Bunting, Melanie Brown, Melanie Chisholm and Geri Halliwell, who soared to fame in the 1990s. They soon became nicknamed 'Posh', 'Baby', 'Sporty', 'Scary' and 'Ginger'. In 1998 the Galoob Toy company issued a well-modelled vinyl set of the girls, bearing quite a good likeness, but they were very expensive for the time, especially if the whole set was required. Galoob issued more sets, though dropped Geri when she announced she was leaving the group. Spice Girl dolls were also made by Hasbro.

Steps

Pop group Steps was formed in 1997 and became very popular. Group members were Lisa Scott-Lee, Faye Tozer, Claire Richards, Ian 'H' Watkins and Lee Latchford-Evans. As with many of the late 1990s groups, dolls were made of the members. These dolls were made by YaBoom, and as well as the standard versions, there was a set containing musical chips.

Star Trek
The cult science fiction series of television programmes and films, *Star Trek*, was created by Gene Roddenbury. The first episode was shown in 1966. The original series followed the interstellar adventures of the starship *Enterprise*, under the guidance of Captain James T. Kirk and the alien Mr Spock. Over time, many dolls and action figures have been produced, not only of the original crew but also of the additional characters from the later series and from the films. Makers include Mego, Mattel and Playmates.

Star Wars
Created by George Lucas, the first in the *Star Wars* series of science fiction space adventure films was released in 1977, subsequently followed by two sequels. The early films followed the adventures of Luke Skywalker, Han Solo, Princess Leia and the two droids C-3PO and R2-D2. Sixteen years later, the first in a series of three prequel films was issued. All the films spawned merchandise, amongst them 12in dolls and numerous figures. Some of the dolls from the 1970s are rare. They were manufactured by Kenner, Palitoy, Hasbro and others.

Stinky Pete
'Stinky Pete' was the Prospector doll in *Toy Story 2*. He was still mint in his box, a collector's item, and wore a red top, blue dungarees, black hat and had a white beard. Various plastic and plush figures have been made of the character.

Strawberry Shortcake
The design for a little girl, 'Strawberry Shortcake', and 'Custard' her cat, was the work of Muriel Fahrion for a greetings card at the American Greetings Card Company in 1977. Later, Muriel's sister, Susan Trentel, made a doll of the character, and the AGCC were so taken with the concept that by 1980 there was a huge collection of dolls in the Strawberry Shortcake range, most of them fruit-scented. The dolls were licensed under Those Characters from Cleveland (TCFC) and sold through Kenner and Palitoy.

Sunny Jim
A major advertising rag character was Sunny Jim, aka 'Mr Force'. Sunny Jim made his debut in the twenties, based on an idea submitted by two young girls to the manufacturers of Force breakfast cereal. This highly successful rag doll was produced in Britain for several decades. He was a 'sideways-on' design, a walking figure representing a jovial, or sinister, depending on your point of view, Georgian gentleman, resplendent in white trousers, red jacket and with his wig tied back in a queue (pigtail). Under his arm he clutched his packet of Force breakfast cereal. Over the years, countless small boys were nicknamed 'Sunny Jim', and various verses appeared on posters and cereal packets, the most famous being: 'High oe'r the fence leaps Sunny Jim, Force is the food that raises him!'

Sunny Jim.

Tressy, Palitoy.

Worzel Gummidge and
Aunt Sally, Bendy Toys.

Take That
The boy group Take That made their first television appearance in 1990. The members were Gary Barlow, Robbie Williams, Jason Orange, Howard Donald and Mark Owen. They became highly successful, and 12in dolls were made of them by Vivid Imaginations during the 1990s.

Teletubbies
Teletubbies were four strange characters that began life in 1997 on a BBC programme aimed at toddlers. Their names were 'Dipsy', 'Tinky Winky', 'Laa-Laa' and 'Po', and each had an antenna on its head and a television screen on its stomach. The programme caused some controversy, due to the babyish language used, but it became cult viewing with many adults, especially students. When the first plush dolls were issued just before Christmas 1997, shops sold out instantly, and many dolls changed hands for vastly-inflated sums on the secondary market. Teletubbies dolls have been made by Golden Bear, Tomy and others.

Temple, Shirley
Shirley Temple was a child star whose likeness in doll form is still much loved, just as it was when the dolls first appeared in the 1930s. Dolls representing Shirley have been made by various companies, though are especially linked to Ideal, and the smiling youngster with her hair in ringlets is instantly recognisable. Collectors' companies such as Danbury Mint and Ashton-Drake still occasionally produce her today.

Tetley Tea Folk
A series of animated characters, representing factory workers at the Tetley Tea Company, usually wearing white coats. The Tetley Tea Folk soon found themselves stars of a major campaign and it wasn't long before collectables appeared, including plush and vinyl dolls. Amongst the characters were 'Gaffer', 'Sydney', 'Maurice', 'Clarence' and 'Archie'. The television adverts combined animation with live-action sets and 'props', such as real tea bags, cups, saucers and spoons. The characters were first introduced in 1973, and continued till 2001 when they were 'retired' – only to reappear again in 2010.

Tiny Tears
Tiny Tears was a baby doll that was introduced in 1965, made by Palitoy at Coalville, Leicestershire. The doll, with its drink, wet and crying actions was an instant success, and has become one of Britain's classic dolls. The first Tiny Tears was 16in high, with small blue sleep eyes and fine baby-blonde hair. She had a slightly pursed open mouth which could take a bottle or dummy and was sold wearing a pink or blue checked gingham romper suit and a bib. Other dolls in the series were later introduced, such as 'Teeny Tears' and 'Teeny Weeny Tiny Tears'. In 1970 Tiny Tears was given a makeover, and suddenly seemed much older, with thicker hair. Over the next few years various other facial alterations

appeared. The doll was then taken over by Tonka, which introduced 'Timmy Tears' and 'Big Sister Katie'. Various other makers then took over, including Hasbro, Ideal and Playmates. The doll is still in production today, under the Toy Brokers brand.

Toni (*See* Pin-Up)

Topsy Doll
A 'Topsy' doll is the name often given to a black bent-limbed baby doll with three clumps of hair 'growing' from holes in the head, frequently tied with ribbon. The dolls were usually made in composition, though after the Second World War plastic versions appeared. The name is thought to have been derived from the child Topsy in the novel *Uncle Tom's Cabin* by Harriet Beecher Stowe.

Topsy-Turvy Doll
Topsy-turvy dolls have a head at each end of their bodies instead of legs, so one might have a black head, but if the skirt is flipped it reveals a white doll. Often they tell a fairy tale, such as Red Riding Hood and her Grandmother, or Poor Cinderella and Rich Cinderella. These dolls have been popular for over a hundred years, and are usually made from composition, cloth or plastic. They are still favourites today.

Tots TV
The three rag dolls, 'Tom', 'Tilly' and 'Tiny', starred in the *Tots TV* television programme made by Ragdoll Productions in the 1990s. All the dolls featured brightly coloured wool hair; spectacle-wearing Tom had blue hair, French Tilly had red and Tiny, green. Various companies produced the dolls including Ravensburger and Golden Bear.

Tottie
Tottie was a small wooden-peg-doll character in a book by Rumer Godden called *The Dolls' House*. In the 1980s the book was made into a successful television cartoon, animated by Peter Firmin and Oliver Postgate, and the programme was called *Tottie, The Story of a Dolls' House*. In the book Tottie shared her home with the delightful celluloid doll Birdie, a snooty wax doll called Marchpane and a toddler known as Apple.

Tressy
Palitoy issued 'Tressy' under licence from the American Character Doll Company in 1964. She was a 12in teen with growing hair, activated when a button was pushed. A key rewound the hair into the head. The first UK doll had painted, side-glance eyes looking towards the right. She was jointed at the neck, hips and shoulders and her straight legs didn't bend. Her hair was rooted mid-length in various colours, without a fringe. The plastic was poor quality, and had a tendency to fade. The first Tressy was dressed in a blue, lemon or pink

straight shift dress with a belt. Several versions of Tressy were issued over the eighteen years or so that she was produced, and there were many outfits available separately. In 1965 she was given a younger sister, 'Toots' and in 1967 a friend, 'Mary Make-Up'. The 1969 Tressy had front facing eyes and a fringe, and though her hair still grew, it was shorter. In 1973 another version appeared, a hard plastic doll with a vinyl head, jointed elbows and wrists and a twist waist. Her key was permanently fitted to her back. The final Tressy came in 1979. This was a pretty doll with soft poseable vinyl arms and jointed hands. Her legs were bendable and she had a twist waist. Her key was permanently fixed.

Tudor Rose

The Tudor Rose company became well-known for its range of hard plastic small dolls with solemn faces and downturned palms. The company was located in Wales from 1948 to 1978, and owned by Rosedale Associated Manufacturers Ltd., who later also used the name Rosedale Rose. The company made several small dolls, as well as a range of various toys, during the fifties and sixties. It was purchased by Mettoy in 1978 who resold it five years later.

Twiggy

Renowned as a model in the 1960s, Twiggy (real name Lesley Hornby) now models for Marks and Spencer. The earliest Twiggy doll appeared in 1966, and was a plastic type made by Mattel. In 2001 Franklin Mint released a porcelain Twiggy doll which stood 16ins high and was dressed in a psychedelic trouser suit, with other outfits available. Twiggy dolls were also issued by Medicom in the mid 2000s. They came in two sizes – the 10ins doll wore various outfits including a black and white mini dress, while the smaller, 4" dolls had moulded plastic outfits.

Upton, Florence

Born in 1873, Florence Upton is famed for her book *The Adventures of Two Dutch Dolls*, mainly because it introduced the golly concept. Written in 1895, it told in verse the tale of a golly and some wooden dolls. There were many other books in the series, most of them written in collaboration with Bertha, her mother.

Wallace

Wallace is a rather absent-minded inventor who lives in Wigan, Lancashire, together with his long-suffering dog, Gromit, and is addicted to Wensleydale cheese. The pair appear in four short, animated cartoons, as well as a feature-length film, *The Curse of the Were-Rabbit*, by Nick Park of Aardman Animations. The characters are made from plasticine modelled over wire armatures and filmed using stop-go animation. The voice of Wallace is provided by veteran actor Peter Sallis. A spate of mainly soft-bodied character dolls from the films has appeared since the series was first televised. 'Human' characters include Wallace and Wendolene.

Weg (*See also* Chapter 1)
Doll character in a series of books by Bertha and Florence Upton.

Westlife
Irish boy band Westlife was formed in 1998. The line-up was Nicky Byrne, Mark Feehily, Shane Filan, Kian Egan and Bryan McFadden. Enormously successful, the group has gone from strength to strength, though announced they would disband in 2012. Bryan McFadden left in 2004. Several sets of dolls featuring the group were made by Yaboom, and some contain music chips.

Willow and Daisy
'Willow' and 'Daisy' was a pair of collectors' dolls launched in 1999, designed by Doug James and Laura Meisner. Doug worked as a fashion designer for film and television and Laura was a fashion doll historian. The Willow and Daisy dolls were leggy 16in teens dressed in a variety of often outrageous outfits, supposedly based on 1960s fashion, and known as 'The Mod British Birds'. They were produced by the American company Knickerbocker. Daisy was an exotic dark-haired beauty, while Willow was a sophisticated blonde, and they both had wigged hair, rather than rooted which made it easier to create intricate hairstyles. Unfortunately, by 2001, Knickerbocker had developed financial problems and so was taken over by Marie Osmond, but the Willow and Daisy line wasn't reintroduced. Laura Meisner died in 2003. Doug James went on to produce a new range of 19½in-high quality fashion dolls known as CED dolls, later creating a series of teens based on the original Willow and Daisy. He called the new girls 'Gabby' and 'Violet', and they were launched in 2007.

Winky doll (*See* Carnival Dolls)

Woody
'Woody' was the cowboy doll from the three *Toy Story* films; *Toy Story* (1995), *Toy Story 2* (1999) and *Toy Story 3* (2010). Originally he was intended as the main character, though was overshadowed in the toy market by Buzz Lightyear, the spaceman. Tom Hanks played the voice of Sheriff Woody who was operated by a pull-cord, saying such things as 'Reach for the sky', 'There's a snake in my boot' and 'This town ain't big enough for the two of us'. However, when no humans were around, Woody, just like the other toys, spoke normally. He was an old-fashioned cowboy doll with, according to *Toy Story 2*, 'an original hand-painted face, natural dyed-blanket-stitched vest, and hand-stitched poly-vinyl hat'. He had always been Andy's favourite and felt jealous when Buzz Lightyear arrived. Various dolls of different sizes have been released since 1995, including an 11in version by Thinkway Toys, complete with pull-cord voice.

Worzel Gummidge (*See also* Aunt Sally)
Originally not a doll but a scarecrow that first appeared in the book *Worzel Gummidge*, by Barbara Euphan Todd, published in 1936, and subsequently in

 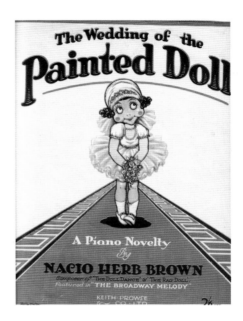

many more. Worzel Gummidge had interchangeable heads – a swede, a mangel worzel and a turnip – to suit his moods, and was able to walk and talk. In 1979 a television series appeared produced by Southern Television for ITV, written by Keith Waterhouse and Willis Hall and starring Jon Pertwee as Worzel Gummidge, with Una Stubbs playing the part of Aunt Sally, a wooden fairground doll. Pedigree issued dolls of the two characters when the television series appeared, with vinyl faces and cloth bodies. There was also a series of rubber 'bendy' dolls, with, in the case of Worzel Gummidge, removable heads, as well as various fabric types. Worzel Gummidge dolls are now regarded as classic character dolls and becoming collectable.

Waugh, Sylvia
Sylvia Waugh was born in Gateshead, County Durham, in 1935, and her first book, *The Mennyms*, was published in 1993. It told the story of a family of life-size rag dolls. The book had such good reviews that she went on to write *Mennyms in the Wilderness* (1994), *Mennyms Under Siege* (1995), *Mennyms Alone* (1996), and *Mennyms Alive* (1996).

Wilkin, Eloise
American illustrator and writer Eloise Wilkin was responsible for producing many books, including dozens of classic Golden Books over her long career. Born in 1904, she had an instantly recognisable gentle style of drawing and became famed for titles such as *Baby Dear*, *We Help Mommy* and *My Little Golden Book About God*. Some of the books that she illustrated were written by other authors, including Patricia Scarry. The baby doll illustrated in *Baby Dear* and

other books was put into production by The Vogue Doll Company which issued the first 'Baby Dear' vinyl and fabric baby doll in 1960. The doll was signed on its left leg by Eloise Wilkin as a sign of authenticity. Various other dolls in the Baby Dear range were subsequently manufactured by Vogue. Eloise Wilkin died in 1987.

Wright, Dare
Dare Wright was a Canadian children's author and photographer born in 1914, and who became renowned for her series of *The Lonely Doll* books, which featured stories and photographs of her childhood Lenci doll, Edith. The first book was published in 1957, and many others followed, often about the Lenci doll and her two teddy bear friends. Various 'Lonely Doll' dolls have been manufactured, notably by R. John Wright and Madame Alexander.

Zapf (*See also* Baby Born)
The Max Zapf company was founded by Max and Rosa Zapf in 1932 and managed by their son, Willie, who converted it into a German partnership known as Max Zapf puppen-und Spielwarenfabrik GmbH. For 60 years the company was a family affair, until in 1992, Zapf Creations was taken over by TA Spietund Freizeit Holding GmbH, a member of the Triumph Adler Group. In the early1980s, the Max Zapf company dolls decided on a UK sales-drive and as a result, became popular in Britain. Suddenly stores were full of beautiful, large play dolls made from an exceptionally heavy, good quality vinyl. The dolls sported thick, silky, long hair, which was imported from Italy because the consistent quality made it perfect for brushing, combing and styling. The eyes, too, were Italian, and they featured great depth of colour. Zapf was of the opinion that people would always pay for quality, and though its products might be slightly dearer than the average doll, they were far superior. Later, they launched a large, bald-headed baby which was amazingly successful, and this led in turn to the 1990s Baby Born ranges, which today still dominate toyshops. Other successful Zapf ranges include 'Annabelle' and 'Chou Chou'. They also introduced a 'Colette' range of dolls, which were superior play dolls with extra well-made shoes and clothing. Zapf also produced a range of top quality designer dolls during the 1990s and early 2000s. These collector's dolls included creations from artists including Nel De Man, Bettine Klemm, Roland Heimer, Brigitte Lehman, von Waltraud Hanl and Wiltrud Stein.

Zwergnase
Zwergnase dolls are the creation of German artist Nicole Marschollek, who was born in Rauenstein, near Sonneberg. She studied at the Sonneberg College of Toy Design and Mechanical Engineering, and then worked for a doll manufacturing company before finally designing for herself. The Zwergnase dolls are extremely distinctive, often bearing character expressions such as faces distorted with joy. They are very well made.

Doll Songs and Music

Are My Ears On Straight? (Montclare Music) 1953
Baby Doll (Harry Von Tilzer) 1909
China Doll Parade (Fox/Prowse) 1922
Dainty Doll (Keith Prowse) 1929
Dance Of the Wooden Dolls (Laurence Wright) 1929
Dance Of The Paper Dolls (M. Witmark) 1928
Dance With a Dolly (Campbell) 1954
Dances Of the Dolls Shostakovitch (B&H) 1965
Doll Dance, The (Keith Prowse) 1936
Doll House (Bamboo Music) 1960
Doll Medley (Keith Prowse) 1937
Dolls House, The (Lareine and Co) 1929
Dutch Doll Dance (Warren & Phillips) 1931
Fairy on the Christmas Tree (Keith Prowse)
Hello Dolly (Edwin H. Morris) 1963
I'd Like To Build That Doll House (Mastercraft) 1927
I Had a Black Dolly called Topsy (Traditional)
I Want A Doll (Harry Von Tilzer) 1918
Kewpie Doll (Leeds Music) 1958
Little Dolly Daydream (Francis, Day and Hunter) 1897
Living Doll (Peter Maurice) 1959
Mama Doll Song (Leeds Music) 1954
My Kewpie Doll (Nat Goldstein) 1913
Oh You Beautiful Doll (Jerome H. Remick) 1911
Paper Doll (Peter Maurice) 1942
Party Doll (Patricia Music) 1957
Punch and Judy Polka (Noel Gay Music) 1944
Rag Doll (Phillips) 1964
Serious Doll Elgar (Oup) 1931
Sick Doll Tchaikovsky (Wise) 1978
Wedding of the Painted Doll (Prowse) 1929

Doll Stories for Children

Enid Blyton, *Mary Mouse and the Dolls' House* (and others in the series). Brockhampton Press 1942

Enid Blyton, *Noddy Goes To Toyland* (and other in the series). Sampson Low 1949

Enid Blyton, *Naughty Amelia Jane* (and others in the series). Newnes 1939

Carine Cadby, *The Dolls' Day*. Mills and Boon 1915

Helen Clare, *Five Dolls in a House*. Bodley Head 1953

Rachel Field, *Hitty, Her First Hundred Years*. Macmillan 1929

Rumer Godden, *The Story of Holly and Ivy*. Macmillan 1959

Rumer Godden, *The Fairy Doll*. Macmillan 1956

Rumer Godden, *Little Plum*. Macmillan 1963

Rumer Godden, *Miss Happiness and Miss Flower*. Macmillan 1961

Rumer Godden, *Home is the Sailor*. Macmillan 1964

Johnny Gruelle, *Raggedy Ann Stories* (and others in the series). Volland 1918

Ann Matthews, *Martin Karen's Doll*. Hippo 1995

Ann Matthews, *Martin Karen's Doll Hospital*. Hippo 1998

Hiawyn Oram and Ruth Brown, *The Wise Doll*. Andersen Press 1997

Beatrix Potter, *The Tale of Two Bad Mice*. Warne 1904

Patricia Scarry & Eloise Wilkin, *My Dolly and Me*. Golden Press 1960

Modwena Sedgwick, *The Adventures of Galldora*. Harrap 1960

Modwena Sedgwick, *The New Adventures of Galldora*. Harrap 1961

Modwena Sedgwick, *A Rag Doll Called Galldora*. Harrap 1971

Esther Wilkin & Eloise Wilkin, *Baby Dear*. Golden Press 1962

Esther Wilkin & Eloise Wilkin, *So Big*. Golden Press 1968

Barbara Euphan Todd, *Worzel Gummidge* (and others in the series). Burns, Oates & Co 1936

Bertha and Florence Upton, *The Adventures of Two Dutch Dolls*. Longmans, Green and Co, 1895

Dare Wright, *Edith The Lonely Doll*. Doubleday 1957

Dare Wright, *Edith and the Duckling*. Doubleday 1981

Dare Wright, *Edith and Midnight*. Doubleday 1978

Dare Wright, *Gift From the Lonely Doll*. Random House 1966

Dare Wright, *Edith and Mr Bear*. Random House 1964

Dare Wright, *Doll and the Kitten*. Doubleday 1960 (and others in the series)

Bibliography

Susan Brewer, *Girls' Toys*. Pen and Sword
Susan Brewer, *Dolls of the 1950s*. Pen and Sword
Susan Brewer, *Dolls of the 1960s*. Pen and Sword
Susan Brewer, *Tiny Tears and First Love*. Virtual Valley
Carolyn Cook & Others, *I Had That Doll!* Park Lane Press
Lester and Irene David, *The Shirley Temple Story*. Robson Books
Kenneth & Marguerite Fawdry, *Pollocks History of Dolls and Toys*. Ernest Benn
    Ltd
Mary Hillier, *Pollocks Dictionary of English Dolls*. Crown
Suzanne Kraus-Mancuso, *Shirley Temple Identification and Price Guide To Shirley
    Temple Collectables* (Vol I & II). Hobby House Press
Colette Mansell, *The Collector's Guide to British Dolls since 1920*. Hale
Neil Miller, *The Dean's Rag Book Company; The First Hundred Years*. Dean's
Patsy Moyer, *Modern Collectable Dolls* series. Collector Books
Peggy Nisbet, *The Peggy Nisbet Story*. Hobby House Press
Edward R. Pardella, *Shirley Temple Dolls and Fashions*. Schiffer

Photo Credits

Acknowledgements

Special thanks go to my husband Malcolm for his support, photography and for fetching and carrying boxes of dolls from storage; son Simon for his technical help and advice, and daughter Jenna for the many hours she spent sorting out the dolls and looking out for new ones to add to the collection.

Index